Growing Apart?

Since the end of the Cold War, the United States has seemed to be growing apart from its democratic neighbors and allies. Why has this happened? The answers to this question are found in the social, political, and economic forces that shape advanced democratic states, rather than the current policies of particular governments. This book brings together a set of leading scholars who examine the evolution of different social, political, and economic forces shaping Europe and America. It is the first book to unite the international relations scholarship on transatlantic relations with the comparative politics literature on the varieties of capitalism. Taken together, the chapters in this book address whether the "West" will continue to remain a coherent entity in the twenty-first century.

Jeffrey Kopstein is Professor of Political Science and Director of the Centre for European, Russian, and Eurasian Studies at the University of Toronto. He is the author of *The Politics of Economic Decline in East Germany 1945–1989* and coeditor of *Comparative Politics: Interests, Identities, and Institutions in a Changing Global Order*.

Professor Sven Steinmo holds the chair in public policy and political economy at the European University Institute (EUI) in Florence, Italy. He is also a professor at the University of Colorado, Boulder, and an honorary professor at Odense University, Denmark. His writing includes *Taxation and Democracy* (winner of the 1994 Best Book Prize, Political Economy Section of the American Political Science Association), *Structuring Politics* (coedited with Kathleen Thelen), and *Political Evolution and Policy Change* (coedited with Bo Rothstein).

Growing Apart?

America and Europe in the Twenty-First Century

Edited by

JEFFREY KOPSTEIN
University of Toronto

SVEN STEINMO
European University Institute

CAMBRIDGE
UNIVERSITY PRESS

CAMBRIDGE UNIVERSITY PRESS
Cambridge, New York, Melbourne, Madrid, Cape Town, Singapore, São Paulo, Delhi

Cambridge University Press
32 Avenue of the Americas, New York, NY 10013-2473, USA

www.cambridge.org
Information on this title: www.cambridge.org/9780521879316

First published 2008

Printed in the United States of America

A catalog record for this publication is available from the British Library.

Library of Congress Cataloging in Publication Data

Growing apart? : America and Europe in the 21st century / [edited by]
Jeffrey Kopstein, Sven Steinmo.
    p.   cm.
Includes bibliographical references and index.
ISBN 978-0-521-87931-6 (hardback) – ISBN 978-0-521-70491-5 (pbk.)
1. Political culture – United States.   2. Political culture – Europe.   3. United States –
Politics and government – 21st century.   4. Europe – Politics and government – 21st
century.   5. Comparative government.   6. United States – Relations – Europe.
7. Europe – Relations – United States.   I. Kopstein, Jeffrey.   II. Steinmo, Sven.   III. Title.
JK1726.G76   2008
327.7304 – dc22   2007013755

ISBN   978-0-521-87931-6 hardback
ISBN   978-0-521-70491-5 paperback

To our professors at the University of California, Berkeley

Contents

Contributors

Mark Blyth is an associate professor of political science at the Johns Hopkins University in Baltimore and visiting professor at the Center for International Business and Politics at Copenhagen Business School. His research interests lie in the fields of comparative and international political economy. He is the author of *Great Transformations: Economic Ideas and Institutional Change in the Twentieth Century* (New York: Cambridge University Press, 2002) and is currently working on three projects. The first is a book on party politics and political economy in advanced welfare states called *The New Political Economy of Party Politics*. The second is a book on constructivist theory and political economy. The third project is a series of papers on randomness in the social sciences, which may or may not end up a book. His articles have appeared in the *American Political Science Review*, *Comparative Politics*, *Perspectives on Politics*, *West European Politics*, and *World Politics*.

Christopher Cochrane is a Ph.D. candidate in the Department of Political Science at the University of Toronto. His research focuses on patterns of public opinion in advanced industrial countries.

Laurent Cohen-Tanugi is a Paris-based partner of the international law firm Skadden Arps and the author of several books on European affairs and transatlantic relations, including *An Alliance at Risk: The United States and Europe after September 11* (Baltimore: Johns Hopkins University Press, 2003). He is a director of Notre Europe, a European think tank founded by Jacques Delors, and a visiting professor on European affairs at the Ecole Normale Supérieure, Paris.

Daniel W. Drezner is Associate Professor of International Politics at the Fletcher School of Law and Diplomacy at Tufts University. He is the author of *All Politics Is Global* (Princeton: Princeton University Press, 2007), *U.S. Trade Strategy* (New York: Council on Foreign Relations, 2006), and *The Sanctions Paradox* (New York: Cambridge University Press, 1999), as well as the editor of *Locating the Proper Authorities* (Ann Arbor: University of Michigan Press, 2003). His work has appeared in numerous scholarly journals, as well as the *New York Times, Wall Street Journal*, and *Foreign Affairs*. He has previously held positions at the University of Chicago, the University of Colorado, Boulder, the Civic Education Project, the RAND Corporation, and the U.S. Treasury Department. He has received fellowships from the German Marshall Fund of the United States, the Council on Foreign Relations, and Harvard University. He received his B.A. from Williams College and his Ph.D. in political science from Stanford University. He keeps a daily Web log at www.danieldrezner.com.

Randall Hansen is Associate Professor and Canada Research Chair in Immigration and Governance in the Department of Political Science at the University of Toronto. His published works include *Citizenship and Immigration in Post-War Britain* (New York: Oxford University Press, 2000); *Towards a European Nationality* (with P. Weil; London: Palgrave, 2001); *Dual Nationality, Social Rights, and Federal Citizenship in the U.S. and Europe* (with P. Weil; New York and Oxford: Berghahn, 2002); *Immigration and Asylum from 1900 to the Present* (with M. Gibney; Santa Barbara: ABC-CLIO, 2005); and articles on immigration, citizenship, and asylum published in *Comparative Political Studies*, the *European Journal of Political Research*, and *World Politics*. His Web site is www.randallhansen.ca.

Daniel A. Kenney is a Ph.D. candidate in politics at Brandeis University. A former Gordon Public Policy Fellow and Callner graduate fellowship recipient at Brandeis, he has recently presented conference papers on "Seizing Domestic Tranquility: Federal Military Intervention During Reconstruction" (2006) and "Executive Use of Force and Industrialization: Military Intervention in Late 19th Century America" (2007). His dissertation offers a theory on when states are likely to use military force internally to pacify social discord.

Jeffrey Kopstein is Director of the Centre for European, Russian, and Eurasian Studies and Professor of Political Science at the University of

Toronto. He is the author of *The Politics of Economic Decline in East Germany 1945–1989* (Chapel Hill: University of North Carolina Press, 1997) and coeditor of *Comparative Politics: Interests, Identities, and Institutions in a Changing Global Order*, 3rd edition (New York: Cambridge University Press, 2007). His recent articles have appeared in *Comparative Politics*, *German Politics and Society*, *Political Theory*, *Theory and Society*, *The Washington Quarterly*, and *World Politics*.

Donald Morrison is a contributor to *Time* magazine in Paris. He has worked on four continents for the magazine and has held nearly every editorial position at *Time*, from national affairs reporter to editor of its European and Asian editions. He is the editor and coauthor of five books, and he also writes for the *Financial Times* and the *New York Times*.

Neil Nevitte is Professor of Political Science at the University of Toronto. His research interests are in public opinion and voting behavior. He is also coinvestigator of the Canadian Election Study and the principal investigator of the Canadian World Values Surveys. His most recent publications include *Value Change and Governance* (Toronto: University of Toronto Press, 2002) (as editor) and *Anatomy of a Liberal Victory* (Toronto: Broadview Press, 2002).

Steven Pfaff is an associate professor of sociology at the University of Washington and director of the Center for West European Studies. His research interests include comparative and historical sociology, politics, and the sociology of religion. Author of *Exit-Voice Dynamics and the Collapse of East Germany* (Durham: Duke University Press, 2006), he has also published articles in the *American Journal of Sociology*, *Comparative Political Studies*, *Journal for the Scientific Study of Religion*, and *Social Forces*.

Sven Steinmo holds the Chair in Public Policy and Political Economy at the European University Institute (EUI) in Florence, Italy. He is also a professor at the University of Colorado, Boulder, and an honorary professor at Odense University, Denmark. His writing includes *Taxation and Democracy* (New Haven: Yale University Press, 1993) (winner of the 1994 Best Book in Political Economy Prize from the American Political Science Association); *Structuring Politics* (New York: Cambridge University Press, 1992) (coedited with Kathleen Thelen); and *Political Evolution and Policy Change*, coedited with Bo Rothstein (London: Palgrave 2002).

Steven Teles is Visiting Lecturer in Law and Political Science at Yale University. He has taught or visited at Boston University, Brandeis, Hamilton, Harvard, Holy Cross, Princeton, and the University of London. He is the author of *Whose Welfare? Elite Politics and AFDC* (Lawrence: University Press of Kansas, 1996) and *The Rise of the Conservative Legal Movement* (Princeton: Princeton University Press, 2007). He is the coeditor of *Ethnicity, Social Mobility and Public Policy* (with Tariq Modood and Glenn Loury; New York: Cambridge University Press, 2005) and *Conservatism and American Political Development* (with Brian Glenn, forthcoming). He is beginning work on a new book examining the role of political analysis in legal and policy design.

Stephen White is a Ph.D. candidate in the Department of Political Science at the University of Toronto. His research focuses on political socialization and comparative electoral behavior.

Acknowledgments

Like all intellectual endeavors, this book should be situated in its specific historical context. Our original idea was to bring together a group of North American and European scholars who were each asked to explore an aspect of "American Exceptionalism." We essentially wanted to know how and why the United States continued to appear so different from its democratic allies.

In our two days of meetings, under the auspices of the University of Colorado's Tocqueville Initiative, we repeatedly found that our conversations were driven in two directions that we had not anticipated. On the one hand, the discussions of differences and similarities between the United States and its allies inevitably led to disagreements and sometimes heated arguments about American foreign policy. On the other hand, we were continually confronted by the fact that it was almost as difficult to talk about America as a single or coherent social and political entity as it is to talk about "Europe." As our group discussion evolved, we soon came to understand that these two phenomena are related: The growing political and social divisions *inside* the countries of the West are profoundly shaping the meanings and agendas of the West.

Clearly these ideas merited further consideration. We quickly agreed to reconvene later that year at the University of Toronto's Institute of European Studies with the generous support of the European Commission. Here we delved more deeply into the social evolution of American and European societies and specifically asked ourselves how these changes are refracted in the obviously difficult relationship between America and its democratic friends. We all agreed that the policies and personalities of individual American and European leaders, especially after September 11, 2001, rendered transatlantic relations more fraught than they otherwise would have been.

Yet what was dividing the West was clearly more than a few personalities or a handful of policies.

At this point, we realized we were working on a project that was unique. This is neither a book just on American exceptionalism, nor is it yet another wistful remembrance of transatlantic opportunities lost. Instead, this book offers a deep and thoughtful study of the evolution of countries that so obviously share common ideals and beliefs *and* an analysis of how and why these countries are growing apart.

We are deeply grateful to the friends and colleagues who have contributed to the development of this project. We would especially like to thank the several colleagues who offered careful readings of the papers at each of our workshops. Michael Adams, Vanessa Baird, Kenneth Bickers, Colin Dueck, Desmond King, and Renan Levine should not be blamed for what we did not include in this book, but they can be rightly commended for some of the better ideas that did make it into this book. We would also like to express our gratitude to two anonymous readers for Cambridge University Press. These reviewers' comments and criticisms were helpful in their details, but we especially appreciate their encouragement to engage the "bigger arguments" that this book develops. Andy Saff, our copy editor, did a wonderful job melding the styles and voices of so many different authors. Finally, we would like to thank our editor, Lew Bateman, for his confidence and good judgment.

Jeffrey Kopstein (Toronto)
Sven Steinmo (Florence)
June 8, 2007

Growing Apart?

INTRODUCTION

Growing Apart?

America and Europe in the Twenty-First Century

Sven Steinmo and Jeffrey Kopstein

As the Cold War drew to a close, most students of international politics had come to believe that the relationship between the United States and Europe was much more than an alliance of interest. The "West" was also a set of ideas: liberal democracy, human rights, and welfare state capitalism were more than just temporary expedients. Taken together, they were the key institutional expressions of the shared values of the West. It is true that the West has never been a unified and homogeneous entity. Still, most of us believed that there was a common project and, whatever our differences, what held us together was far more important than what divided us. Indeed, many of us believed that the countries of the industrialized West were also becoming more alike in their basic values, their models of political economy, and their modes of foreign policy.

Of course, it was never politically correct to assert this, and many of us offered ritual critiques of "the end of history" thesis.[1] Yet it was sometimes difficult to see things otherwise. The louder the protests against the assertion of the final triumph of liberalism, the more inevitable it all seemed. It was hard to deny that Western democratic liberalism won out because this system was simply better than all the alternatives. Consequently, the American–European alliance would dominate the world for as long as any reasonable analyst could foresee. The attacks of September 11, 2001, drove home this consensus. When terrorists brought down the World Trade Center in New York, it was understood that this was not just an attack on America. It was an attack on the very idea of the West.

Who would have thought that only a few years later this basic consensus would be brought into question? Rather than confidently predicting the

[1] Francis Fukuyama, *The End of History and the Last Man* (Glencoe: Free Press, 1992).

inevitable spread of liberal values and institutions across the globe, many
have come to question whether these institutions are even appropriate for
much of the world.[2] Whereas the 9/11 attacks at first invoked enormous
support for the United States, a sense of common identity and declarations
from European allies that "We are All Americans," such sentiments gave
way within a few short years to blossoming anti-Americanism and a new
"Transatlantic Divide."[3] Relations between the United States and its traditional European allies quickly recovered from the low point reached in the
months before the war in Iraq in early 2003, but the periodic attempts since
then to recapture the lost essence of the Cold War partnership have only
highlighted the fact that something has changed.

The purpose of this book is to offer a deeper understanding of the sources
of cohesion and division both within and between the developed democracies in North America and Europe. To explore these issues, we have brought
together a diverse group of experts, each of whom has been asked to examine
various dimensions of the growing divide between America and its historical friends and ideological allies. This book does not offer a singular and
straightforward answer to complicated questions. Instead it offers a set of
fascinating essays, each of which probes different dimensions underlying
America's increasingly strained relationship with its democratic neighbors.

Typically, those who have written on the strained relationship within the
West focus on foreign policy and speak to these issues as if they were exclu-
sively problems of international relations. The central idea motivating this
book is different. This book is premised on the belief that in order to explain
what is happening *between* democratic states of the West, one must first
understand what is happening *inside* these countries. By focusing our analysis

---

[2] This is especially true of the disappointment with democracy promotion. See Thomas
Carothers, "The End of the Transition Paradigm," *Journal of Democracy*, vol. 13, no. 2, 2002,
pp. 5–21; idem, *Critical Mission: Essays on Democracy Promotion* (Washington: Carnegie
Endowment for Peace, 2004).

[3] The literature is large. On the attitudes preceding the invasion of Iraq, a good statement
is Charles Kupchan, "The End of the West," *Atlantic Monthly*, November 2002; on the
impact of the Iraq War, see Philip H. Gordon and Jeremy Shapiro, *Allies at War: America,
Europe, and the Crisis over Iraq* (New York: McGraw-Hill, 2004); Laurent Cohen-Tanugi,
Alliance at Risk: The United States and Europe since September 11 (Baltimore: Johns Hopkins
University Press, 2003); Charles A. Kupchan, *The End of the American Era: U.S. Foreign
Policy and the Geopolitics of the Twenty-First Century* (New York: Knopf, 2002); Peter H.
Merkel, *The Distracted Eagle: The Rift between America and Old Europe* (London and New
York: Routledge, 2005); Bruno Tertrais, *La Guerre Sans Fin: L'Amérique Dans L'Engregage*
(Paris: Édition du Seuil et La République des Idées, 2004); on anti-Americanism, see Andrei
Markovits, *Uncouth Nation: Why Europe Dislikes America* (Princeton: Princeton University
Press, 2006).

on what is happening inside Western democratic states and exploring the divergent trends within them, we can gain far greater insight into how, why, and whether the West is truly growing apart.

We approached the design and contents of this book in an intuitive way. We asked ourselves: what are the most important social forces and policy areas shaping democratic capitalist states today? The answers were obvious: the persistence of religion as a force in public life in America and Europe; changing social values within democratic states; the decline of traditional news media and the growth of "new" media in its many forms; the increasing economic competition between states for capital, labor, and jobs in a globalizing world economy; the role of neoliberal economics and the privately financed think tanks that promote free-market ideals; immigration and the consequent growth of ethnic diversity in rich democracies; and last, but certainly not least, the divergent interests and identities of different North Atlantic Treaty Organization (NATO) nations after the demise of the Soviet Union. We believed that only by looking deeply into each of these different policy issues and social trends could one truly gauge whether the United States and its democratic allies are in fact growing apart. But from the outset, we understood that no single author could examine all of these diverse issues in anything but a superficial manner. Thus, we sought out some of the world's leading experts in each of these social and policy arenas and specifically asked them to explore how, why, and whether America is different from its democratic neighbors and also where they saw these countries heading.[4]

Are we growing apart? All of our contributors point to differences between the United States and Europe that were in place well before the crisis in transatlantic relations of 2003 over the invasion of Iraq. The different place of religion and immigration in the United States and Europe, the different level of trust in the market as the primary means of distributing resources, and the varying degree of commitment to multilateralism all reflect long-term institutional, creedal, and power differentials across the Atlantic.

Where our contributors disagree is on the matter of trajectory. For the most part, those who concentrate on domestic politics and society maintain that the divide is in fact growing. The United States and Europe are increasingly different. At the same time, however, these domestic analyses also stress deep divides *within* the societies of the West that in some ways rival those between them. On the other hand, our two contributors who

---

[4] This group met first in Boulder, Colorado, in early June 2005, and again in Toronto, Ontario, in October of that same year.

focus on transatlantic relations maintain that the divide on foreign affairs between the two continents exists, but the evidence of it deepening is scant at best. In short, the story is one of the United States and Europe growing apart as societies and polities but also managing to find enough common ground to survive, not only as an alliance but even as a community of nations on the global stage.

Whether divergent societies will be able to sustain their close alliance into the future must remain an open question. It is worth thinking through, however, the forces that caused the question to be posed in the first place. What we find is not the narcissism of small differences between the United States and its democratic allies but a reconsideration of the meaning and importance of these differences in light of a changed world at the end of the Cold War.

After the Cold War

The collapse of the Soviet Union was certainly a victory for liberal democracy. It was, however, a victory especially for the United States, the leader of the West and the most significant exemplar of the liberal creed. In the eyes of many, it was American liberalism, not European social democracy, that brought down the Berlin Wall. This fact (or at least this interpretation of the facts) has carried enormous consequences. In the United States, the end of the Cold War demonstrated the essential benevolence of the American way of doing things and proved how much the rest of the world needed U.S. leadership.[5] For Americans, this point in time marked the beginning of a new era in which U.S. influence could guide the world toward ever greater peace, prosperity, and freedom. Indeed, for most Americans, the defeat of communism was proof that market economies are not just more efficient than state-dominated ones, they are also morally superior. The economic and political collapse of communism reaffirmed American faith in individual liberty and economic liberalism. Clearly, not everyone saw it exactly this way, but this was the dominant view in the United States.

Europeans, it turned out, drew quite different conclusions from communism's demise. For many, the end of the Cold War engendered a profound ambivalence about America's role in the world and a deep concern for the future of their social order. Yes, the West had become rich under benevolent American hegemony. But what would the world look like with only one superpower? Would the United States always use its unchallenged power

---

[5] In the words of the Clinton administration, the United States was the "indispensible nation."

wisely? Who would stand up for the welfare state if there were no systemic rival challenging the market economy? Who would preserve the hard-won victories of social and Christian democracy in Europe? With these questions in mind, many Europeans came to view the European Union not merely as a large market but as a potential economic, political, and perhaps even military counterpoise to the United States.[6] In short, the victory of the market over the state at the end of the Cold War created a profound intellectual and moral challenge within the West. It is precisely this challenge that raised the question of whether Europe and America are growing apart.

These dilemmas of domestic politics and society were mirrored in the realm of foreign policy. In an ironic twist of fate, at the very moment when American power appeared to be at its zenith, it became superfluous for many Europeans. Absent the threat from the East, Europeans soon questioned the need for the American shield that had so long protected them. Moreover, although it was obvious that capitalism was victorious over communism, it was far from obvious that America's version of capitalism was preferable to European social democracy. The spread of the American economic model (under the rubric of "globalization") was increasingly perceived by many (although not all) Europeans as a threat to the embedded capitalism that had stabilized politics and society after World War II. What was before considered American political leadership was now seen in many parts of Europe as American unilateralism and what was considered American economic leadership was now thought by many to be rapacious neoliberalism. Of course, not everyone perceived the American unipolar moment as a threat, and not all European leaders shared then French Foreign Minister Hubert Védrine's characterization of the United States as a *hyperpuissance*, but many, perhaps most, did.

A New Great Transformation?

The end of the Cold War laid bare a set of political, economic, and social challenges that in important ways recalls those of an earlier era so brilliantly described by Karl Polanyi in his seminal work *The Great Transformation*.[7] In that study, Polanyi showed that the triumph of liberal capitalism in the nineteenth and early twentieth centuries was the product of political will and economic interest. He argued that capitalism did not win out because

---

[6] Jürgen Habermas, "Why Europe Needs a Constitution," *New Left Review*, September–October 2001.

[7] Karl Polanyi, *The Great Transformation* (Boston: Beacon Press, 2001).

it was simply more "natural," or because it better reflected human nature, but because those who promoted this system had become economically and politically more powerful than their opponents. Perhaps Polanyi's greatest insight was to show that the victory of liberal capitalist ideas and institutions was destined always to remain partial. Capitalism's victory engendered its own antithesis in the form of the twin rejectionist ideologies of communism and fascism. In the long run, after two world wars, the desire for a pure liberalism was blunted and the global order could be stabilized by international institutions, democratic politics, and social policies, the historic compromise that political scientists referred to as embedded liberalism.

There are of course crucial differences between the post–Cold War world and that of the first half of the twentieth century. But there are important parallels, too. Once again, there are those with significant political and economic power at their back who see this moment as a time to push forward to an ever more ideal version of what has made modern capitalism so successful. And once again there is a countermovement. These forces should not be understood as simply America versus the rest of the world. In contrast to this, the evidence within this book points to the existence of a "two-track movement"; the centrifugal and centripetal forces playing themselves out today can be seen not only between but also within the states of the democratic West.

Are we once again in the 1930s? Clearly not. One of the key differences is that at this moment free-market capitalism is typically identified with one country, the United States. Furthermore, even within the United States, liberal capitalism has been restrained by calls for social justice. Like its European counterparts, the United States also witnessed an historic social compromise in the last half of the twentieth century. But America's compromise was always different from Europe's. The vast open spaces, unimaginable natural resources, and the near constant flow of disaffected European immigrants seemed to confirm the belief that it was the market itself, unguided by the state, that created wealth. Thus even while a compromise was struck, the balance in the United States always tilted in favor of the market.

The Europeans, by contrast, never shared the Americans' unbridled enthusiasm for the market. Yet, as long as the Soviet Union remained a threat to Western Europe, the differences between the American and European models of capitalism seemed more differences in degree than in kind. The Soviet threat also made American leadership, and especially American military power, a matter of existential importance for most Europeans. In short, notwithstanding transatlantic differences in views about how society should be organized, throughout the 1980s and even the beginning of the 1990s, the American economic model appeared to be particular to the United States and American power seemed to most citizens on both sides of the Atlantic to be benign, even benevolent.

Yet, just as Polanyi could discern a countermovement against market society, a countermovement that took on multiple ideological forms from left to right, so too can one now identify a multifaceted countermovement to the victory of the American economic model and the singularity of American power that started to take shape towards the end of the 1990s and in the first decade of the twenty-first century. Instead of opposition to market society alone, however, the new countermovement encompasses opposition to a much broader array of freedoms that have developed since Polanyi's time. Although outside of the West this opposition has occasionally taken on violent forms, even within the West it is precisely the questions of how free, how liberal, and how democratic society should be that are at the core of our understanding of the divide within the West.

Perhaps most illustrative of the new countermovement is the reshuffling occurring in the conventional views of what is "left" and "right" in both America and Europe. Consider, for example, the continuing debates over free trade, immigration, democracy promotion, and religion. Much of the most biting criticism of outsourcing and wage competition now comes not from its traditional home on the left but from the populist right. Perhaps more surprising, much of the most sustained criticism of immigration and the free movement of people across international borders has emerged not on the nativist right but on the environmentalist left. Democracy promotion has become the bête noir not only of the anti-imperialist left but of the realist right. Finally, on questions of religion, it is not only the right that argues for a place for religion in public life (for Christianity) but also the multicultural left (for Islam).

European and American populism, of both the right and the left, appear increasingly cut from the same cloth. Democrats and liberals across America have gnashed their teeth over Thomas Frank's polemic "What's the Matter with Kansas?" The problem set out by Frank is that people in the middle of the country apparently vote against their self-interest. The conservatives have duped these hapless red state voters, Frank maintains, by talking about moral values but enacting policies that these people should not favor.[8] Rarely do these same liberals wonder what is the matter with France (or Norway or Denmark), where economic nationalists of the left and xenophobes of the

---

[8] Thomas Frank, *What's the Matter with Kansas? How Conservatives Won the Heart of America* (New York: Henry Holt and Co., 2004).

right are leading some of the most popular parties in these countries. This suggests that American fans of Lou Dobbs on CNN and working-class Jean-Marie Le Pen supporters in France are products of the same phenomenon, a backlash against the triumph of liberalism. The key differences in political expression are not so much the products of different frustrations, but of different political institutional structures that channel these sentiments in different ways.

Of course, from the standpoint of Africa, Latin America, or Asia, what potentially divides America and Europe may seem trivial compared with what unites them. Both are rich and powerful compared to the other continents. The bulk of world trade flows back and forth across the Atlantic between Europe and North America. Yet, even with a smoothly functioning West in the eyes of much of the rest of the world, the opponents of the West remain keenly aware of the fissures within and between the societies of America and Europe. Whether they are able to exploit these fissures to divide the West from without will depend, in part, upon whether the West is already growing apart from within.

Religion and Public Values

One of the most surprising trends across the West has been the sustained and even growing impact of religion on political life. In the United States, a country founded with a constitutional separation of church and state, religious leaders are both active and influential in political campaigns and public policy. Indeed, politicians seem compelled to profess their faith in order to get elected. In Europe, the growing appeal of Islam among immigrants from the Muslim world has become one of the most difficult political and moral challenges facing these putatively Christian nations.

These developments are surprising because modernity and secularism were supposed to go hand in hand. Judeo-Christian teachings may have helped lay the groundwork for capitalist modernity, but social theorists since Max Weber have maintained that organized religion would decline in importance across the West. This expectation was founded on the belief that as societies modernize, citizens should become more rational and less superstitious. Though rarely stated explicitly, the implicit argument here is that religion *is* superstition: Religious belief grows out of the unknown and, as science advances, people should look for increasingly rational explanations for the natural world around them rather than mystical or "irrational" ones. The inevitable result, so the argument goes, is that religion would slowly die off everywhere.

In Europe we do indeed see a secular decline in religious institutions, church attendance, and the role of organized religions in public life. But we also see a countermovement. To be sure, political Islam may currently constitute a small ripple in Europe's political landscape, but scholars and journalists alike now view this as a potential tsunami due to both demographic trends and because Christianity *is in fact* deeply institutionalized into European politics and identity. In institutionally secular America, one can also see the rise of politicized religion as a countermovement to the social liberalism that has dominated cultural life since at least the 1960s. Although it is not true that Americans on the whole are more religious today than they were several decades ago, it is clearly the case that religion is an increasingly powerful force in American public life. Whereas churches in Europe are more likely to be filled with tourists than worshipers, American churches are thriving, many offering four or five services every Sunday to congregations that measure in the thousands.

What accounts for these differences? Steven Pfaff's fascinating analysis begins by noting that there is no evidence that Americans have become more "spiritual" in recent years. Neither do they value spirituality more than their European counterparts. On the contrary, he believes that there is a market for "spiritual goods" in every society. This demand is met outside of traditional churches in most of the advanced world. In the United States, with its unregulated religious marketplace and fierce interdenominational competition for adherents, spiritual leaders are more likely to satisfy the needs of their constituents. In Europe, on the other hand, traditional church leaders draw a state salary whether they meet these needs or not. As a result, Americans go to church and Europeans do not.

These institutional differences are important because they may have political consequences. As anyone who has attended fundamentalist religious services in America will know, pastors do not restrict their sermons to spiritual matters. Of course, people of all denominations attend church at least in part because they want to understand the world in which they live. In the United States, however, religious leaders increasingly use the pulpit to espouse political and not simply worldly advice. (This was equally true of Reverend Martin Luther King as it was of Reverend Jerry Falwell and the local imam.)

What do people "learn" in churches? What should we make of the fact that Americans go to church more often than Europeans, but both are equally spiritual? We want to suggest that the prominence of religion in America is important not only because of the political activism of its religious leaders, but also because of what happens *in* the church. In other words, religious leaders convey social and political messages. As Pfaff notes, in America religiosity is closely correlated with positive attitudes toward the free market, whereas in Europe religiosity tends to correlate with critical attitudes toward the market.[9] The exact explanation for this difference is unclear, but it is certainly reasonable to think that churches that provide a large number of social services and educational facilities in the United States regard the state provisions of these services as competition.

The logic of this analysis casts an entirely new light on the growing religious divide in Europe. If we accept that the separation between church and state has made American religious entrepreneurs more competitive and better at catering to the needs of their "customers," then it stands to reason that the institutional discrimination against the Islamic leaders in Europe will also work to sharpen their entrepreneurial skills. Moreover, at the same moment when the traditional welfare state is under intense fiscal strain (as Mark Blyth discusses in Chapter 5), these newly emerging Islamic "religious firms" stand waiting in the wings anxious and willing to fill in the void. As the American case shows, once their customers are in the pews (or on their prayer mats), spiritual leaders do not restrict themselves to matters of spirtuality. As this is the case, we may indeed be "growing apart," but in ways that might make Europeans just as uncomfortable as any liberal American.

The increasing sophistication of political/religious leaders helps explain why American politics has become so polarized in recent years. American values are in fact dividing into two broad groups. Significantly, as the chapter by Christopher Cochrane, Neil Nevitte, and Steve White demonstrates, the values within each group are becoming *more coherent*. Whereas for Christians in Europe religiosity and moral values have essentially decoupled, in the United States those who define themselves as religious have become ever more traditionalist in their moral outlooks while those with secular orientations are growing more permissive.

Cochrane et al. convincingly demonstrate that people with strong religious beliefs are systematically different from their secular counterparts on a broad palette of cognate values, and these differences are increasing. Perhaps most significantly, the relationship between traditional religious values and attitudes toward distributive justice is diverging in America. While in Europe there does not appear to be an association, in the United States "left" and "right" are increasingly "bundled" with traditional religious values. As they note:

[K]nowing where an American stood on moral values meant that one could predict with increasing accuracy where he or she stood on economic justice, left-right

[9] Cochrane et al.'s findings in Chapter 2 of this book support this contention.

location or levels of religiosity.... Indeed, the United States is the only country in our analysis where moral outlooks predict attitudes toward economic egalitarianism more effectively than income!

Of course, we do not know exactly why we see this correlation. There is no logical reason why those who self-identify as devout should be less tolerant and forgiving of economic failure and more hostile toward public generosity than secular indivuduals. But apparently this is what the data show in the American case. The evidence suggests, moreover, that these divisions within the United States are likely to be with us for a while.

We do not mean to suggest that the rightward turn in the United States is simply a product of the growing power of religious fundamentalists. If it is true that the views of "middle" Americans, at least, have moved away from those of Europe, certainly the media also play a role. In Chapter 3, Don Morrison, the former senior editor of European and Asian editions of *Newsweek* magazine, offers a nuanced reading of the media's position in the United States and Europe. In response to the question of whether the press "has been sowing the seeds of mistrust between Europe and the United States," Morrison answers, "possibly, yes, to a limited degree, but not enough to matter." Although the war in Iraq and the policies of the Bush administration undoubtedly worsened relations and made it easy for the media on both sides of the Atlantic to whip up emotions, "well before the United States arrived in Baghdad," Morrison reminds us, "there were factors driving the U.S. and European opinion apart." The problem, Morrison maintains, is that the media on both sides of the Atlantic are increasingly driven by market forces on the one hand and by fear of the new media technologies on the other. As Michael Kinsley has recently argued, "The newspaper industry is having a psychic meltdown over the threat posed by the Internet."[10] Citizens everywhere in the West can easily read any number of different news sources and see whatever they want to see and hear whatever they want to hear – and apparently they want to hear and see different things. At the same time, the media are businesses and in order to maximize advertising revenue, publishers and broadcasters need to reach as large an audience as possible and are therefore tempted to "report" what their viewers, listeners, and readers already believe. Perhaps, as Morrison suggests in his discussion of the run-up to the war in Iraq, "Europeans and Americans are being given different versions of reality."

The counterintuitive result of these trends is that the press in America appears to be becoming more partisan while the press in Europe is less so – or

[10] Michael Kinsley, "The Twilight of Objectivity," *Daily Camera*, April 3, 2006.

at least such is the case if we interpret "partisan" as the left-right divide that has traditionally defined European politics. Perhaps we should not be so surprised, however. Our first three chapters suggest that America *is* dividing, whereas there appears to be substantially greater consensus in Europe and that consensus is increasingly anti-American. We will return to this theme later on, but certainly one of basic facts of life today in Europe is that these societies increasingly define themselves in contrast to America. If the role of the media is to be skeptical of power, then it is their duty to be skeptical of America. And in Europe (and Canada), this skepticism also sells papers.

Globalization, Americanization, and the End of the Good Life?

For many Europeans, the victory of market competition poses a threat to their generous welfare states. The fear is that economic competition will depress wages, erode employment security, and decrease the power of nation-states to regulate the economy. Although people may want social protection and redistributive policies in many democratic countries, market society, it is believed, will render such policies unworkable. In other words, globalization (the free movement of goods, services, and people across borders) will inevitably bring about not just "convergence," but more ominously a "race to the bottom" in government revenues and the provision of social services. For example, in a recent article in *Foreign Policy*, titled "The Let Us Eat Cake Generation," Elisabeth Eaves articulated what many already believed about the student protesters in France. These protesters are "people who are out of touch with the world beyond France ... who are intent on protecting the privileges of a bygone era."[11] Lulled into their "delicious life," as columnist David Brooks described it, Europeans are unwilling to accept the need to adapt to the realities of the new world economy. Margaret Thatcher summed it up with the acronym *TINA*: there is no alternative. Either adjust to the rigors of the new competitive world economy by producing as cheaply as possible and by cutting back on taxes and social welfare spending or suffer the fate of long-term economic decline.[12]

Mark Blyth's chapter, "One Ring to Bind Them All," argues that the convergence thesis is wrong. In fact, he finds a "growing divergence" between Europe and America over the kinds of societies that they want to build and sustain, "and such divergence lies at the core of why the United States and

---

[11] Elisabeth Eaves, "The Let Us Eat Cake Generation," *Foreign Policy*, Web exclusive, April 4, 2006.

[12] David Brooks, "Fear and Rejection," *New York Times*, June 2, 2005.

Europe are indeed growing apart today." Noting the profound challenges facing all advanced capitalist nations, Blyth tells us that Europeans not only do not want to accept the hyperliberalism of the American model, *but also that they do not have to.* Blyth contradicts the convergence thesis with his own thesis, that economic policy is not a matter of necessity but, rather, a battle over ideas.

To be sure, in the last years of the twentieth century, neoliberal economics seemed hegemonic. Not only did Democratic U.S. President Bill Clinton embrace these new ideas, but European governments from Sweden to Portugal seemed to be following suit. Blyth reminds us, however, that although Europe may have looked as though it were adopting the new orthodoxy, the continent is not a single political economy with a singular set of problems. Global economic competition (to say nothing of demographic change) has undoubtedly helped change the background music of many policy discussions across Europe. But this does not mean that all Europeans must dance to the same (American) tune.[13]

Some might interpret the 2007 victory of French President Nicholas Sarkozy as evidence that "even the French" are finally giving up on their hallowed social model. Such an interpretation would be wrong. Throughout his campaign, Sarkozy was very careful to tell voters that his government would not threaten the basics of the French social welfare state, even while he promised significant reforms of that welfare state. There is of course plenty of room for reform, but scholars have yet to find evidence in France of plans to abandon foundational programs such as universal health care or even most of France's job protections. Indeed, Sarkozy's views can be seen as a prime example of the mixed attitudes held by many Europeans toward America and the "American model." On the one hand there is a deep admiration for the creativity and independence of Americans, and at the same time a deep dismay and patent distaste for the many of the social outcomes produced by the "American model." Why do so many Europeans reject the new neoliberal orthodoxy? One answer, of course, could be that Europeans are simply deluding themselves and will eventually come around

---

[13] It is also interesting to consider the differences within the United States. The differences among Sweden, Poland, and Germany, for example, are certainly great, but are they greater than the differences among Alabama, New York, and Minnesota? Some comparisons are useful here: Per capita income (2005) in the United States ranged from $53,102 in Connecticut to $26,257 in Mississippi, and from $69,736 in Luxembourg (or $45,674 in Ireland) to $15,981 in Portugal. The official unemployment rate in America ranged from 2.4 percent in Hawaii to 9.9 percent in Mississippi and from 4.3 percent in Ireland to 9.6 percent in Greece.

to the American model. Another explanation is that they simply don't have to accept it. A growing body of evidence demonstrates that this "cut back or die" argument is simply wrong. Although the continental welfare states ran into trouble in the first years of the twenty-first century, the impressive performance of many European countries defies the notion that economic competition *requires* low taxes and small governments. In fact, *there is no correlation between economic performance and tax burdens and/or social spending.*[14] Surely, many believe that there is such a connection, but real evidence for this connection is simply absent. Moreover, the fiscal reality is that not even the United States has scaled back the size of its government. Notwithstanding the antigovernment philosophy of the Republican Party, which controlled both houses of Congress for twelve years between 1994 and 2006, public spending did not decrease. Even excluding military spending, U.S. government outlays *increased* during the Bush administration. Apparently, the pressures identified by Polanyi to soften capitalism's rougher edges impose themselves on Republicans as well as social democrats.

Steven Teles and Daniel Kenney, in Chapter 5, "Spreading the Word," systematically explore the remarkably conscious effort to spread these neoliberal ideas around the world. Their chapter opens with a basic introduction to what might be called the "vast right-wing conspiracy," but it quickly cautions the reader not to assume that this conspiracy has been successful or even competent. In fact, the subtitle for this chapter could well be "Why Neoliberal Ideas Fail in Europe But Succeed in America." In their answer to this question, they also offer insight into one of Cochrane et al. and Pfaff's surprising findings, namely that "traditionalists" in America (but not Europe) accept free-market ideas. They show that there has been a concerted and well-funded effort to connect traditional values and free-market ideas in the United States, but that for institutionally bounded reasons this connection simply does not stick in Europe (or for that matter in the developing world). Part of the reason for this divergence brings us back to the different role of the state in Europe. Just as church leaders find themselves bound to the state, so too in Europe (and much to the chagrin of European neoliberals) corporate and business leaders are integrated into the state through corporatist

---

[14] See Peter H. Lindert, *Growing Public: Social Spending and Economic Growth since the Eighteenth Century* (Cambridge and New York: Cambridge University Press, 2004); Philipp Genschel, "Globalization and the Welfare State: A Retrospective," *Journal of European Public Policy*, vol. 11, no. 4, 2004, pp. 613–36; Duane Swank and Sven Steinmo, "The New Political Economy of Taxation in Advanced Capitalist Democracies," *American Journal of Political Science*, vol. 46, no. 3, 2002, pp. 642–55.

arrangements.[15] As a result, European business interests are simply less hostile to government than the same interests in America.[16]

Falling Apart?

In the spring of 2006, mass protests broke out across America. In a response to congressional efforts to close the borders and punish illegal immigrants, hundreds of thousands of people went to the streets to demonstrate and claim their American identity. In what the *New York Times* described as a "precious cause," many of these protesters stood on the U.S. Mall and recited the Pledge of Allegiance, "reading from yellow sheets printed in English and in a crude phonetic spelling to help Spanish speakers pronounce the unfamiliar words. Something about the latter version – with its strange sense of ineloquent desire – was enough to provoke tears."[17]

Ai pledch aliyens to di fleg
Of d Yunaited Esteits of America
An tu di republic for wich it estands
Uan naishion, ander Gad
Indivisibol
Wit liberti an yostis
For oll.[18]

The reason that the *Times* and so many other Americans found this moment moving is that America's long history of offering foreigners homes would seem to give immigration a special place in the American psyche. To be sure, the United States has lapsed into long periods of nativism and outright racist discrimination.[19] But the Statue of Liberty is still a powerful symbol in American political culture. And if "ideas" matter, as Blyth, Teles, and Kenney argue, then it is not surprising that the idea of America as a land of immigrants should still have an important role to play in the story.

Randall Hansen's Chapter 6, "Work, Welfare, and Wanderlust: Immigration and Integration in Europe and North America," thus addresses one of

---

[15] Peter Hall and David Soskice, eds., *Varieties of Capitalism: Institutional Foundations of Comparative Advantage* (Oxford: Oxford University Press, 2001).

[16] Peter A. Swenson, *Capitalists against Markets: The Making of Labor Markets and Welfare States in the United States and Sweden* (Oxford and New York: Oxford University Press, 2002).

[17] "People Power," *New York Times*, April 12, 2006.

[18] Ibid.

[19] Desmon King, *Making Americans: Immigration, Race and the Origins of the Diverse Democracy* (Cambridge: Cambridge University Press, 2000).

the most difficult and politically explosive issues facing liberal democracies today. Again, the expectation in this case is that outcomes should be different on each side of the Atlantic. For most of the past three hundred years, people emigrated from Europe to America, whereas it has only been in the latter half of the twentieth century that economic growth in Europe afforded these countries the ability to be net importers rather than exporters of labor.[20]

Many may find it surprising to discover that Europe and America are more alike today than expected. In fact, by the 1990s, the demographic makeup in Europe and America looks "broadly similar." Indeed, some countries in Europe have a substantially higher immigrant population than does the United States.[21] But although they may look somewhat similar demographically, the political implications of growing ethnic diversity are quite different on each side of the Atlantic. This is because European nations, Canada, and the United States are pursuing widely different strategies both with respect to whom they let in and what they do with these newcomers once they arrive. The Canadians, for example, have an explicit policy of encouraging immigration of highly skilled and/or wealthy immigrants. Historically, America recruited precisely this type of individual in what was known as the great "brain drain," but today U.S. policy for the most part shuts out such immigrants. Thus the vast majority of those who do arrive are low-skilled workers with low levels of education.

The great fear in the United States, as the debate over immigration in Congress demonstrates, is that these new low-skilled immigrants do not integrate into "mainstream" American culture and instead concentrate themselves into cultural and linguistic enclaves. This, sadly, is precisely the pattern witnessed in Europe. Europeans have attempted to close their borders to all but political refugees and "family unification" in recent years. Today in Europe there are significant efforts to move away from the multiculturalism of earlier years toward a more explicitly integrationist approach. Europeans are increasingly adopting policies designed to develop immigrants' language

---

[20] Interestingly, as the United States took measures to close its borders (or at least steeply restrict entry), the demand for labor in Europe grew to the point where labor started to arrive from the very parts of the world from where the United States attempted to restrict immigration.

[21] Indeed, seven OECD countries have larger foreign-born populations (as a percentage of the population) than does the United States. See http://titania.sourceoecd.org/vl = 10969590/ cl = 12/nw = 1/rpsv/factbook/01-03-01.htm. In fourteen nations, immigrants account for 10 percent or more of the population. They account for approximately 12 percent of the United States population. See Jean-Christophe Dumont, and Georges Lemaitre, "Counting Immigrants and Expatriates in OECD Countries: A New Perspective," in OECD, ed., *Directorate for Employment, Labor and Social Affairs (DELSA)* (Paris: OECD).

skills and tests their acceptance of European liberal values.[22] It is ironic that as European nations have moved toward more explicitly integrationist policies, the United States Congress has debated legislation that would have created a new and legal class of temporary *Gastarbeiter*.

Perhaps the most important difference between the European strategy for integrating immigrants and that of the United States and Canada, however, is that in the more market-oriented United States, new immigrants must make it on their own. Little help awaits them upon arrival and they must rely on family and friends to find work, which they almost always do. In Europe, whether or not integrationist policies are successful, generous welfare states mean that new immigrants are less dependent on the labor market. "The result," Hansen notes,

is that a legal migrant arriving in Europe will face the choice between, on the one hand, seeking a job in an often less-than-buoyant market and (because her qualifications will likely not be recognized) accepting a poorly paid and unrewarding position and, on the other, accepting comfortable, clean social housing and sufficient monthly support to eke out a living. The choice should be clear. In the United States, a legal migrant will face the choice between work and starvation.

And where does this leave Europe? In a bind. Given an aging population, Europe needs to import labor and most likely increase the average age of retirement. Yet, with more highly regulated labor markets and more expensive tax regimes, it is far from clear that Europeans can compete effectively for high-skilled workers. If, on the other hand, they change strategies and begin to import low-skilled workers, these immigrant workers are quite likely to fill the ranks of the structurally unemployed. To make matters even more difficult, as Pfaff might point out, these young immigrants become easy targets for religious entrepreneurs, who may well interest them in extremist politics.

The Transatlantic Divide

When we think about the West, we mean not merely the existence of a common political, social, and economic model. We also mean the relations *between* the United States and its democratic allies in Europe and Canada. Are relations between America and Europe growing more distant, as they appear to be in their diverging domestic paths of development? The dispute

---

[22] For example, immigrants to Germany must take a test that contains questions about German institutions, history, society, and culture and in some cases asks the immigrant about their attitudes toward homosexuality, forced marriage, and women's rights. In the Netherlands, prospective immigrants must take a test based on a video about Holland that shows pictures of nudity and two men fondly kissing one another.

between the United States on one side and France and Germany on the other over the war in Iraq certainly seemed to point in that direction.

To avoid any undue sentimentality, it is important to ask, just how close was the relationship in the first place? The simple answer is: very close. This is the case whether one considers volume of trade, military cooperation, the movement of students and tourists back and forth across the Atlantic, the reverence that American elites continue to have for European high culture, or simply the similarity of tastes and patterns of consumption. In the decades following World War II, the societies on both sides of the Atlantic became so intertwined that Karl Deutsch quite plausibly posited the existence of a "security community" between the old and new worlds.[23] What he meant by this is that whatever conflicts might occur between the Western allies, one could be sure that these would be settled peacefully. Genuine military conflict between the old and new continents had become unimaginable. This security community was cemented by the broad range of international regimes and institutions in which the United States and its European allies were charter members. Taken together, these multilateral institutions and regimes constituted the international counterpart to the domestic settlements that stabilized liberalism at the domestic level after World War II.

Daniel Drezner, in Chapter 7, "Lost in Translation: The Transatlantic Divide over Diplomacy," does not question the existence of a security community and the importance of multilateralism, but he does show that Americans and Europeans value multilateral institutions for different reasons. The United States is the global hegemon. "Because of the importance of reputation," Drezner tells us, "the American view of multilateralism differs from most other countries. For the United States, multilateralism serves only as a means to an end." Europeans, by contrast, tend to see multilateralism as an end in itself. This leads to very different diplomatic styles, something that became evident in 2003 during the dispute between the United States and many of its European allies over the war in Iraq.

Using the insights of game theory, Drezner argues that the Bush administration's disdain for traditional diplomacy and its tendency to issue ultimatums to longstanding allies followed a specific logic, which he labels the

---

[23] Karl W. Deutsch, Sidney A Burrell, Robert A. Kann, Maurice Lee, Jr., Martin Lichterman, Raymond E. Lindgren, Francis L. Loewenheim, and Richard W. Van Wagenen, *Political Community and the North Atlantic Area: International Organization in the Light of Historical Experience* (Princeton: Princeton University Press, 1957). For a modern update and elaboration of the idea, see Emanuel Adler and Michael Barnett, "A Framework for the Study of Security Communities in Theory, Comparison, and History," in Emanuel Adler and Michael Barnett, eds., *Security Communities* (New York: Cambridge University Press, 1998), pp. 29–65.

"grim trigger" strategy. The idea here is that states that do not follow the rules of multilateral commitments (not process but substance) should be relentlessly punished. Any means necessary should be used to enforce the norms underlying the multilateral institutions. "Multilateral institutions that fail to enforce their own norms – such as the United Nations – end up becoming the object of scorn." The logic and purpose of this strategy is to elicit cooperation from states that would otherwise not respond to traditional diplomatic practice. Drezner points to two successes of the Bush administration's grim trigger strategy: the increased cooperation of Pakistan after 9/11 and Libya's renunciation of its nuclear program.

The problem with the grim trigger strategy as employed by the Bush administration with its European allies, however, is that it precludes nurturing the relationship through dialogue and diplomacy, places too much stock in the importance of reputation, and, perhaps most important, lacks flexibility. It never forgives and never forgets. To take the most obvious example, German Chancellor Gerhard Schröder's declaration that Germany would not participate in the Iraq War even if it were given the green light by the United Nations was meant more for domestic consumption during an election campaign than as a once-and-for-all proposition. It was not meant to provoke a crisis in relations with the United States, but the grim trigger strategy left the United States no alternative but to treat it that way.

Still, in the end, Drezner is an optimist. "The transatlantic tiffs over diplomatic style make great headlines," Drezner notes, "but they do not fundamentally alter the transatlantic relationship." Certainly the current rift is difficult, but it can also be temporary. Perhaps the United States has used up the bullets in the grim trigger's gun. The quagmire in Iraq, volatile oil prices, rising American debt, and the appearance of new Asian powers suggest that America will have to reengage diplomatically and multilaterally. Drezner finds evidence for this in the second term of George W. Bush. Whether, having pulled the grim trigger, the United States can go back to being a cooperator remains to be seen. Successful cooperation depends upon trust between the players and, as evolutionary game theory teaches us, trust is easy to destroy but very difficult to reconstruct.

Drezner's optimism about the future of transatlantic relations is shared by his French colleague Laurent Cohen-Tanugi. As Cohen-Tanugi makes clear in Chapter 8, "The Atlantic Divide in Historical Perspective: A View from Europe," the end of the Cold War has exposed a divergence in interests between the United States and Europe that the need for unity during the Cold War had hidden. In his view, much more so than in the four decades before 1989, relations between the two continents will need to be managed carefully – on both sides – and it cannot be assumed that the Americans and the Europeans will share the same vision. Cohen-Tanugi appears to agree with Blyth when he says that the roots of the current of anti-Americanism in Europe are to be found in different worldviews. The disagreements, then, are fundamentally about what kinds of societies we should become. "As the memory of World War II and of the East/West confrontation faded among the younger generations," Cohen-Tanugi maintains, "asserting European 'values' and collective preferences, generally in opposition to the 'American model,' became one of the key justifications of European unification in the political discourse."

He also suggests that the changes *within America* help explain the current conflict. Although he does not put it this way, certainly these change of loci of power in America are also related to the cultural shift (a return to religion and/or traditionalism and a reaffirmation of the market over state redistribution) that Cochrane et al. and Pfaff describe. "At the same time, the shift of America's centers of economic and political power from the East Coast elites of European descent and Atlanticist culture toward the South and the West of the country further distanced the two longstanding allies from one another." In some ways, then, the dispute over how to proceed with the war on terrorism after 9/11 represented the perfect storm in which the latent differences between the two continents laid bare by the end of the Cold War could become manifest. Americans believed that 9/11 changed the world; European believed that what it really changed was America.

Still, Cohen-Tanugi remains an optimist, reminding us that even while the United States and Europe may look like we are "on different planets," the bonds that bind us are resilient.[24] We are still each other's greatest trading partners and "we face a common threat," Islamic fundamentalism and its challenge to the basic values that Americans and Europeans (whatever our differences) clearly share.

Cohen-Tanugi also believes that the fear of Americanization and the spread of the American neoliberal economic model is overdrawn. Where Blyth sees Europeans balking at the Americanization of their economies and societies, especially at the underlying implication that growing inequality is both inevitable and healthy, Cohen-Tanugi takes a broader view. "However pertinent it might be, the objection nevertheless omits the freely accepted and

---

[24] The reference is to Robert Kagan's influential work *Of Paradise and Power: America and Europe in the New World Order* (New York: Knopf, 2003), which built on an earlier article that highlighted important differences of U.S. and European views of the world by characterizing Americans as from "Mars" and Europeans as from "Venus."

very broadly positive character throughout Europe of the transformation of closed and administered economies into open and competitive markets."

Cohen-Tanugi is most fearful of what he calls a "self-fulfilling prophesy" in which the desire to be different forces us to forget that we are mostly alike. Echoing a theme brought out in Morrison's essay, he warns "[t]he principal threat to transatlantic solidarity lies rather in the insidious indoctrination of public opinion by politicians and the media in favor of the separatist argument." Surely, differences will persist, but they need not threaten what he sees as "the civilizational unity of the West."[25] America and Europe do have increasingly different interests and identities that lead them to have different views about the world. These differences need to be understood and carefully managed so as to prevent a vicious cycle of "diplomatic incompetence, nationalistic excess, and popular acrimony." This emphasis on "management" suggests that in contrast to the chapters on domestic politics and society, Cohen-Tanugi believes there is no reason to characterize the United States and Europe as growing apart.

A careful reading of both Drezner's and Cohen-Tanugi's contributions indicates that the security community of the Cold War era may not be dead, but it is a community that we can no longer assume will persist into the future without concerted effort on both sides of the Atlantic to rebuild a common purpose. Much will depend on whether the two sides can agree on a common definition of the primary security threats and whether they can agree on a common set of means to address the threats. If these two tasks can be accomplished, these contributions suggest there is a good chance that the transatlantic alliance and its institutionally based security community can remain healthy even as the economies, polities, and societies of the United States and Europe grow apart.

Conclusion

How are we to square the discordant findings of this book? Can the West really hold together as a security community even if its constituent societies are growing apart?[26] We do not have a set answer to this question. It stands

---

[25] For a systematic rebuttal of the thesis of a "clash of civilizations" within the West, see Cohen-Tanugi, *An Alliance at Risk*, pp. 119 et seq.

[26] See the excellent debate on whether the U.S.-European divide over the war in Iraq represents an erosion of the North Atlantic security community in Michael Cox, "Beyond the West: Terrors in Transatlantia," *European Journal of International Relations*, vol. 11, no. 2, 2005, pp. 203–33; and the response by Vincent Pouliot, "The Alive and Well Transatlantic Security Community: A Theoretical Reply to Michael Cox," *European Journal of International Relations*, vol. 12, no. 1, 2006, pp. 119–27.

to reason, however, that if the divergence in domestic politics and society continues unabated, there will come a time at which the values that bind the West together will no longer be shared. At that point, the West will no longer be a community but merely an "alliance."

We do not appear to be near that point yet and there are several indications that even if the West continues to grow apart, it will not *fall* apart any time soon. For one thing, even where trust in the market diverges sharply, the level of commitment to civic and democratic liberal freedoms remains strong on both sides of the Atlantic. For another, as several of our contributors demonstrate, the divergences within European and North American societies are perhaps just as strong, and in some ways even stronger, than those between them.

In framing this book, we have drawn on Polanyi's imagery of a "double movement" and maintained that one important source of discord within the West is the movement toward ever-freer political and economic markets on the one hand, and the countermovement against it on the other. The end of the Cold War unleashed an unprecedented series of agreements and treaties expanding the scope of the market internationally. The European Union (EU) deepened its market integration and widened its membership in the two decades following 1989. The North American Free Trade Agreement (NAFTA) came on line in 1994. The creation and enlargement of the World Trade Organization (WTO) seemed to be the crowning achievement of liberalism's final victory.

It is now clear, however, that the post–Cold War liberal project generated its own countermovement. Outside of the West, that movement has ranged from the politics of antiglobalization, to a new semi-authoritarianism in many parts of the developing world, to that of radical Islam. Within the West, liberals and populists have squared off against each other on free trade, the welfare state, immigration and integration, and social values. In the short run, the populists have succeeded in stalling, and in some respects even derailing, the post-1989 liberal project. The populist countermovement has ensured that NAFTA is unlikely in the near future to expand farther into South America or develop into a customs union among its existing members. The EU is equally unlikely to deepen integration or broaden its membership to include Turkey in the near future. The failure of the Doha round of WTO negotiations ensured that open agricultural markets will not soon threaten the livelihood of farmers in Europe and America.

Economic populism has been tracked by similar trends in politics. Concern over immigration as a source of wage competition and cultural decline has become a mainstream political issue on both sides of the Atlantic. Populist parties have served in government throughout Europe, and many European countries have openly repudiated their earlier commitment to multiculturalism and embarked on serious assimilationist drives. In the United States, populism has been carried not only by politicians but perhaps more importantly by a new nativism in the media. On both sides of the Atlantic, the liberal universalism of democracy promotion as the cornerstone of foreign policy (on both the left and the right) has come under attack.

Where will this end? Will the domestic countermovements against the liberal project undermine the transatlantic relationship as well as intensify centrifugal forces within these societies? It is difficult to predict the long run, but one might look at politics within the United States as it lurches through the first ten years of the twenty-first century as evidence of a countermovement against the idealism of the early post–Cold War years. It was this idealism that launched the neoliberal project that sought to cut back on government in America and bring democratic freedoms to the oppressed of the world. But as we approach the century's second decade, much of that idealism is gone. Does this imply that we should see a "growing together" in the years ahead as Europeans and Americans find some sort of common ground halfway between their highest ideals and deepest fears? Although it is too early to offer firm predictions, the contributions to this book provide the conceptual and empirical materials for mapping out the road ahead.

I

The Religious Divide

Why Religion Seems to Be Thriving in the United States and Waning in Europe

Steven Pfaff

Introduction

In the decades following the Second World War, most social scientists expected convergence among the Western industrial democracies. Modernization was expected to bring prosperity and opportunity, initiating a "culture shift" to posttraditional values and lifestyles.

However, in recent years observers have remarked on a growing divide between Europeans and Americans. This divergence may be nowhere greater than in the religious sphere. While faith is loudly proclaimed and a bustling diversity of religious organizations jostles for attention in all arenas of public life in the United States, the European Union (EU) is described as thoroughly secularized, comprised of societies in which religion occupies an ever-shrinking private role.

Secularization theory was long the dominant perspective on religious change.[1] It maintains that modernization erodes religion's plausibility, intensity, and authority. Further, the theory posits the retreat of sacred institutions, the privatization of faith, and the "progressive shrinkage and decline of religion" in public life.[2] As political scientist Ronald Inglehart explains, "Modernization theorists ... have argued that the world is changing in ways that erode traditional values. Economic development almost inevitably brings the decline of religion, parochialism and cultural differences." In fact,

---

[1] Steve Bruce, *God Is Dead: Secularisation in the West* (Oxford: Blackwell's Press, 2001); Grace Davie, "Europe: The Exception That Proves the Rule?" in P. Berger, ed., *The Desecularization of the World: Resurgent Religion and World Politics* (Grand Rapids: Eerdmans, 1999), pp. 65–83.

[2] José Casanova, *Public Religions in the Modern World* (Chicago: University of Chicago Press, 1994).

crossnational research suggests a negative association between development and religiosity.[3]

Nevertheless, the contemporary vitality of religion in the United States and other countries has led to a reappraisal. Peter L. Berger, once a prominent proponent of the secularization thesis, recently announced, "Our age is *not* an age of secularization. On the contrary, it is an age of exuberant religiosity, much of it in the form of passionate movements with global outreach."[4] More bluntly, sociologist Rodney Stark advised that the thesis be left to "rest in peace"; contrary evidence and theoretical shortcomings effectively consigning it to the dustbin of history.[5]

The United States seems to present a particular problem for secularization theory. Although by nearly every indicator it is among the most modern of societies, nearly all measures of religious identification and involvement place the United States far above most European counterparts. For sure, this is not a novel development. In the nineteenth century, Alexis de Tocqueville already noticed an Atlantic religious divide, declaring religion America's "first institution." Rather than echoing Tocqueville, however, we have to explain the basic reasons why religion either thrives or wanes historically. First, this is because the contrast between Europe and the United States is a partially misleading one. Not all of Europe is equally secular, and religion in the United States can be described, to paraphrase sociologist Christian Smith, as both thriving *and* embattled.[6] Even as "exuberant religiosity" makes itself felt, a growing proportion of Americans (more than 10 percent) has fully disaffiliated, and another eschews organized religion while identifying spiritually.[7] Second, we need an explanation of variation in religiosity that specifies social mechanisms rather than merely asserting cultural differences.

This chapter seeks to identify the factors that shaped religious differences between the United States and the EU countries and explore the resulting

---

3 Ronald Inglehart and Wayne E. Baker, "Modernization, Cultural Change, and the Persistence of Traditional Values," *American Sociological Review*, vol. 65, no. 1, 2000, pp. 81–2.
4 Peter L. Berger, "Globalization and Religion," *Hedgehog Review*, vol. 4, no. 2, 2002, pp. 7–20.
5 Rodney Stark, "Secularization, R.I.P.," *Sociology of Religion*, vol. 60, no. 3, 1999, pp. 249–73.
6 Christian Smith et al., *American Evangelicalism: Embattled and Thriving* (Chicago: University of Chicago Press, 1998).
7 Michael Hout and Claude S. Fischer, "Why More Americans Have No Religious Preference: Politics and Generations," *American Sociological Review*, vol. 67, no. 2, 2002, pp. 165–90; Penny Long Marler and Hadaway C. Kirk, "'Being Religious' or 'Being Spiritual' in America: A Zero-Sum Proposition?" *Journal for the Scientific Study of Religion*, vol. 41, no. 2, 2002, pp. 289–300; Brian J. Zinnbauer et al., "Religion and Spirituality: Unfuzzying the Fuzzy," *Journal for the Scientific Study of Religion*, vol. 36, no. 4, 1997, pp. 549–64.

political implications. I contend that differences in religiosity are not the result of inherent differences in the spiritual values or cultural needs of Americans and Europeans. Drawing on an expanding literature in the political economy of religion, I will show that we can think of religious groups as if they were business enterprises – firms that compete with one another for customers by satisfying demand for religious (and often social) goods and services. Hence, much of the difference in religiosity across societies can be explained by the relative competitiveness of the firms that comprise a religious "marketplace" and by the extent to which governments regulate that marketplace.

Understanding the Political Economy of Religion

Fundamentally, I am arguing that American religious firms have become more competitive and hence more successful because of the predictable consequences of the constitutional separation of church and state. Conversely, where the state regulates religious activities and (perhaps worse) subsidizes particular religions, those firms lose touch with their "customer" base and cease adapting to the changing marketplace through innovation in organization, products, and services. As a result, where religious monopolies and oligopolies have been established, churches tend to be empty despite very great expenditures to support them. Where priests, pastors, preachers, imams, and rabbis must persuade people to become and remain involved, they adapt, innovate, and market their products in ways that attempt to satisfy spiritual demands.

In discussions of religion, the ambiguous concept of church–state separation usually confuses matters. Europeans see the frequent intrusion of religion into American public affairs and declare that there is no separation of church and state. "Faith statements" by political candidates, official prayers for the well-being of the republic, and debates over such matters as prayer in the public schools or the teaching of evolution are cited by many Europeans as proof of a polity that, if not quite a theocracy, is nevertheless one in which religion plays an outsized and unseemly part.

European claims to church–state separation leave many Americans no less puzzled. They point out that many European countries have a church establishment that benefits from public funds and a host of privileges, makes Christian festivals official calendar holidays, and discourages "sectarianism" by suppressing cults and new religions. They may even discourage religion through secularizing policies and laical ideologies (as in France). The insistence by many European elites that religion remain a merely private sentiment is seen as an intrusion upon religious liberty by many American observers. Headscarf bans in France, Germany, and other countries surprise many Americans for whom the *hijab* is a legitimate expression of personal conviction.

To move beyond normative debates, let us say that institutional separation of state and religion obtains where government does not provide religious goods through an established firm, where there is minimal restriction on the public activities of religious groups, and where no particular religious organization is officially privileged or disprivileged through regulations or subsidies.[8] As I will demonstrate in this chapter, because competition is the key factor that explains religious vitality, we should expect that where state involvement in religious markets is modest, religious life will be vital. Where religion is strictly controlled or where religious monopolies have been established, religiosity will be wan.

Focusing on the state as regulator also helps us to understand how religion influences politics on both sides of the Atlantic. Political mobilization on the basis of religion is often triggered by the efforts of political elites to reduce the public role of religion (institutional secularization) or extend governmental authority to domains previously organized by religious organizations. As suggested by sociologist Michael Hechter's theory of cultural politics, state penetration into areas once dominated by religion should provoke conflict, especially where it threatens the influence of religious authorities.[9] "Reasonable" government regulation of religious expression or activities is often viewed as an attack on religion by those whose interests and status would be diminished. Religious leaders mobilize politically to preserve their autonomy and status, decrying the regime for "compelling" believers to compromise their faith and values.

Again, the nature of religion–state institutions is important in this respect. Where religion is organized voluntarily, the everyday functioning of the organization promotes collective action; in other words, in congregational religion, if members don't produce religious goods collectively, they aren't provided. So where religion is based on voluntary association, an active religiosity readily becomes a central feature of public identity and citizenship. Religious leaders form interest groups to protect their position, enhance their competitiveness, and seek a share of public resources. The power of

---

[8] In fact, religious economies are regulated to varying degrees in most countries around the world. In a comparative study of the extent of separation of religion and state, Jonathan Fox found that about three-quarters of governments make no substantial effort to separate state and religion and that at least some restriction on religion is ubiquitous – only the United States has no substantial state restrictions on religion. See Jonathan Fox, "World Separation of Religion and State into the 21st Century," *Comparative Political Studies*, vol. 39, no. 6, 2006, pp. 537–69.

[9] Michael Hechter, "From Class to Culture," *American Journal of Sociology*, vol. 110, no. 2, 2004, pp. 400–45.

any particular religious group is held in check chiefly by the simultaneous mobilization of its competitors. This scenario corresponds roughly to the situation that evolved in the United States.

It stands to reason that where religious goods are largely provided by an established authority, there should be less collective action on that basis (many formal church members will be tempted to free-ride). In those societies, the laity is mostly passive and religious group membership becomes associated with membership in the state. Only when growing pluralism (as through immigration) or institutional reforms threaten the resources and privileges to which the established faiths are accustomed will their leaders mobilize politically or challenge the state. This scenario corresponds to most countries of the EU. This chapter will now explore these propositions in light of the comparative sociology of religion and the historical development of the United States and the EU countries.

Religion, Belief, and Social Values in Europe and the United States

Survey evidence indicates that we should not be content with a stylized contrast between a godless Europe and a pious America. Surveys show that weekly religious attendance among Americans has been relatively high and stable throughout the twentieth century. Although there are indications that reported attendance may be inflated due to social desirability effects,[10] Gallup surveys conducted for the last six decades consistently find that about 40 percent of American adults report weekly attendance.[11] Membership in religious organizations has been more variable. Census and polling data show that a century ago less than half of Americans belonged to a religious organization. Reported church membership rose to about three-fourths of the population by 1960. It has declined since, but surveys and church records indicate that it remains at about 60 percent of Americans.[12] In this light, the recent experience of the country with evangelicalism can be understood as part of the longer-term trend of the "churching of America" that has been under way since the early nineteenth century.[13] That process made American

[10] Kirk C. Hadaway, Penny Long Marler, and Mark Chaves, "What the Polls Don't Show: A Closer Look at U.S. Church Attendance," *American Sociological Review*, vol. 58, 1993, pp. 741–52.

[11] U.S. Department of Commerce, *Statistical Abstract of the United States* (Washington: U.S. Department of Commerce, 1997); Robert Wuthnow, *The Restructuring of American Religion* (Princeton: Princeton University Press, 1988).

[12] Robert Putnam, *Bowling Alone: The Collapse and Revival of American Community* (New York: Simon and Schuster, 2000).

[13] Roger Finke and Rodney Stark, *The Churching of America, 1776–1990* (New Brunswick, NJ: Rutgers University Press, 1992).

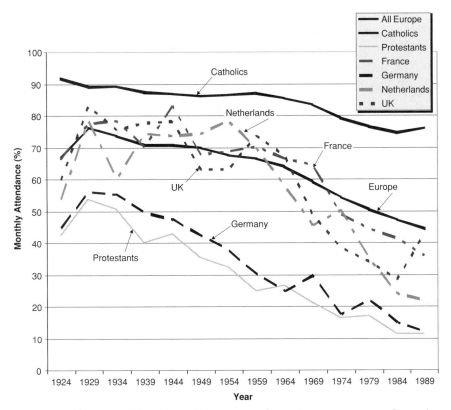

FIGURE 1.1. At Least Monthly Religious Attendance in 16 European Countries, 1920s–1980s, Based on Retrospective Data. *Source*: WVS 99–01.

religion diverse, well organized, and effectively marketed such that the majority has a voluntary attachment to organized faith.

Because it is very difficult to find comparable data on religious participation for several societies over time, the most recent "European Values" component of the World Values Survey (WVS) enables us to estimate the churchgoing rate based on how often respondents reported attending services when they were about twelve years old. Assuming that children usually attend with their parents, we can construct a picture of religious change in a population grouping respondents into five-year cohorts. Focusing on the older EU countries (pre-2004 expansion), the data indicate declining organized participation in religion. Figure 1.1 presents retrospective data on at least once-a-month religious attendance between the 1920s and 1980s reported by respondents.

TABLE 1.1. *Indicators of Religiosity in European Union Countries and North America (% Respondents Reporting)*

Country	Religion Important	Church Attendance Never	Church Attendance Once or more per month
Pre-2004 EU Countries (Group Mean)	**49.0**	**41.9**	**32.1**
Austria	54.8	31.6	44.9
Belgium	47.6	50.5	27.8
Denmark	27.1	50.0	11.9
Finland	42.0	47.4	12.5
France	36.4	67.0	12.3
Germany	28.2	52.4	24.3
Greece	68.3	5.2	33.6
Ireland	76.3	10.6	74.6
Italy	72.1	17.0	53.6
Netherlands	39.7	54.2	37.9
Portugal	76.1	33.4	53.1
Spain	46.2	43.5	35.6
Sweden	35.0	58.7	8.8
United Kingdom	36.8	64.7	18.7
New EU Member Countries (Group Mean)	**45.5**	**31.2**	**30.5**
Czech Republic	21.4	56.1	12.8
Estonia	21.6	38.3	10.8
Hungary	41.6	44.0	17.8
Latvia	44.3	34.6	15.0
Lithuania	56.8	17.5	28.9
Poland	83.9	6.0	78.1
Slovakia	57.4	23.1	49.8
Slovenia	36.6	30.1	30.7
North American Countries (Group Mean)	**78.6**	**15.8**	**57.6**
Canada	64.9	26.4	38.3
Mexico	87.6	6.5	73.6
United States	83.2	14.4	61.1

Note: Italicized countries have a Roman Catholic majority.
Source: WVS 99–01.

In these societies, figures for attending at least once a month fell from about 70 percent in the 1930s to less than 50 percent at the end of the 1980s. However, confessional differences are immediately evident; decline is much more conspicuous among Protestants (–40 percent) than Roman

Catholics (−16 percent). The changes are highlighted by some of the larger countries. Figures for attending at least once a month fell from about 80 to 40 percent in the UK, from 70 to 40 percent in France, from about 70 to 20 percent in the Netherlands, and from over 50 to just 15 percent in Germany.

Religion as a feature of the private lives of Europeans is highly variable. Although more than 80 percent of Americans report that religion is personally important in the most recent WVS, just 36 percent of the French, 35 percent of Swedes, 28 percent of Danes, and one-fifth of Czechs and Estonians consider religion of personal importance (see Table 1.1). Yet citizens of Catholic majority countries generally report greater importance of religion, often in proportions comparable to Americans: 84 percent of Poles, 76 percent of Portuguese, 76 percent of the Irish, and 72 percent of Italians.

Table 1.1 also indicates that there are a number of European countries where the proportion of the population that *never* attends religious services, a good indicator of disaffiliation, is substantially greater than regular attendance. Attendance is more robust in predominantly Catholic countries, with the exception of France, whereas the proportion never attending is highest among predominantly Protestant countries of Northern Europe. In North America, the United States falls in between Canada and Mexico, with fewer than 15 percent of Americans never attending services. As we'd expect, the subjective importance of religion and regular church attendance are very highly correlated across countries (.867),[14] however, there are a number of countries where the stated importance of religion exceeds regular attendance. This is notable in the United States, where the gap is fully 37 percent. Americans attach a very great importance to religion, an opinion that extends beyond the ranks of regular churchgoers.

Interestingly, Americans and Europeans do not seem fundamentally different in personal faith or spirituality (see Table 1.2). In the United States, belief in God is nearly universal (95.9 percent) and reported incidence of private prayer is very high (78.5 percent). However, the United States is not an isolated bastion of faith; solid majorities believe in God across most of Europe and North America, with more than 90 percent of the public in Mexico, Canada, Poland, Portugal, Italy, and Ireland professing belief. Across Europe and North America, there is a high correlation between rates of private prayer outside of religious services and belief in God (.851) and rates of the subjective importance of religion and prayer (.946). There are

---

[14] The Pearson's correlation value between the two variables is .867. A correlation describes the extent of the linear association between variables, meaning that the value of one variable can be predicted to some extent by that of another.

TABLE 1.2. *Indicators of Public and Private Religiosity in the EU Countries and North America (% Respondents Reporting)*

Country	Belong to Church Organization	Confidence in Churches	Believe in God	Pray Outside of Services (*Once or More per Week*)
Pre-2004 EU Countries (Group Mean)	10.45	49.1	76.5	41.5
Austria	25.0	38.9	87.4	44.6
Belgium	12.2	43.1	71.9	35.6
Denmark	11.9	59.2	68.9	20.3
Finland	–	56.5	80.9	37.4
France	4.6	45.4	61.4	19.3
Germany	12.6	35.4	54.0	28.8
Greece	6.7	54.8	91.0	53.3
Ireland	19.1	57.5	96.8	74.5
Italy	10.3	67.1	93.5	62.1
Netherlands	5.3	28.6	59.5	33.1
Portugal	6.3	79.1	95.5	63.4
Spain	6.6	42.3	85.0	39.9
Sweden	–	44.9	53.3	–
United Kingdom	4.8	34.3	72.5	27.5
New EU Member Countries (Group Mean)	8.2	53.7	71.3	42.0
Czech Republic	7.3	20.4	40.3	19.3
Estonia	7.1	43.8	50.7	17.8
Hungary	12.7	45.3	67.6	37.0
Latvia	5.3	92.4	79.5	34.3
Lithuania	4.6	66.3	85.8	53.0
Poland	5.4	66.7	97.1	78.2
Slovakia	16.5	68.9	82.9	–
Slovenia	6.7	25.4	65.2	54.2
North American Countries	37.2	72.7	94.9	72.5
Canada	30.5	61.7	91.0	59.8
Mexico	23.4	80.7	97.8	79.2
United States	57.8	75.7	95.9	78.5

Note: Italicized countries have a Roman Catholic majority.
Source: WVS 99–01.

only a handful of countries – Sweden, Germany, Estonia, and the Czech Republic – in which less than 60 percent of the population professes belief.

We can interpret this as indicating that there is less variation in religious demand than we might expect from attendance figures. What strikes me as the most important difference between the United States and the EU countries is the high proportion of Americans – about 60 percent – who report belonging to a religious organization. I will demonstrate how this is a direct result of the denominational structure of American religion and its congregational style of organization. Europeans, by contrast, commonly limit themselves to passive enrollment in established religious confessions that do not require continuous participation.

Nevertheless, confidence in churches as public institutions seems to be largely independent both of the level of religious involvement in the country and whether or not Protestants or Catholics predominate. Presumably, where churches perform charitable services, maintain national traditions, and do not presume to meddle in private lives or public affairs, they are generally approved. A survey conducted in Germany in July 2005 illustrates this. A greater proportion of Germans find churches important for kindergartens and medical services (77 percent) or weddings and funerals (70 percent) than for the teaching of the Word of God (46 percent).[15]

Religious affiliations and beliefs are consequential for social values on both sides of the Atlantic (see Table 1.3). The proportion of respondents who agree with the statement "abortion is never justified" was more than half in Mexico and Ireland, and 30 percent or more in Italy, Portugal, Hungary, Latvia, Poland, Canada, and the United States. This is highly correlated (.726) with the proportion of the population that considers religion important. Interestingly, categorical opposition to divorce ("divorce is never justified") is quite uncommon in the United States, despite its religiosity and social conservatism on other issues. The greatest disapproval of divorce is apparent in strongly Catholic countries such as Mexico (37 percent), Ireland (26.7 percent), Poland (26.4 percent), and Italy (18.5 percent).

Each of the countries in which strong disapproval of homosexuality is a majority position – Hungary (88.5 percent), Lithuania (77.1 percent), Latvia (76.9 percent), Poland (61.3 percent), and Estonia (56.3 percent) – is a recent member of the EU and was a communist society until 1989 or 1991. These are not uniformly pious countries but all were part of the Soviet bloc, where homosexuality was portrayed as among the worst forms of cultural

---

[15] Mario Kaiser, Ansbert Kneip, and Alexander Smoltcyzk, "Das Kreuz mit den Deutschen," *Der Spiegel*, vol. 33, July 2005, pp. 135–51.

TABLE 1.3. *Indicators of Social Values in European Union Countries and North America (% Respondents Reporting)*

Country	Religious Leaders Should Not Influence Politics	Abortion Is Never Justifiable	Divorce Is Never Justifiable	Homosexuality Is Never Justifiable
Pre-2004 EU Countries (Group Mean)	76.1	23.4	11.0	24.1
Austria	84.7	23.5	11.6	27.2
Belgium	80.3	28.7	12.9	28.2
Denmark	84.6	12.9	7.0	20.7
Finland	67.9	10.2	2.9	26.8
France	86.3	14.9	7.7	23.8
Germany	73.7	23.2	12.7	21.7
Greece	78.4	18.4	6.6	24.0
Ireland	77.9	54.7	26.7	37.8
Italy	78.7	31.7	18.5	29.9
Netherlands	66.4	15.3	4.7	6.9
Portugal	81.4	34.7	15.9	40.7
Spain	66.5	28.4	11.8	16.9
Sweden	66.8	5.2	2.3	8.6
United Kingdom	71.7	25.7	12.4	24.6
New EU Member Countries (Group Mean)	80.7	27.7	17.4	56.5
Czech Republic	79.8	13.4	6.9	26.4
Estonia	84.5	20.7	10.9	56.3
Hungary	78.1	32.5	23.7	88.5
Latvia	83.9	36.7	25.2	76.9
Lithuania	81.9	29.1	18.7	77.5
Poland	85.4	44.7	26.4	61.3
Slovakia	74.1	25.1	13.5	23.8
Slovenia	77.7	19.5	14.2	41.6
North American Countries (Group Mean)	68.6	42.7	18.3	35.7
Canada	77.9	31.1	10.5	25.9
Mexico	64.5	66.9	37.0	49.8
United States	63.3	30.2	7.4	31.5

Note: Italicized countries have a Roman Catholic majority.
Source: WVS 99–01.

degeneracy and where discussion of sexuality was highly taboo. Otherwise, there is no strong association between opposition to homosexuality and religion, with opposition only somewhat more common in the United States (31.5 percent) than in most Western European countries.[16]

Explaining Religious Variation: The New Paradigm in the Study of Religion

How do we explain the startling differences in participation and commitment across countries? Previously, social scientists relied on secularization theory for comparative insight. Yet there is no unified theory of secularization, and its mechanisms remain obscure.[17] In addition, it is not clear why indicators of "secularization" are high in some modern societies – for instance, in many Western European societies – but lower in others such as the United States, or why some countries that are far less developed than the Western industrial democracies are more irreligious. The generally high levels of belief in God and frequency of private prayer across Europe could suggest that these are societies with substantial (unmet) demand for religion.

Social scientists have developed a "new paradigm" in the scientific study of religion that offers a rival to secularization theory.[18] The paradigm has been described as offering "supply-side" or "rational choice" explanations of religion. Advocates have garnered support through studies of religion in Western Europe, Eastern Europe, and the Americas.[19] These studies pay

---

[16] Readers may be worried that my reliance on descriptive statistics and bivariate correlations could lead to spurious conclusions. In a collaborative project with Anthony Gill on religion and politics in the new Europe, we conducted multivariate ordinary least squares (OLS) regression with standard controls on samples drawn from sixteen EU member countries included in the WVS 99–01. We found that monthly and weekly church attendance in Europe was positively associated with political conservatism on a standard left-right scale, as has been demonstrated in the United States. Likewise, OLS regression analysis reveals that, as in the United States, Europeans who are active members of churches are also more likely to be involved with other civil society organizations. Unlike America, however, in Europe regular churchgoing is negatively correlated with economic libertarianism on a standard scale of economic ideology. We suspect that this is the legacy of Catholic social teachings critical of free markets and economic inequality.

[17] See Bruce, *God Is Dead*; Stark, "Secularization."

[18] Stephen R. Warner, "Work in Progress toward a New Paradigm for the Sociological Study of Religion in the United States," *American Journal of Sociology*, vol. 98, no. 5, 1993, pp. 1044–93; Rodney Stark and William Sims Bainbridge, *A Theory of Religion* (New York: Peter Lang, 1987); Rodney Stark and Roger Finke, *Acts of Faith* (Berkeley: University of California Press, 2000).

[19] Ted G. Jelen and Clyde Wilcox, "Context and Conscience: The Catholic Church as an Agent of Political Socialization in Western Europe," *Journal for the Scientific Study of Religion*, vol. 37, no. 1, 1998, pp. 28–40; Rodney Stark and Laurence R. Iannaccone, "A Supply-Side

attention to competitive pressures that force religions to be more responsive to "consumers" (adherents and potential adherents), thereby improving the quality and range of their goods and services. To be sure, critics have offered theoretical, methodological, and empirical challenges to the new paradigm.[20] Yet the new approach, by identifying the central role played by church–state institutions in causing variation across societies, does much to explain the differences in religiosity that we have observed.

Religious Regulation and Its Consequences

In the *The Wealth of Nations*, Adam Smith observed,

The teachers of [religion] . . . may either depend altogether for their subsistence upon the voluntary contributions of the hearers; or they may derive it from some other fund to which the law of their country may entitle them; such as a landed estate, a tythe or land tax, an established salary or stipend. Their exertion, their zeal and industry, are likely to be much greater in the former situation than the latter.

The result of establishing churches was evident in their poor performance:

. . . the clergy, reposing themselves upon their benefices, [that] had neglected to keep up the fervour of faith and devotion in the great body of the people; and having given themselves up to indolence, were become altogether incapable of making any vigorous exertion even in defence of their own establishment.

Smith went on to imagine a society without state regulation of the religious sphere:

There would in this case, no doubt, have been a great multitude of religious sects. Almost every different congregation might probably have made a little sect by itself, or have entertained some peculiar tenets of its own. Each teacher would no doubt have felt himself under the necessity of making the utmost exertion, and of using every art both to preserve and to increase the number of his disciples.[21]

Reinterpretation of the 'Secularization' of Europe," *Journal for the Scientific Study of Religion*, vol. 33, no. 3, 1994, pp. 230–52; Paul Froese and Steven Pfaff, "Replete and Desolate Markets: Poland, East Germany, and the New Religious Paradigm," *Social Forces*, vol. 80, no. 2, 2005, pp. 481–507; Paul Froese, "After Atheism: An Analysis of Religious Monopolies in the Post-Communist World," *Sociology of Religion*, vol. 69, no. 1, 2005, pp. 57–75; Anthony Gill, *Rendering unto Caesar: The Catholic Church and the State in Latin America* (Chicago: University of Chicago Press, 1998).

[20] Bruce, *God Is Dead*; James D. Montgomery, "Contemplations on the Economic Approach to Religious Behavior," *American Economic Review*, vol. 86, 1996, pp. 443–7; Mark Chaves and Phillip Gorski, "Religious Pluralism and Religious Participation," *Annual Review of Sociology*, vol. 27, 2001; David Voas, David Olson, and Alisdair Crockett, "Religious Pluralism and Participation: Why Previous Research Is Wrong," *American Sociological Review*, vol. 67, 2002, pp. 212–30.

[21] Adam Smith, *An Inquiry into the Nature and Causes of the Wealth of Nations* (Oxford: Oxford University Press, 1976), vol. II, pp. 788–92.

Smith's theory predicts that where churches are established and sectarian challengers suppressed, the zeal of the clergy fades over time, the quality of religious goods declines, and the cost of producing religious goods soars. Under such circumstances, only subsidies and discouragement of rival sects could prop up the established churches.

Smith's formulation may seem too simple a foundation to help us explain something as complex as religion. And yet a basic exercise in comparison demonstrates the plausibility of his insights. Comparing the Lutheran church in the United States to that in Europe two centuries after Smith, allows us to approximate the sort of natural experiment common in other fields. This comparison holds constant much of what might influence religiosity – doctrine, liturgy, size of the church, and so on – while focusing on the effect of church–state institutions. Thinking of religious groups as firms allows us to consider the cost-effectiveness of the mainline Evangelical Lutheran Church in America (ELCA) and its official counterparts in the Evangelical Lutheran People's Church in Denmark, the Evangelical Lutheran Church in Finland, and the Evangelical Lutheran Church in Sweden. Dividing total annual expenditures by the number of newly baptized members (child and adult), the congregations of the ELCA (whose membership numbers about 5 million, comparable to the Nordic churches) spent about U.S. $25,000 per baptism in 2002. Expenditures by baptism for the Danish, Finnish, and Swedish churches were $2.3 million, $1.6 million, and $1.7 million respectively.[22] One could argue that there aren't enough targets for baptism in these historically Christian countries with their low birthrates. Although perhaps this is true, indicators of member commitment relative to costs tell a similar story: Weekly attendance rates for the Nordic churches are all 5 percent or less compared to about 30 percent for the ELCA.

Of course, one cannot make too much of this comparison because the extent and quality of services provided by these churches may be very different. Nordic churches maintain expensive historic buildings and monuments in city centers. They employ numerous clergypeople, social workers, cultural functionaries, and administrators. In fact, despite its recent official "disestablishment," the Swedish church remains the country's tenth largest employer with about twenty-five thousand employees. The point is that, as Smith would have predicted, the focus of the Nordic churches appears to have shifted from the production of religious goods to other purposes. In the United States, by contrast, Lutherans had to compete with rival churches in

---

[22] David J. Barrett, George T. Kurian, and Todd M. Johnson, *World Christian Encyclopedia*, 2nd edition (Oxford: Oxford University Press, 2001).

a new institutional environment without the advantages of state-collected tithes, subsidies, and laws designed to support them or suppress the competition. Accordingly, they largely adapted to the circumstances of a pluralistic marketplace.[23]

Smïth's brilliant insight has informed past research demonstrating that established churches in Europe tend to be weak.[24] Put simply, the new paradigm contends that religious commitment should grow when firms actively compete to offer the best incentives – spiritual, social, and material – for membership. Rodney Stark and Roger Finke summarize a core proposition of the model:

> To the extent that pluralism or regulation are adequate inferential measures of competition, the overall level of religiousness will be higher where pluralism is greater or where regulation is lower.[25]

Drawing from this proposition, the very great vitality of American religious life, characterized as it is by a very low degree of state regulation and by a very diverse, competitive market, would seem to provide ideal conditions for religion to flourish and for religious entrepreneurs to seek out every potential niche within the distribution of religious demand. In most European countries, by contrast, extensive and intrusive regulation by the state combined with limited religious pluralism should be expected to depress religious vitality and limit the range of options available to consumers.

Modern German history can help illustrate central insights of the theory. Following the Reformation struggles, dynastic rulers decided what would become the official religion in their realms (*cuius regio euis religio*). Central European princes either established a Protestant church (Lutheran or Reformed) or the Roman Catholic Church. Established churches benefited from entitlements, whereas religious minorities suffered a variety of disadvantages, including legal discrimination.[26] Church policies often reflected interests of state; for instance, following unification under Prussian leadership in 1871, Calvinists and Lutherans were unified on the Prussian model.

Consistent with supply-side expectations, the available data on weekly church attendance in the late nineteenth through the mid-twentieth centuries

---

[23] Rodney Stark, "German and German-American Religiousness: Approximating a Crucial Experiment," *Journal for the Scientific Study of Religion*, vol. 36, no. 2, 1997, pp. 182–93.

[24] Laurence Iannaccone, "The Consequences of Religious Market Structure," *Rationality and Society*. vol. 3, no. 2, 1991, pp. 156–77; Stark and Iannaccone, "A Supply-Side Reinterpretation."

[25] Stark and Finke, *Acts of Faith*, p. 297.

[26] Eric W. Gritsch, *A History of Lutheranism* (Minneapolis: Fortress, 2002).

reveal declining participation.[27] In the old Reformation heartland, church attendance fell dramatically: In Saxony, weekly church attendance fell from about 70 percent in 1862 to half that level in 1913, and to just over a fifth of the population on the eve of the Second World War. An industrial region such as Saxony might be taken as indicative of the inevitable link between modernization and religious decline. However, the more proximate cause may have been poor performance by religious monopolies; Protestant districts of Germany had among the lowest rate of clergy to parishioners in Europe.[28] A geographer of imperial Germany notes: "With industrialization country parishes with tax-supported clergy might have only a handful of families left on the land, while the new cities might struggle with a proportion of one clergyman to 30,000 souls."[29]

As with the Latin American Catholicism analyzed by Anthony Gill, indolent, established Protestant churches did little to serve the interests of their adherents.[30] They sided with the crown, alienated the poor, deployed few clergymen, and became both unattractive and vulnerable to attack from ideological rivals. Anticlerical sentiment grew widespread, particularly among workers.[31] By 1912, hundreds of thousands had joined the Social Democratic Party (SPD) and more than a million people read its newspapers and journals. Socialism became an "alternative culture" directed against the state, the church, and the elite.[32] A similar pattern obtained across the Nordic countries.[33] Nevertheless, growing dissatisfaction with state-supported religious firms does not seem to have resulted in complete abandonment of faith. The large majority of Protestants continued to have its children baptized and confirmed, to marry in a church, and to have a religious funeral.[34] Despite the appeal of Marxist-inspired socialism, atheist associations failed to thrive.[35]

---

[27] Hugh McLeod, *Secularisation in Western Europe: 1848–1914* (New York: St. Martin's Press, 2000); Evangelische Kirche in Deutschland, *Kirchliches Jahrbuch für die evangelische Kirche in Deutschland 1950* (Gütersloh: Bertelsmann, 1951).

[28] Emile Durkheim, *Suicide: A Study in Sociology* (London: Routledge and Kegan Paul, 1952), pp. 160–1.

[29] Franklin Littell, *Historical Atlas of Christianity* (New York: Continuum, 2001), p. 239.

[30] Gill, *Rendering*.

[31] Alfred Kelly, *The German Worker* (Berkeley: University of California Press, 1987).

[32] Vernon Lidtke, *The Alternative Culture: Socialist Labor in Imperial Germany* (New York: Oxford University Press, 1985).

[33] Flemming Hemmersam, ed., *To Work, to Life, to Death: Studies in Working Class Lore* (Copenhagen: Society for Research in the History of the Labour Movement in Denmark, 1996).

[34] Evangelische Kirche in Deutschland, *Kirchliches Jahrbuch*.

[35] Lidtke, *The Alternative Culture*.

Throughout the period, the Catholic Church fared better than the Protestant churches, largely because Prussian anti-Catholic legislation prompted defensive mobilization supported by Rome. Opposing Bismarck's *Kulturkampf* energized the faithful and directed them against discrimination and secularization. In fact, the Catholic Center grew to be the second largest parliamentary party after the SPD by 1912. The zeal of Catholicism despite its position in a religious oligopoly should not surprise us since competition – whether through political conflict or through the rivalry among religious firms – accounts for religious vitality according to the new paradigm.[36]

Various changes of political regime in the twentieth century failed to profit religion. The fall of the monarchy in 1918–19 did not lead to religious deregulation or to lasting revitalization of the churches.[37] Although the Weimar constitution pledged the religious neutrality of the state, the two great confessional churches were not disestablished and remained highly political.[38] Later, the Nazi regime attacked independent clergy and tried to undermine Christian culture and beliefs. And in communist East Germany (1945–89) antireligious regulations and the promotion of an exclusive, socialist-inspired atheism devastated organized religion.

The post-war Federal Republic restored the church law of 1919, reaffirming the privileged position of the established confessions. Regulation of religious groups, alongside state subsidies for recognized confessions, remains a feature of the religious market.[39] New religions and sects routinely find themselves denounced as cults, subject to discriminatory laws, and placed under police surveillance. Recently, regulations have provoked conflicts with new religious movements such as the Scientologists and with evangelical Christians.[40] Despite the Muslims' expanding share of the population, as of this writing no Islamic religious organization has been granted state recognition as an official religious body.[41]

---

[36] For an excellent analysis of the struggle between Catholicism and liberal reform, see Andrew C. Gould, *Origins of Liberal Dominance: State, Church, and Party in Nineteenth Century Europe* (Ann Arbor: University of Michigan Press, 1999).

[37] Daniel Borg, *The Old Prussian Church and the Weimar Republic: A Study in Political Adjustment, 1917–1927* (Hanover and London: University of New England Press, 1984).

[38] Horst Groschopp, ed., *Kein Jenseits ist, kein Aufersteh'n: Freireligiöse in der Berliner Kulturgeschichte* (Berlin: Koenigsdruck, 1998).

[39] Thomas Gandow, "New Religious Movements in Germany," in Helle Meldgaard and Johannes Aagaard, eds., *New Religious Movements in Europe* (Oxford: Aarhus, 1997).

[40] Steven Erlanger "U.S.-Style Evangelical Drive Rouses Germany," *New York Times*, January 17, 2002.

[41] Steven Pfaff and Anthony Gill, "Will a Million Muslims March? Muslim Interest Organizations and Political Integration in Europe," *Comparative Political Studies*, vol. 39, no. 7, 2006, pp. 803–28.

I do not mean to generalize from the history of a single country. The German case points more broadly to the very great weaknesses of what may be called *state churches*. A state church, established by law, has little material basis for independence, relying upon the state to defend it from potential competitors ("cults," "sects," and "heresies") and offer loyalty and support to the regime in exchange for these privileges. Historical examples of this type of church abound: the Lutheran Churches in the Nordic and German states, Orthodox churches of Eastern Europe, Latin American Catholicism, the Church of England, and so on.[42] In societies dominated by state churches, ordinary people have incentives to maintain membership in the established religion but little reason to take active part. Religion becomes an appendage of state membership; where this institutional form predominates, we should expect widespread affiliation with little voluntary commitment.

Clearly, any religion could become a "state church," but the Catholic Church has distinctive institutional features that often protect it from becoming fully subordinated. These are its external source of supreme organizational and doctrinal authority (the papacy) and substantial mechanisms for establishing dependence and control among its clergy. These features protect a certain level of autonomy even under oppressive regimes. This is why dictators have often found the Roman Church a fickle ally and have had to contend with it playing a substantial role in cultivating opposition or brokering a political transition when it no longer perceives that an alliance with the regime is in its interest (as in the Philippines, Spain, and Poland).

In contrast to state churches, there are also cases of what might be called *national churches*. Social conflicts in which religious organizations become highly visible advocates of subaltern groups provide competitive pressure in the absence of pluralism. We see the effect in colonial Ireland, in Poland under communism, in the Shah's Iran, and in the Jim Crow South. Clearly, if the members of a social group are divided among several religions, a nationally identified church is unlikely to take shape.[43] Churches serve as organizational vehicles for national conflict only when they have some degree of institutional autonomy. If there is no real difference between a church and the state, dissident forces will not strongly identify with religion because the church can offer no great advantage. National churches thrive during political conflicts; however, once tension ends or abates, commitment should weaken.

[42] Sabrina P. Ramet, *Nihil Obstat: Religion, Politics, and Social Change in East-Central Europe and Russia* (Durham: Duke University Press, 1998); Gill, *Rendering*.

[43] Steve Bruce, *Choice and Religion* (Oxford: Oxford University Press, 1999), p. 116.

In sum, national churches will retain their potency so long as they do not become state churches. If they or their allies take power, national churches begin to weaken. They tend to lose members and commitment because they will no longer function as an alternative to the state and will likely move toward establishing monopoly status. Although Catholic churches have an institutional advantage over those fully identified with the state, the decreases in religiosity reported in postconflict Catholic societies are consistent with the logic of the new paradigm.

Moving from Supply to Demand

Much of the secularization debate comes down to this: Are low levels of religiosity explained by supply-side or demand-side deficiencies? So far, I have endeavored to explain the differences between observed religiosity in the United States and the EU by reference to supply-side factors. However, it is also worth considering the "demand side," that is, the preference for religion. Religious economy theorists define religious demand as a basic existential need for meaning and understanding common to all cultures. Religion provides immanent goods or rewards that are unavailable elsewhere, so religious demand is assumed to be relatively constant.[44] Secularization theorists disagree, contending that enlightenment, prosperity, technology, and multiculturalism create a "crisis of credibility" for religious believers.[45]

I have shown why the religiosity of many European societies declined in the nineteenth and twentieth centuries because established churches enjoyed monopolistic advantages and failed to rise to the challenges of evangelizing newly urbanized populations. Even as religious attendance plummeted, membership declined much more gradually because of the services that the churches provided and the lack of viable alternatives to which to exit. The resulting pattern was one of affiliation without commitment.

It may be that poor supply eventually made these churches vulnerable on the demand side. Historically, weakening demand is observable both in popular indifference toward religion and successful inroads into popular opinion by anticlerical and atheist political movements. In France and other countries, radical republicans engaged in fierce battles against the clergy and religious "superstitions." And, in practice, bound to conservative interests, the established churches largely lived up to their reactionary reputation. Marxist-inspired parties fought bitter battles against clericalism and preached scientific atheism. Facing anemic state churches, they had

44 Stark and Bainbridge, *A Theory of Religion*.
45 Peter L. Berger, *The Sacred Canopy* (New York: Doubleday, 1967); Bruce, *God Is Dead*.

much success in deterring religious participation and promoting skepticism. Above all, the instrumentalization of Darwinism bore fruit. As historian Alfred Kelly documents, even though Marxist indoctrination largely failed, "popular Darwinism" became influential; God was replaced by "Nature" and an "anti-Christian evolutionary monism."[46]

Even if Europeans resented state churches, the popular appeal of Marxist-inspired "scientific" atheism was limited even as skepticism and indifference spread. Atheist entrepreneurs effectively decreased religious demand during the communist era because they enjoyed state support, sanctioned believers, and competed against already weakened and discredited state churches.[47] In East Germany, where an accommodating Protestant Church was seen as a bulwark of discredited conservatism, religion declined sharply in the face of atheist campaigns. A similar dynamic obtained in the Czech territories. But in Poland, where the Church built on its reputation as a defender of national interests, countermobilization affirmed popular Catholicism.[48]

In the United States, there were also strong pressures toward institutional secularization in the late nineteenth and early twentieth centuries. Christian Smith has shown how "secularizing activists" intent on challenging the Protestant establishment altered the institutions of public life, including the press, schools, universities, and legal system.[49] Their goal was to overthrow mainline custodianship of public morality, to promote "objective" science and education, and to buttress church–state separation. They largely succeeded, Smith argues, because only a fifth of the population belonged to mainline denominations, because of the overconfidence and laxity of those denominations, because of the interest of business elites in greater economic freedom (such as opposition to the Comstock law), and finally because of the very strong divisions between the mainline clergy and dissident evangelicals.

So why didn't the "secular revolution" in American life lead to weaker demand for religion in the long run, as it seems to have done in Europe? The answer may lie in the social movements behind institutional secularization. In Europe, secularization occurred largely from the bottom up. Elites created and defended religious establishments that widening sectors of the population simply ignored or abandoned. By the end of the twentieth century, these

---

[46] Alfred Kelly, *The Descent of Darwin: The Popularization of Darwinism in Germany, 1860–1914* (Chapel Hill: University of North Carolina Press, 1981), p. 181.

[47] Daniel Peris, *Storming the Heavens: The Soviet League of the Militant Godless* (Ithaca and London: Cornell University Press, 1998).

[48] Maryjane Osa, *Networks of Solidarity* (Minneapolis: University of Minnesota Press, 2003).

[49] Christian Smith, ed., *The Secular Revolution* (Berkeley and Los Angeles: University of California Press, 2003).

churches became so anemic that the political elites no longer relied on them for purposes of legitimacy or popular mobilization, and disestablishment was even discussed. The situation was very different in the United States, with its decentralized and plural religious culture.

In the United States, secularization was largely a struggle between rival factions of the educated elite. Liberalizing elites largely succeeded, yet it is telling that two great periods of elite-driven secularization in the United States, 1910–20 and 1960–80, were followed by the great upsurges of popular fundamentalism and evangelicalism. The many-headed denominational structure of American religion meant that there was little secularizing that elites could do to affect grass-roots mobilization. Conservative churches shaped popular dissatisfaction with secular institutions and liberal norms, forging new political constituencies.[50]

One result of these different paths of historical development is that Americans expect religion to play an apparent role in the public life of adherents. Public religion thrives because American denominationalism transforms every religion, regardless of its origins or doctrines, into voluntary associations. Unlike religious organizations in most societies around the world, American congregations are democratically organized. Christian, Jewish, and Muslim communities that originally had authoritarian clerical traditions generally adapt to this reality and are governed by locally selected congregational councils. Even in traditional religious organizations, the laity rebels when the religious hierarchy violates local interests, as in the clerical abuse scandals in the American Catholic Church. Government plays its part in encouraging congregational attachments and denominational pluralism through the indirect subsidies of tax exemptions for religious organizations and the deductibility of individual charitable donations from taxable income.

This makes American religion a ready foundation for interest groups that jostle for influence in the public sphere and in the making of government policy. And, unlike in many European contexts where confessional groups are formally included in a corporate polity, these religious identities are as plural as the denominational structure itself. Responding to various demand niches, denominations become arrayed along a liberal-centrist-conservative continuum. As sociologist José Casanova observes of American public religion, "the majority of Americans tend to be humanists, who are simultaneously religious and secular," and "both religious 'fundamentalists' and

---

[50] See e.g., Kristin Luker, *Abortion and the Politics of Motherhood* (Berkeley: University of California Press, 1984).

'secular humanists' are cognitive minorities."[51] Religion is no obstacle to entering the agora, but rather a thread in the toga that most citizens wear. In fact, religious identification may serve as an essential marker of moral qualifications for public life. Sociologists have found that Americans are more universally hostile and distrustful toward professed atheists than members of nearly any other culturally recognizable group.[52]

The last feature that can affect demand for religion involves the host of incentives beyond the spiritual that religious firms offer to attract and retain adherents. As sociologists Darren Sherkat and Christopher Ellison note, religious groups often "serve as conduits for a variety of secular privileges (e.g. social support, access to mating markets, daycare, and economic activities), and social ties to co-religionists provide solitary incentives for participation in religious organizations."[53] For some, social incentives may well be the primary motivator of adherence.

Again, the importance of religion as a source of social assistance divides the United States from many EU countries. With the rise of the welfare state, many governments displaced churches as providers of social goods. In fact, in a crossnational analysis of per capita welfare spending and religiosity, political scientists Anthony Gill and Eric Lundsgaarde found a negative association between state-provided welfare and religious involvement.[54] In the context of anemic monopoly churches, undermining religious groups and charities as providers of welfare benefits may have contributed to disaffiliation. In the United States, where the reach of the welfare state is limited, religious firms became specialists in providing a restless people with resources, family support, and community assistance.

Will the patterns I have described persist? There is little reason to expect the demand for religion to disappear. However, given low intergenerational transfers of spiritual capital (that is, religious training, devotions, catechism, hymnody, and other forms of human investment in producing religious goods) and weak constraints – social, economic, or political – on religious choices, individuals will likely assemble eclectic, personalized religious worldviews. As is becoming apparent in Europe, if demand remains

---

[51] Casanova, *Public Religions*, p. 38.

[52] Penny Edgell, Joseph Gerteis, and Douglas Hartmann, "Atheists as 'Other': Moral Boundaries and Cultural Membership in American Society," *American Sociological Review*, vol. 71, no. 2, 2006, pp. 211–34.

[53] Darren E. Sherkat and Christopher G. Ellison, "Recent Developments and Current Controversies in the Sociology of Religion," *Annual Review of Sociology*, 1999, p. 381.

[54] Anthony Gill and Eric Lundsgaarde, "State Welfare Spending and Religiosity: A Cross-National Analysis," *Rationality and Society*, vol. 16, no. 4, 2004, pp. 399–436.

but denominational and confessional attachments weaken, religious preferences become more individualized and the status of orthodox authorities
diminishes.[55] As Philip Gorski aptly puts it, "the weakening of traditional
Christianity appears not as a decline of religion per se . . . but as a return to
polysemism, since the new worldviews are not uniformly theistic."[56] In fact,
even in the most highly "secularized" societies, supernatural beliefs persist.
For example, the WVS reveals that although only 60 percent of the Dutch
believe in God, nearly 70 percent believe in "supernatural forces." In Estonia, where only half of the population believes in God, more than 60 percent
believe in the supernatural.

There are social mechanisms that tend to promote or contain this spiritual diversity. Childhood socialization often reinforces religious commitment
by providing an initial stock of spiritual capital that increases returns to
subsequent religious involvement. Ongoing involvement adds to the stock,
and increasing returns create denominational loyalty. However, that does
not mean that all individuals prefer an exclusive investment in a particular "asset class." Most people tend to diversify unless compelled to invest
in exclusive or incommensurable varieties of spiritual capital. Unless orthodoxy is binding, the diverse and pluralized worldviews that Gorski describes
will predominate. Free from constraint, people tend to create a "mixed
ideological portfolio" – a diverse set of beliefs drawing upon rationalist
ideas, religious doctrines, and personal spirituality.[57] A recent survey of
Germans underscores this point. Only two-thirds of professed Christians
believe in life after death in heaven, and only a third in the omnipotence of
God; yet many believe in non-Christian spiritual concepts, such as Buddhist
reincarnation.[58]

There are parallel developments in the United States. More than a tenth of
Americans describe themselves as spiritual but not religious. As new forms of
spirituality develop and the old mainline denominations struggle, the weakening grip of traditional religious organizations also becomes evident in the
growing appeal of nondenominational churches. A highly individualized and
diverse religiosity may not require exclusive, lifelong membership in a particular religious firm. This makes it doubtful that it will generate social capital

---

[55] Yves Lambert, "A Turning Point in Religious Evolution in Europe," *Journal of Contemporary
Religion*, vol. 19, no. 1, 2004, pp. 29–45.

[56] Philip Gorski, "The Return of the Repressed: Religion and the Political Unconscious of Historical Sociology," in Julia Adams, Elisabeth Clemens, and Ann Shola Orloff, eds., *Remaking
Modernity* (Durham: Duke University Press, 2005).

[57] Laurence Iannaccone, "Risk, Rationality, and Religious Portfolios," *Economic Inquiry*, vol.
32, 1995, pp. 285–95.

[58] Kaiser, Kneip, and Smoltcyzk, "Das Kreuz mit den Deutschen."

in a fashion comparable to exclusive religions. The consequence may be that as contemporary people diversify spiritually, their social capital, and hence their capacity for collective action, will diminish. One result might be that although belief persists, committed religious membership declines.

The Return of the Repressed? Religion and the Future of Politics

Democratic theorists since Tocqueville have identified religious attachments as providing a resource for democracy. Religion can be an important source of the social capital identified as making democracy work.[59] But the influence of religion need not limit itself to generating consensus; religious sentiments also generate political conflict. The potential influence of religiosity on politics is evident in comparing public opinion on religion and politics in the United States and the EU. Substantial majorities in every one of the democracies included in Table 1.3 oppose the direct involvement of religious leaders in politics. It is telling, however, that in the United States the *lowest* proportion of respondents – just over 60 percent – insists that religious leaders stay out of politics. Precisely because religion is an important focus of public life and interest group politics, there is a weaker consensus in the United States favoring political secularism.

Even so, religion's capacity to motivate political action has not entirely disappeared in Europe. In particular, two challenges to political secularism and the suppression of public religion have provoked conflict. The first is conservative mobilization in the new member states of the EU against pressures for institutional liberalization. The second is the pressure on existing church institutions and the consensus on privatized religion from increasingly assertive Muslim minorities.

In a recent scene that might be familiar to Americans, an anti-abortion protest in the halls of the European Parliament in Strasbourg led to scuffles and angry confrontations among parliamentarians. Asked to explain why he staged the protest, Maciej Giertych, member for the League of Polish Families Party, declared, "We want to see Europe based on a Christian ethic. We accept the teachings of the Catholic Church on all moral issues. If you want to know our opinions, read the opinions of the Catholic Church." One of the opponents, Ana Gomes of the Portuguese Socialist Party, complained, "I would rather we had moved on but if we have to have that ideological and political fight [over abortion policy], then I am ready." Her colleague, a member for the British Labour Party and a gay rights activist, explained,

---

[59] Robert D. Putnam, *Making Democracy Work: Civic Traditions in Modern Italy* (Princeton: Princeton University Press, 1993).

"New groups have come [into the EU] from Poland, the Czech Republic, Latvia, and Catholicism is certainly becoming a very angry voice against what it sees as a liberal E.U. On women's rights and gay equality, we are fighting battles that we thought we had won years ago."[60]

As the EU expands territorially and exerts pressure on member states to institute reforms, such episodes may become more common. Conservatives perceive the EU as promoting an agenda at odds with European traditions. Pope Benedict XVI has called for "spiritual reawakening" in Europe that would affirm its identity as the center of Western Christendom. Backed by the Vatican, conservatives from Poland, Italy, and other countries lobbied hard for references to Christianity in the preamble to the proposed EU constitution. And Vatican diplomats have signed concordats with governments in countries such as Poland, Slovakia, Lithuania, Portugal, and Italy, seeking common ground on issues such as abortion rights, reproductive technologies, and gay rights.

Catholic mobilization has borne some early fruit. In 2005, the conservative Law and Justice Party came to power in Poland, winning both the office of president and the prime minister (held by twin bothers, as it happens). Law and Justice initially governed with the support of two small parties, the populist Party of Self-Defense and the League of Polish Families. The de facto coalition is cemented by opposition to what conservatives see as the permissive liberalism of the EU and its attempted interference in national sovereignty. The Polish government's strict anti-abortion law, its opposition to homosexual unions, and its abolition of the women's ministry from the cabinet have rankled EU politicians. The conservatives welcome the confrontation. Andrege Monka of the League of Families explains, "Sooner or later one of the cultures will win out. Either we get influenced by Western European values or with time we'll go back to the roots of Europe that are illustrated clearly in Poland."[61]

Conservatives in the "new Europe" often find themselves closer to Washington than Brussels. After 1945, the countries east of the Elbe came under Soviet domination and communist governments embraced the ideology of Marxism-Leninism, imposing coercive secularization from above.[62] Regimes attacked the churches and promoted "scientific atheism" in place of religion. Religious groups generally suffered severe persecution, and in most

---

[60] Graham Bowley, "Conservative Poland Roils E.U.," *New York Times*, December 29, 2005.

[61] Rachel Martin, "EU Uneasy with Poland's Move to Right," National Public Radio, February 19, 2006.

[62] Froese and Pfaff, "Replete and Desolate Markets."

TABLE 1.4. *Religiosity of Postcommunist Poland compared with the United States, Italy, and Hungary, 1990*

	% of Population Stating That Religion Is "Very Important" to Them	% of Population Who Consider Themselves Religious	% of Population Who Believe in God	% of Population Who Attend Church Weekly
Poland	52.5	95.3	96.6	65.2
United States	53.5	83.8	96.0	65.2
Italy	30.7	84.5	89.9	37.9
Hungary	23.2	56.8	65.4	20.7

Source: WVS 90–93.

countries organized religion became very weak. Yet in some, especially where the Roman Catholic Church refused to make damaging concessions to the state and cast itself as a patriotic defender, Catholicism became a beacon of national autonomy and tradition. Indeed, the clergy helped to preserve precommunist loyalties both to the churches and to conservatism.[63] Subsequently, in the peaceful revolutions, churches and religious leaders played a large role in negotiating democratic transitions, particularly in Poland.

As a result of this experience, popular attachment to the Church remains surprisingly strong across the region. It is telling that Poles, in particular, were very close to Americans in terms of several indicators of religiosity at the close of the communist era (see Table 1.4). Churches and religious leaders have continued to play an important role in the political life of Poland and other postcommunist societies and were often among the most important advocates of EU membership. And now, with the EU intervening in the social and cultural affairs of member states, a mounting *Kulturkampf* between Eurocrats and Catholic conservatives may help the Roman Catholic Church to stave off the otherwise predictable consequences of its near monopoly status.

Even so, in asserting religiously driven politics, the Catholic "theo-cons" face long odds. As part of his campaign to reevangelize Europe and affirm loyalty to the Church, Pope Benedict visited his homeland in the summer of 2005 to coincide with the World Youth Congress of the Church. The festival drew some eight-hundred thousand participants, suggesting that interest in spirituality has not vanished among European youth. Yet in reasserting the

---

[63] Jason Wittenberg, *Crucibles of Political Loyalty: Church Institutions and Electoral Continuity in Hungary* (Cambridge and New York: Cambridge University Press, 2006).

authority of the Church, the dogmatist faces an uphill struggle in Western Europe. A survey in July 2005 found that just over half (56 percent) of Germans aged eighteen to twenty-nine now profess belief in God. And, even among the faithful, few have doctrinaire beliefs, with most assembling a diverse conception of spirituality.[64] Like other Western Europeans, Germans value the churches less for their role in promoting religion than for providing social services, maintaining cultural traditions, and stimulating general moral uplift.

In Western Europe, it is an assertive Islam that may do the most to challenge the secular consensus on the private role of religion. European Muslims are not as well organized as their Catholic counterparts; for the most part, the roughly 20 million Muslims in Europe have yet to become an organized political force. Yet this is not because of a lack of salient political issues, as the 2005 riots outside Paris and the furor over the Danish cartoons of Muhammad indicate. Across Europe, anger over media depictions, police scrutiny, tightening restrictions on immigration, chronic unemployment, restrictions on the wearing of religious attire, and the availability of Islamic instruction in public schools have charged political debate.

Conflict may be exacerbated by European church–state institutions ill suited to Muslim religious organizations and practices.[65] Although European states have traditionally worked with hierarchically organized religions with definitive leaders, Islam – particularly the Sunni varieties prevalent in Europe – is highly decentralized and nonhierarchical, with a variety of competing legal and theological traditions. Europe's Muslims are also cleaved along lines of ethnicity, national origin, and citizenship status, making the Islamic sector of the European religious market somewhat like the American denominational structure. Most mosques have their own imam and are responsible for their own administration, including clerical salaries. Although some are associated with denominational groupings based on shared theology or ethnic origin, there is no overarching hierarchy. Sunni Islam does not have the equivalent of a pope, bishops, or superintendents with final doctrinal authority. Today, building on their own well-organized milieu, many Muslim leaders promote religion as an alternative source of social identity and a defender of immigrant interests.

In accord with the supply-side model, both the plural organization and outsider status of Islam in Europe appear to increase its vitality. Yet it also

[64] Kaiser, Kneip, and Smoltcyzk, "Das Kreuz mit den Deutschen."
[65] Joel S. Fetzer and Christopher Soper, *Muslims and the State in Britain, France, and Germany* (New York: Cambridge University Press, 2005).

makes Muslims difficult to integrate into European polities. European authorities want Islam to be organized into hierarchical groupings, with "responsible" leaders at the top. Yet the cost for any Muslim leader, representing a fraction of all adherents, to enforce doctrinal or organizational unity is remarkably high and "spoilers" are difficult to suppress. Moreover, although privileges and subsidies may offer an attractive incentive for cooperating with the state, government ties limit the autonomy of religious firms.

Given these realities, the general pattern is of low- and mid-level Muslim organizations. This, in turn, makes it difficult for officials to manage immigrant affairs and for Muslims to assert their religious interests through ordinary political channels. If second- and third-generation Muslims continue to feel estranged, then Islam may well remain an ersatz homeland, displacing the nation of residence. And the unwillingness to reform religious institutions or accommodate greater pluralism may well prove a factor in European opposition to Turkey's bid to join the EU.

Conclusion

My argument in this chapter can be summarized in terms of three underlying theoretical propositions. The first is that to the degree that a religious economy is competitive, average levels of religious participation will be high. The second is that political rivals to established religions can suppress religious demand by raising the cost of consumption. The third is that regulations that impinge on the doctrinal authority or organizational autonomy of religious firms provoke countermobilization that challenges the secularism of the polity.

It is evident that in the spiritual realm, the United States and Europe have grown far apart. This does not mean that religion in Europe will continue to decline with each passing year or that American religion will continually extend its grasp. Nor does it mean that secular government is seriously threatened by religious activism. In coming decades, EU states will face pressure to accommodate traditional and conservative values and a larger public role for religion. European polities will also be stretched to integrate new religions and especially Islam, indicating a serious challenge to the tolerant, multicultural, but secular consensus that has been at the heart of European politics since 1945. Recently, parties with anti-immigrant platforms and expressing suspicion of Islam have done well in Denmark, the Netherlands, and other countries. These positions are sometimes framed in terms of a defense of the cultural homogeneity and secular values putatively underlying the democratic welfare state.

New forces may reawaken a Europe that is growing more religiously plural. Catholicism is being reenergized by confronting expanding EU authorities. Countermobilization by religious conservatives may limit extension of social and cultural policies from Brussels to the member states. New religious movements such as Buddhism, reflecting diverse and intimate spiritual cravings, may thrive. Protestant sects are making substantial inroads against the historic confessions in some parts of Europe.[66] And Europe's expanding Muslim population is not only more pious on average than its neighbors, but beginning to demand religious liberties and a voice in public affairs.[67]

The United States faces challenges of its own. In his antebellum travels, Tocqueville perceived that the vitality of American religious life lay in its self-reliance and independence from state control. He observed, "Free and powerful in its own sphere, satisfied with the place reserved for it, religion never more surely establishes its empire than when it reigns in the hearts of men unsupported by aught beside its native strength."[68] Today, the "empire of faith" so desired by American evangelicals may be its own undoing. The growing political clout of Christian conservatives may in the long run undermine the appeal of religion as an alternative to a secular politics. Evangelicals profited by opposing the "establishment"; now they are becoming it. Their power to institute regulations or grant subsidies that privilege their interests or impose their values through the mechanisms of the state may associate religion with oppressive conformity, intolerance, and illegitimate entitlement in broadening circles of American opinion. As this chapter has shown, religion and the state are tightly intertwined. Both state intrusion into the religious sphere and the temptation to use state power to promote public piety have driven cycles of secularization and revival through history and may do so again.

---

[66] Nate Anderson and Leah Anderson. "Under Reconstruction: How Eastern Europe's Evangelicals Are Restoring the Church's Vitality," *Christianity Today*, October 13, 2005.

[67] Pfaff and Gill, "Will a Million Muslims March?"

[68] Tocqueville, quoted in Raymond Aron, *Main Currents in Sociological Thought* (New York: Anchor, 1968), vol. I, p. 255.

2

Value Change in Europe and North America

Convergence or Something Else?

Christopher Cochrane, Neil Nevitte, and Stephen White

Introduction

A large body of empirical evidence demonstrates that the basic values of mass publics in advanced industrial societies have changed over the last three decades.[1] The same research also shows that there are significant and persistent crossnational differences in values. This chapter considers whether the trajectory and pace of value change in advanced industrial countries is leading to convergence or divergence in the values of publics in Europe and North America.

The question of value convergence or divergence can be conceptualized and addressed empirically in at least two ways. The most straightforward approach entails identifying common value domains among European and North American publics and then asking, Have these become more, or less, alike over the two decades for which we have data? A second approach, however, is to explore the internal dynamics of value change by examining how North American and European publics organize their core values. After outlining some different perspectives on value change and describing our data and methodological approach, we present the basic crossnational

---

[1] Russell J. Dalton, *Citizen Politics*, 2nd edition (Chatham, NJ: Chatham House, 1996); Neil Nevitte, *The Decline of Deference: Canadian Value Change in Cross-National Perspective* (Peterborough: Broadview Press, 1996); Ronald Inglehart, *Modernization and Postmodernization: Cultural, Economic and Political Change in 43 Societies* (Princeton: Princeton University Press, 1997); idem, *Cultural Shift in Advanced Industrial Society* (Princeton: Princeton University Press, 1990); idem, *Silent Revolution: Changing Values and Political Styles* (Princeton: Princeton University Press, 1977); Scott Flanagan, "Changing Values in Advanced Industrial Societies Revisited: Towards a Resolution of the Values Debate," *American Political Science Review*, vol. 81, 1987, pp. 1303–19; idem, "Changing Values in Advanced Industrial Societies," *Comparative Political Studies*, vol. 14, 1982, pp. 403–44.

and crosstime evidence of change on single-value dimensions for publics in Europe and North America. The focus then shifts to consider the matter of how publics on both continents bundle their basic value outlooks. Do the publics in North America and Europe organize their basic value outlooks in similar or different ways? And are there discernible patterns in the way in which these core values have changed over the same period?

On balance, the evidence suggests that Europeans and North Americans are moving in the same direction when it comes to their core value outlooks. But the evidence also shows that the publics in Europe and North America are moving in opposite directions when it comes to the dynamics of how these core values are bundled. Between 1981 and 2000, the American values divide tightened and it expanded across a greater range of value dimensions. Americans who disagreed on one issue became gradually more likely to disagree on other issues as well. The values divide in Europe, by contrast, increasingly fragmented over the same period.

Perspectives on Value Change

Understanding value change from a crossnational perspective is important for a number of reasons. First, such a vantage point facilitates a more precise understanding of the drivers of value change. Are the sources of value change rooted in the specific histories of advanced industrial societies, or are values being moved by something that these countries share in common? Second, and of more practical significance, the beliefs of mass publics can influence international decision making. As Robert Putnam has noted, national decision makers must always balance domestic and international political considerations in a two-level game[2]; and there are reasons to believe that value compatibility between different publics makes it easier to achieve that balance.[3]

There are two broad schools of thought concerning crossnational shifts in basic values. One suggests that the social and political values of different societies follow similar developmental trajectories.[4] The value composition of any particular mass public at any given moment depends on that country's

---

[2] Robert Putnam, "Diplomacy and Domestic Politics: The Logic of Two-Level Games," *International Organization*, vol. 42, 1988, pp. 429–60.

[3] K. W. Deutsch, *The Nerves of Government* (New York: Free Press, 1963); idem, *Political Community and the North Atlantic Area. International Organization in the Light of Historical Experience* (Princeton: Princeton University Press, 1957); idem, *Nationalism and Social Communication* (Cambridge, MA: MIT Press, 1952).

[4] Daniel Bell, *The Coming of Postindustrial Society* (New York: Basic Books, 1973); Inglehart, *Modernization and Postmodernization*.

level of economic and technological advancement, but value change generally occurs in a comparable and even predictable fashion across Western
nations. According to this line of reasoning, the expectation is that the basic
value landscapes of these two sets of publics will be basically similar because
Western European and North American publics experience similar levels of
"postindustrialism." Different analysts emphasize different consequences of
the processes of postindustrial value change. Some draw attention to the
fact that these publics have become "emancipated from the forces previously dominating society."[5] Others, such as Ronald Inglehart, contend that
such goals as freedom, autonomy, and quality of life are increasingly valued
as people become less preoccupied with such material goals as wealth and
security.[6] Yet others focus on changing authority patterns.[7] To be sure, the
underlying theoretical explanations for these broad shifts in values vary from
scholar to scholar, but the common thread is that publics in advanced industrial states share the same syndrome of value change. From this perspective,
the expectation is that the countries of Europe and North America are on
broadly similar trajectories when it comes to basic values.

A second school of thought suggests that shifts in basic values are rooted in
the specific historical circumstances of societies. The timing and sequence of
such events as massive immigration flows, economic development, and the
establishment of political institutions, they contend, can have a profound
and lasting impact on the evolution of the values of mass publics.[8] This
historical perspective features prominently in most explanations for the cultural and political exceptionalism of the United States.[9] The postindustrial
and historical propositions stand as the major alternative accounts of value
change in late-industrial states. But it is also important to acknowledge an
emerging middle ground. Recent empirical scholarship suggests that the trajectories of change in Europe may be more complex than proponents of the
postindustrialism thesis allow.[10] Wil Arts and Loek Halman, for instance,

---

[5] L. Halman and R. de Moor, "Religion, Churches and Moral Values," in P. Ester, L. Halman, and R. de Moor, eds., *The Individualizing Society* (Tilburg: Tilburg University Press, 1993), p. 299.

[6] See Inglehart, *Moderization and Postmodernization*.

[7] Nevitte, *Decline of Deference*.

[8] Louis Hartz, *The Founding of New Societies* (New York: Harcourt Brace, 1964); Seymour Martin Lipset, *Continental Divide: The Values and Institutions of the United States and Canada* (New York: Routledge, 1990).

[9] See, for example, John Kingdon, *America the Unusual* (New York: St. Martin's/Worth, 1999); Seymour Martin Lipset, *America Exceptionalism: A Double-Edged Sword* (New York: W. W. Norton, 1996).

[10] Jan W. van Deth and Elinor Scarborough, eds., *The Impact of Values* (New York: Oxford University Press, 1995).

find that "country specific characteristics and historic roots... appear to be the most important characteristics in understanding country differences in value orientations."[11] The expectation that flows from this perspective is that value change in different societies across Europe and North America does not conform to a single discernible pattern. Indeed, it is entirely possible that the values of publics in different countries may diverge with the passage of time. Fundamental value changes may move in different directions, and at different rates, in different societies.

Data and Methodology

Measuring value change presents a number of empirical challenges. First, the conventional wisdom is that changes in values take place slowly; they are incremental because under normal conditions they are geared primarily by socialization and population replacement.[12] Consequently, tracking value change directly and reliably calls for directly comparable data that are gathered at regular intervals over a long time span. One possible approach is to cast the widest possible net and to gather data from multiple countries over the longest time span possible. But that approach confronts a variety of potential problems. Different surveys use different strategies for collecting data; survey items may have different metrics, and even questions tapping similar values are rarely asked in exactly the same way. With these kinds of data, it becomes difficult to ascertain whether any apparent crosstime changes in the data reflect genuine shifts in values or whether these changes are simply the result of differences in the question wording of the survey items, response set variations, administration effects, or some combination of instrument effects.

To respond to these challenges, we adopt a more cautious approach and rely on data from the World Values Survey (WVS). The WVS contains data from nationally representative samples of publics from twenty-one countries in 1981–3 (N = 28 764), forty-three countries in 1990–3 (N = 59 169), forty-five countries in 1995–7 (N = 78 574), and sixty-seven countries in

---

[11] Wil Arts and Loek Halman, eds., *European Values at the Turn of the Millennium*, European Values Studies 7 (Leiden: Brille, 2004), p. 51.

[12] M. Rokeach, *The Nature of Human Value* (New York: Free Press, 1973); David Sears, "The Persistence of Early Political Predispositions: The Roles of Attitude Object and Life Stage," in Phillip Shaver and Clyde A. Wheeler, eds., *Review of Personality and Social Psychology* (Beverly Hills: Sage, 1983), pp. 79–116; Paul Abramson and Ronald Inglehart, "Generational Replacement and Value Change in Eight West European Societies," *British Journal of Political Science*, vol. 22, 1992, pp. 183–228; Nevitte, *Decline of Deference*.

1999–2002 (N = 96 296). The WVS is explicitly designed to maximize the crossnational and crosstime reliability of the data. Many of the survey items from the 1981 wave of the survey are asked in precisely the same way in each of the successive waves and in each of the participating countries. To maximize crossnational and crosstime reliability, this analysis focuses only on those countries for which we have data from at least three time-points beginning in 1981. After screening the questionnaires used in each of these countries, we isolated those variables that met two important criteria for inclusion: identical question wording and response set across countries and time-points. That screening disqualifies four country datasets from consideration: Argentina, Japan, Korea, and Mexico. Nonetheless, that screening process leaves us with sixty-three variables for analysis across two decades in fifteen countries: Belgium, Canada, Denmark, Finland, France, Iceland, Ireland, Italy, the Netherlands, Norway, Spain, Sweden, the United Kingdom, the United States, and West Germany (see Appendix A).

The next step involves determining how respondents in all countries organize their core values. To identify these underlying structures in the responses to the sixty-three survey items that met our criteria for inclusion, the pooled data from each of the fifteen countries and four time-points are subjected to exploratory factor analysis (principal components). The initial results reveal eleven components with an Eigenvalue greater than one (Appendix B). Six of these components measure an underlying construct well enough to meet or exceed the minimum threshold of scale reliability,[13] and of these six components, four turn out to be statistically reliable in all countries and at each and every time-point: religiosity (component 1), work motivations (component 2), political protest (component 3), and moral permissiveness (component 6).

Each of the value dimensions emerging from these screening procedures has attracted significant attention from analysts of culture and cultural change: religiosity and moral values,[14] work motivations,[15] and political protest.[16] This analysis focuses initially on two of the most important value dimensions: religiosity and moral values. The second part of the investigation then turns to explore how Europeans and North Americans fold these core values into their conceptualizations of "left" and "right," conceptualizations

---

[13] We used a Cronbach's Alpha of .700 as the minimum threshold of scale reliability.

[14] Emile Durkheim, *The Elementary Forms of the Religious Life*, translated by J. W. Swain (New York: Free Press, 1912); Peter Berger, *A Rumor of Angels* (Garden City, NY: Doubleday, 1969).

[15] Max Weber, *The Protestant Ethic and the Spirit of Capitalism* (New York: Scribner's, 1958).

[16] Samuel Barnes, Max Kasse, and Klaus Allerbeck, *Political Action* (Beverly Hills: Sage, 1979).

that are part of the everyday political discourse among publics in all of these states.

A substantial body of empirical evidence indicates that publics in advanced industrial states clearly can and do employ and respond to "left" and "right" labels.[17] The left–right dimension, however, is not content-specific; it has taken on different meanings for different publics at different historical moments. Left–right considerations become substantively important precisely because they allow us to probe the question of convergence or divergence from a slightly different vantage point: Is the value content that Europeans and North Americans pour into their notions of "left" and "right" the same? Or has it changed? And if so, to what extent has the content of these left–right ideological vessels become more similar or more different with the passage of time?

Our analytical approach to investigating change on these value dimensions begins by taking each survey as the first (1981), second (1990), second plus one-half (1995), and third (2000) time-point and then to plot lines of best fit through the values for those countries.[18] Because the samples are *nationally* representative, the trend lines for Europe and North America are weighted to take into account population differences between the countries within each region.[19] The second stage in the analysis process probes these data more deeply by separately examining three salient value dimensions: religiosity, moral permissiveness, and left–right self-placement.

Findings: The Rate and Direction of Changing North American and European Values: Growing Together or Growing Apart?

Nine survey items load heavily on the single dimension that we label "religiosity." These items include questions about the importance of God and religion in the lives of respondents, whether respondents get comfort and strength from religion, beliefs in God, heaven, an afterlife and hell, rates of

---

[17] Dieter Fuchs and Hans-Dieter Klingemann, "The Left–Right Schema," in M. Kent Jennings and Jan van Deth, eds., *Continuities in Political Action* (Berlin: de Gruyter, 1989); Dalton, *Citizen Politics*.

[18] The slope of the line of best fit represents the trend: ΔValues $= \beta_1$(year), in the equation Values $= \alpha + \beta_1$(year) $+ \epsilon$.

[19] The weighting formula is simply:

$$\frac{\Sigma(\text{Population of } X_{1...n} \div (\mu \text{ Population of Selected European} \mid \text{North American Countries}) * Y_{1...n})}{N}$$

This weighting procedure ensures that the countries within Europe and North America affect the aggregate means on each value dimension in a way that is proportionate to their relative share of the population.

church attendance, and confidence in the churches (see Appendix C for question wording and variable coding). Together, these items constitute a highly reliable and broad scale of religiosity.[20] Figure 2.1 summarizes the trends in religiosity among publics in each country and highlights the weighted aggregate trend lines for Europe and North America. Clearly, the aggregate trends for Europe and North America are relatively stable; there has been a marginal decline in levels of religiosity between 1981 and 2000. In effect, Europeans and North Americans were almost as religious in 2000 as they were in 1981.

A more detailed probing of these data, however, shows that this aggregate stability masks significant within-country variations, particularly in Europe. Levels of religiosity declined in seven European countries, were stable in two countries, and increased in four others (substantially so in three of them). The trajectories in Canada and the United States are stable and identical. Substantial variation between European countries has been documented elsewhere,[21] but it is the stability of aggregate levels of religiosity between 1981 and 2000 that is noteworthy.

The simple intuition is that levels of religiosity among publics might well be responsible for shaping orientations toward other such value dimensions as "moral outlooks." The empirical implication of that line of speculation is that national changes in moral outlooks might mirror the changing levels of religiosity in each country. The data summarized in Figure 2.2, however, provide no support for this hypothesis. Rather, the publics in all but one of the countries included in the analysis became more permissive in their moral outlooks between 1981 and 2000.[22] The weighted trends for moral permissiveness show that European and North American publics have converged during the course of the two decades for which we have data. There is also evidence of the emergence of two distinctive clusters of countries: Britain, the United States, and West Germany, on the one hand, and Belgium, Canada, Demark, Finland, France, Iceland, and Norway, on the other. Taken together, the data reported in Figures 2.1 and 2.2 appear to present a paradox: If levels

---

[20] It would be possible, of course, to dichotomize our scale of religiosity into separate institutional and spiritual components. But factor analysis and reliability checks for the data for each country show that there is no statistical justification for introducing such a dichotomy; the scale measures a single component and is highly reliable in all national contexts and at each time-point.

[21] Loek Halman and Thorleif Petterson, "Individualization and Value Fragmentation," in Ruud de Moor, ed., *Values in Western Societies* (Tilburg: Tilburg University Press, 1995).

[22] Denmark is the only exception. We include Denmark even though we only have Danish data on moral permissiveness for 1981 and 2000.

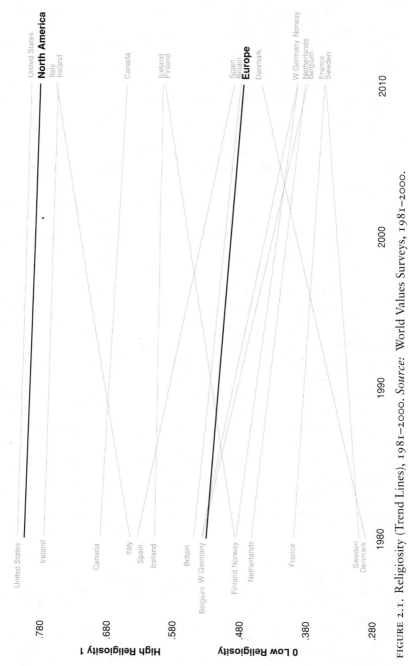

FIGURE 2.1. Religiosity (Trend Lines), 1981–2000. *Source:* World Values Surveys, 1981–2000.

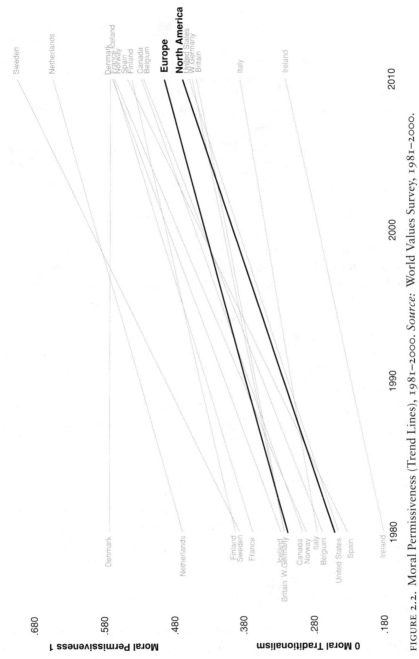

FIGURE 2.2. Moral Permissiveness (Trend Lines), 1981–2000. *Source:* World Values Survey, 1981–2000.

of religiosity are relatively stable over the two decades and there is substantial variability between countries, then what accounts for the seemingly uniform and substantial rise in levels of moral permissiveness? That question will be revisited later in the analysis.

The initial WVS results do indeed point toward common syndromes of value change among North American and European publics: Among both, levels of religiosity are declining slightly and moral permissiveness is increasing. These patterns seem to signify what might conventionally be thought of as a "shift to the left." On all of these value dimensions, as well as on such other value dimensions as political protest, economic egalitarianism, and even political protest potential, publics in Europe and North America appeared more "left-wing" in their value outlooks in 2000 than twenty years earlier.

The WVS has always contained a question asking respondents to place themselves on a standard left–right scale, and so the question of whether these publics have shifted "to the right" or "to the left" can be answered directly. As the data in Figure 2.3 show, the North American and European patterns are in the same direction. Both Canadians and Americans moved significantly "to the left" between 1981 and 2000. This same pattern is evident in eight European countries, including Spain, Germany, and especially Britain. Italy was the only large country to experience a "shift to the right" over the same period, joining Iceland and Denmark as the only European publics to move in the opposite direction. The Dutch and French publics remained in relatively stable ideological space during the course of these two decades. The net results of these national patterns are aggregate continental trends indicating convergence. On balance, North Americans and Europeans moved in the same direction.

Value Dynamics in Europe and North America

To this point, the primary focus has been on the national-level "big pictures" for each of the fifteen countries in the analysis. Exclusive attention to nation-level data, however, sheds no light on the dynamics of value change within each country. Knowing how many people in any national setting hold what particular values is a useful starting point. But it is at least as important to know *who* holds which values, and how some sets of values are bundled with others.

There are two basic strategies available for examining the value dynamics within countries. One is to focus on the extent to which publics within a country disagree or agree on any given value dimension. Knowing how

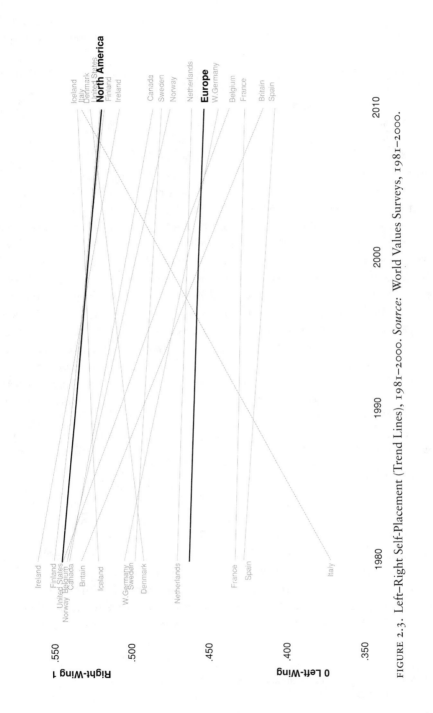

FIGURE 2.3. Left–Right Self-Placement (Trend Lines), 1981–2000. *Source:* World Values Surveys, 1981–2000.

publics are distributed along and across core values is certainly consequential because it is harder to reach consensus on value questions when the country is polarized.[23]

The second approach works from the premise that most people hold more than one value simultaneously. People hold core economic values while also holding moral values, religious values, and work values. Following Philip Converse, the second approach draws attention to why or whether these different values are connected to each other.[24] Do moral values run with economic ones? Are workplace motivations connected to religious outlooks? And are these connections, these values packages, changing or stable?

The second approach is more promising for a combination of empirical and theoretical reasons. First, it turns out that the extent to which publics agree, or disagree, about these basic value outlooks is essentially the same from one population to the next (although these results are not shown here). Moreover, the average distance of each individual from the overall average, the standard deviation, is partly an artifact of the scale construction. "Floor" and "ceiling" effects, for instance, will shrink the standard deviation where the national average is concentrated toward one end of the scale, regardless of whether the national distribution is clustered around the mean or polarized between groups who are far but equidistant from the average. Scales can capture values only up to a certain extreme point. Anything beyond that extreme will get lumped into the highest or the lowest available category on the scale, thus positioning the respondent artificially close to the average position because there was no available category to capture their actual opinion. Since our scales are designed to measure values from a very broad segment of the world's population, "floor" and "ceiling" effects will thus inevitably affect analyses of how values are distributed.

More important, though, the bundling of values is especially germane to an investigation into the extent of the values divide within societies. If people's attitudes on one value dimension tend to be strongly connected to their attitudes on another value dimension, then, ipso facto, there are overlapping disagreements within society. If people who disagree in their religious outlooks also turn out to disagree in their moral outlooks, work motivations, economic attitudes, and protest potential, then the values divide has a greater capacity to sort and possibly mobilize people than would be the case under those circumstances where value orientations are more randomly

---

[23] Anthony Downs, *An Economic Theory of Democracy* (New York: Harper and Row, 1957).

[24] Philip Converse, "The Nature of Belief Systems in Mass Publics," in David Apter, ed., *Ideology and Discontent* (New York: Free Press of Glencoe, 1964).

bundled. Aggregate distributions and across-time trajectories on separate value dimensions reveal one aspect of the value change story in Europe and North America. What they do not reveal, however, is the extent to which value disagreements overlap to divide each society into separate camps.

Value Bundling

Research drawing on the insights of Max Weber suggests that values in advanced industrial countries are becoming increasingly "individualized" and "fragmented."[25] According to Weber, "with the multiplication of life chances and opportunities the individual becomes less and less content with being bound to rigid and undifferentiated forms of life prescribed by the group. Increasingly he desires to shape his life as an individual and to enjoy the fruits of his own abilities and labor as he himself wishes."[26] Empirical research in Europe by Halman and de Moor provides evidence of a contemporary variant of this argument. Halman and de Moor show that "... values, beliefs, attitudes and behaviors are increasingly based on personal choice and are less dependent on tradition and social institutions."[27] As values become increasingly detached from such social structures as the family, church, or even class, individual values become more and more fragmented as the range of possible combinations of values expands considerably. As the values that individuals hold on one value dimension become progressively disconnected from their positions on other value dimensions, religiosity loses its hold on moral outlooks, and the language of "left" and "right" fails to constrain moral or economic outlooks. This conceptualization of individualization predicts increasing levels of value fragmentation.

Weber provides convincing reasons to suppose that the deepening and widening of advanced industrialism will be accompanied by accelerating trends toward individualization in these societies. And this theory can be tested empirically by developing some operational definitions of individualization and exploring crossnational and crosstime data on value change in postindustrial Western countries. Following Halman and de Moor, the focus here is primarily on the linkages between religious and moral outlooks. Religion clearly qualifies as a traditional social institution that historically has provided guidance for the life choices and worldviews of individuals.

---

[25] Halman and de Moor, "Religion, Churches and Values"; Ulrich Beck and Elisabeth Beck-Gernsheim, *Individualization: Institutionalized Individualism and Its Social and Political Consequences* (London: Sage, 2002); Arts and Halman, *European Values.*

[26] Max Weber, *Economy and Society: An Outline of Interpretive Sociology*, edited by Guenther Roth and Claus Wittich (Berkeley: University of California Press, 1978).

[27] Halman and de Moor, "Religion, Churches and Values," p. 72.

And the empirical implication of individualization theory is that religion will progressively lose its hold on the moral outlooks of citizens in Western countries. At issue is not just the question of whether religion itself is becoming less important in modern societies (secularization). Rather, the question is whether individuals are becoming less likely to take their cues from religious outlooks when making decisions about important moral questions. The paradox raised at the beginning of this analysis was this: If religious values are relatively stable over the two decades for which we have data, then what explains the relatively sharp increases in moral permissiveness? One potential answer to that question comes from the dynamics of individualization.

Figure 2.4 graphically displays the connectedness (Pearson's R) between religiosity and moral traditionalism for publics in every country across the two decades. Two striking findings emerge from the data. First, there is convincing evidence for supporting the individualization hypothesis in Europe. The connection between religiosity and moral outlooks has weakened in every single European country over these two decades. In effect, religious and moral outlooks have become increasingly decoupled. Not only are Europeans more secular, but by 2000 there was a greater consensus in moral outlooks between religious and secular Europeans than was the case in 1981.

The second finding concerns clear evidence indicating that the correlation between religiosity and moral traditionalism operates in the opposite direction; it increased in only two countries – the United States and Canada. The pattern is particularly striking within the United States. Between 1981 and 2000, the moral outlooks of secular Americans became far more permissive and they did so quite quickly. The moral outlooks of religious Americans, by contrast, changed rather slowly. The net effect of these changes stands in sharp contrast to the European pattern; the gap between the moral outlooks of religious and secular Americans widened substantially.

Taken together, these data are consistent with the argument that the religious cleavage has become more salient in the United States and less salient in Europe. The significant point to emphasize, however, is that the increased salience of the religious cleavage in the United States is not attributable to a rise in levels of religiosity or a decline in moral permissiveness (see Figures 2.1 and 2.2).

The declining connection between religiosity and moral outlooks is only one element of individualization. If values are moving away from such social structures as religion, then it is also plausible that other value bundles are also experiencing fragmentation. Perhaps individuals are choosing their own value outlooks with little regard for such structuring influences as class,

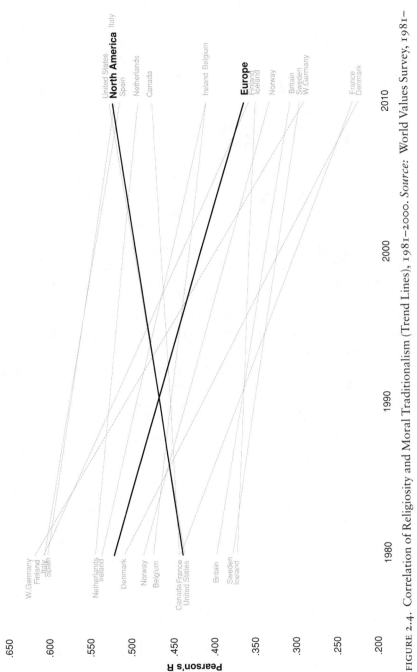

FIGURE 2.4. Correlation of Religiosity and Moral Traditionalism (Trend Lines), 1981–2000. *Source:* World Values Survey, 1981–2000.

religion, or the compartments of "left" and "right." With the WVS data, it becomes possible to explore directly the extent to which individuals organize their value outlooks along the lines of left and right by tracking cross-national and crosstime trends in the ways that left–right self-identification is connected to a variety of different core values.

One possibility to consider is that the categories of "left" and "right" mean different things to Europeans and North Americans – that Europeans and North Americans pour a different value content into their conceptions of left and right. The data provide no support for this line of speculation. According to the WVS data, "right-wing" self-identification is associated with moral traditionalism, and "left-wing" identification connotes moral permissiveness in every single country. When the analysis is expanded to encompass attitudes toward economic egalitarianism in 1990 and 2000, the same basic patterns persist: In every country, publics who see themselves as "left-wing" consistently favor greater income equality. And those who see themselves as "right-wing" are consistently more supportive of income incentives for individual effort.[28] When it comes to the connection of left–right self-identification to both moral and economic values, however, the findings are somewhat less straightforward. If value bundles are falling apart, the expectation is that "left" and "right" are less useful categories for organizing these value outlooks.

Figure 2.5 plots the correlations between moral traditionalism and left–right self-identification. As these data show, the categories of "left" and "right" have taken on increasingly moral connotations in five countries: Canada, Denmark, Finland, Sweden, and the United States. In nine countries, the opposite pattern emerges. Left–right self-identification grew apart from moral values in Belgium, Britain, France, Germany, Iceland, Ireland, Italy, the Netherlands, and Spain. Intriguingly, the North American and European trajectories are nearly identical to the trajectory of the correlations between religious and moral outlooks. For North Americans, that connection became closer between 1981 and 2000, whereas for Europeans that connection weakened. Do "left" and "right" serve more as compartments of moral values in North America and of economic values in Europe?

The WVS findings concerning the links between economic egalitarianism and left–right self-placement are graphically summarized in Figure 2.6. Note that the WVS measures of economic egalitarianism were first introduced in

---

[28] The distributive justice questions were not asked in 1981. We therefore have data for these measures for 1990, 1995, and 2000 only.

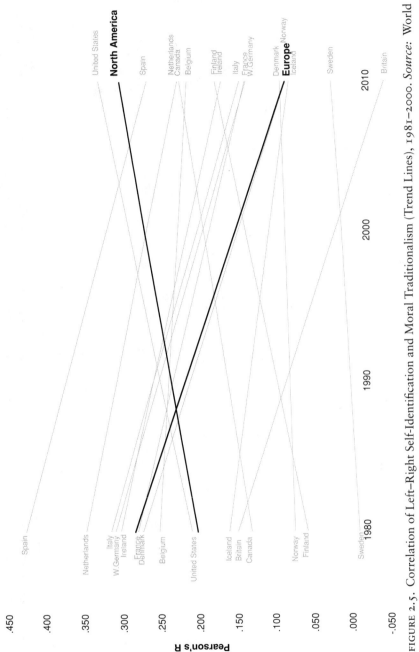

FIGURE 2.5. Correlation of Left–Right Self-Identification and Moral Traditionalism (Trend Lines), 1981–2000. *Source:* World Values Survey, 1981–2000.

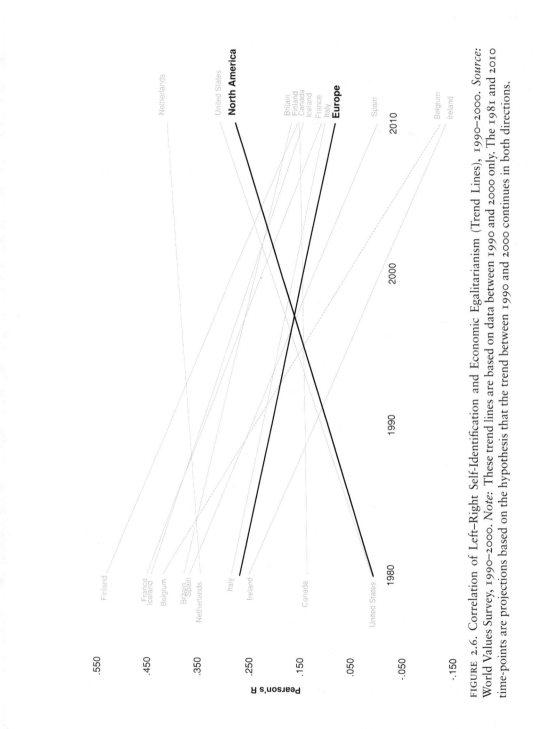

FIGURE 2.6. Correlation of Left–Right Self-Identification and Economic Egalitarianism (Trend Lines), 1990–2000. *Source:* World Values Survey, 1990–2000. *Note:* These trend lines are based on data between 1990 and 2000 only. The 1981 and 2010 time-points are projections based on the hypothesis that the trend between 1990 and 2000 continues in both directions.

1990 and so the three time-points concerned here are 1990, 1995, and 2000 only.[29]

The striking finding once again is clear evidence of divergence between the patterns in Europe and North America. In Canada and the United States, left–right self-identification became progressively more tightly bundled with attitudes toward distributive justice. With the single exception of the Netherlands, in each European country for which we have data, the opposite patterns persisted. In short, the salience of "left" and "right" as bundles of economic and moral values has increased in North America while it has decreased in Europe.

This line of analysis could be extended to other value dimensions as well. Our data suggest that Europe and North America are diverging when it comes to the ways that value outlooks are organized. In Europe, individualization and value fragmentation appear to be occurring across a number of important value dimensions: moral values are less constrained by religious outlooks, and left–right self-identification serves less effectively than it once did as compartments in which economic and moral values are organized. In North America, however, the connection between religious and moral outlooks has increased substantially, as has the extent to which the terms "left" and "right" are filled in with economic and moral values.

Conclusion: Convergence, Divergence, or Something Else?

This chapter began with a question: Does value change among publics in Europe and North America produce convergence or something else? The answer to that question, of course, depends on which values and which countries are under consideration. The approach followed here relies on direct individual level values data from the WVS from 1981 to 2000. The advantage of these data is that a large core of identically worded questions has been repeatedly asked of publics in multiple countries over the course of two decades. From these data we identified eleven core value dimensions and then focused on the very clear value dimensions for which we have reliable scales for each country at each time-point. The approach is conservative but robust. The aggregate answer to the research question is that the patterns of value change do not qualify as "convergence" but rather something else.

When it comes to the distributions of values across countries, North Americans and Europeans are moving in the same direction. Moral outlooks have become more permissive; publics are more tolerant about some behaviors

---

[29] We include for analysis all countries for which we have data for at least 1990 and 2000. For the sake of comparing these trends with those presented in the other figures, we plot the lines of best fit and extend these lines to 1981 and 2010.

that were once considered highly controversial or utterly unacceptable. Similarly, both North Americans and Europeans moved more "to the left" in their political outlooks between 1981 and 2000. The end result of the shared trajectories in both moral outlooks and political self-identification is that Americans and Europeans are moving closer together; their paths converged on these value dimensions.

The trend in religious outlooks, however, is less consistent. In some countries levels of religiosity declined, in others it increased, and in yet others it remained stable. On balance, aggregate levels of religiosity declined very modestly on both continents. But they declined at different rates, and consequently the gap between Europe and North America over the two decades widened slightly. Certainly, publics on both continents became more secular in their religious outlooks in 2000 than they were in 1981, but the pace of secularization was so incremental that it is hardly plausible to identify secularization as a central theme of value change from 1980 to 2000.

The analysis of within-country dynamics, however, reveals that there is quite another dimension to this story. In the United States, value differences became progressively more reinforcing; religious differences are strongly connected with moral differences, as well as with opposing opinions about distributive justice. In effect, if you knew where an American stood on moral values, you could predict with increasing accuracy where he or she stood on economic justice, left–right location, or levels of religiosity. The same applies, but to a lesser extent, to Canadian respondents. Indeed, the United States is the only country in our analysis where moral outlooks predict attitudes toward economic egalitarianism more effectively than income. Poor Americans may not support widespread wealth redistribution, but secular and morally permissive Americans are far more egalitarian in their economic outlooks than their religious and morally traditional co-nationals. In Europe, value disagreements overlap as well, but they do not do so nearly as tightly or as widely. Different moral outlooks overlap with differences in religiosity, but the overlap has weakened with the passage of time and moral outlooks do not run with economic viewpoints.[30]

These data suggest that Americans over the last two decades have settled into two separate but clear value camps. European values, by contrast, are becoming more individualized and fragmented. In America, people who disagree in their religious outlooks are more likely than Europeans who disagree

---

[30] The only two exceptions to this trend are Britain and Italy, where moral outlooks run with economic viewpoints in precisely the opposite direction as the language of left and right would lead us to predict. In both of these countries, "right-wing" economic outlooks are associated with "left-wing" moral outlooks, and "left-wing" economic outlooks are associated with "right-wing" moral outlooks.

in their religious outlooks to share different opinions about moral issues and economic egalitarianism. Americans with right-wing moral values are the same people who also hold right-wing economic values. The same applies to Americans on the left. Europeans think of left and right in the same way as Americans. The significant difference is that Europeans with left-wing moral outlooks are less likely to also hold left-wing economic viewpoints, or vice versa. In Europe, many people hold right-wing economic outlooks and many others hold right-wing moral outlooks. Unlike North Americans, however, comparatively few Europeans hold both at the same time.

The publics in Europe and North America are diverging when it comes to how they bundle their core values together. The American values divide, in effect, amounts to a fault line that is spreading across value dimensions, not widening between them. Americans are no more divided in their religious outlooks than they once were, but religious differences are now more likely to be connected to differing views about distributive justice, morality, and even left–right self-identification. By comparison, the values divide in Europe hardly qualifies as a crack. In the end, the trajectories on individual value dimensions are the same on both continents, but the common ground between people is more navigable in Europe than in America. Whereas Europeans seem to be growing together, North Americans seem to be growing apart.

Appendix A: Countries, Waves, and Sample Sizes

Country	Sample Size			
	1981–3	1990–1	1995–7	1999–2001
1. France	1,200	1,002	–	1,615
2. Britain	1,231	1,484	1,093	1,000
3. Germany (West)	1,305	2,101	1,017	2,036
4. Italy	1,348	2,018	–	2,000
5. Netherlands	1,221	1,017	–	1,003
6. Denmark	1,182	1,030	–	1,023
7. Belgium	1,145	2,792	–	1,912
8. Spain	2,303	4,147	1,211	2,409
9. Ireland	1,217	1,000	–	1,012
10. United States	2,325	1,839	1,542	1,200
11. Canada	1,254	1,730	–	1,931
12. Norway	1,246	1,239	1,127	–
13. Sweden	954	1,047	1,009	1,015
14. Iceland	927	702	–	968
15. Finland	1,003	588	987	1,038
TOTAL:	23,736	19,861	7,897	20,002

Appendix B: Rotated Factor Analysis (Principal Components Factor)

	1. Religiosity	2. Job Traits: Fulfillment	3. Political Protest	4. Institutional Confidence	5. Civil Permissiveness	6. Moral Permissiveness	7. Subjective Well-Being	8. Neighbors: Minorities	9. Job Traits: Economic	10. Military Nationalism	11. Family Life
1. V196: Importance of God	-.868	-.018	-.080	-.019	.066	-.157	-.045	.001	.025	.008	-.049
2. V197: Strength from Religion	.804	.018	.059	.052	-.057	.120	.022	.003	.003	-.040	.076
3. V191: Believe in God	.778	-.009	.094	-.003	-.060	.054	.015	-.004	-.020	.030	.090
4. V195: Believe in Heaven	.769	-.023	.039	.036	.010	.158	.025	-.004	-.058	.119	-.162
5. V186: Importance of Religion	.757	-.003	.105	.008	-.088	.056	.036	.009	.009	.002	.142
6. V185: Church Attendance	.700	.051	.040	.060	-.059	.253	-.033	-.012	.013	-.069	.026
7. V192: Believe in Afterlife	.706	.043	-.056	-.001	.007	.038	.001	-.042	.009	.013	-.103
8. V147: Confidence in the Churches	.687	.007	.095	.243	-.034	.210	.047	.029	.012	.120	.054
9. V194: Believe in Hell	.640	-.003	-.042	.002	.038	.189	-.052	-.010	-.065	.125	-.209
10. V91: Job: Use Initiative	-.025	.723	-.096	-.017	-.029	-.066	.034	.004	-.059	-.018	-.041
11. V94: Job: Responsible Job	-.007	.654	.001	.036	.058	.055	.066	.048	-.146	.061	.019
12. V93: Job: Achieve Something	.077	.616	-.094	-.012	-.073	-.042	.052	-.012	-.057	.139	-.071
13. V96: Job: Meets Abilities	.056	.573	.007	-.001	-.061	-.071	-.037	.015	-.192	-.087	.115
14. V95: Job: Interesting	-.010	.525	-.097	-.009	.012	-.071	.051	-.022	-.177	.131	-.097
15. V89: Job: Respected by People	.089	.483	.074	.051	-.063	.032	-.018	.057	-.316	-.138	.067
16. V136: Attend Lawful Demonstrations	-.101	.085	-.745	-.008	-.034	-.146	-.010	-.082	.025	-.047	.048
17. V137: Join Unofficial Strikes	-.159	-.063	-.717	.014	.113	-.056	-.023	.019	-.064	-.029	-.014
18. V135: Join Boycotts	-.071	.094	-.709	-.047	-.022	-.186	.023	-.060	.029	.075	-.125
19. V138: Occupy Buildings	-.114	-.034	-.660	-.002	.148	-.059	-.052	.018	-.041	-.205	-.027
20. V134: Sign Petition	-.006	.164	-.567	-.039	-.083	-.157	.078	-.085	.083	.218	-.172
21. V155: Confidence: Parliament	.059	.054	.026	.745	-.039	.043	.049	-.017	.062	.032	.032
22. V156: Confidence: The Civil Service	.119	.008	.057	.717	-.034	.065	.054	-.009	.008	.087	-.012
23. V149: Confidence: The Press	.036	-.015	-.027	.601	.016	-.002	-.003	-.022	-.072	-.109	.048
24. V151: Confidence: Labor/Trade Unions	-.017	-.114	-.204	.600	-.039	-.024	.019	-.040	-.134	-.044	.013
25. V152: Confidence: The Police	.137	.037	.153	.569	-.093	.062	.102	-.015	.045	.304	-.057

26. V204: Justifiable: Illegal Gov't Benefits	.075	.047	.069	.006	-.720	.033	.046	.010	.017	.063	-.020
27. V207: Justifiable: Accepting Bribe	.077	.029	-.028	.028	-.698	.130	.042	-.029	.014	.008	-.055
28. V206: Justifiable: Cheat on Taxes	.169	-.003	.072	.115	-.683	.123	.007	-.047	-.003	.010	.018
29. V211: Justifiable: Divorce	.244	-.009	.115	.053	-.027	.766	.027	.050	.018	-.021	.077
30. V210: Justifiable: Abortion	.347	-.022	.110	.016	-.057	.735	.013	.009	-.007	-.032	.008
31. V212: Justifiable: Euthanasia	.259	-.002	.074	.080	-.098	.687	-.018	-.045	-.016	-.060	.000
32. V208: Justifiable: Homosexuality	.174	-.066	.170	-.003	-.014	.683	-.030	.117	-.030	.160	.120
33. V213: Justifiable: Suicide	.206	-.031	.099	.008	-.186	.587	.063	-.024	-.064	.139	.108
34. V81: Life Satisfaction	-.060	-.033	-.024	-.054	.077	-.035	-.828	.017	-.007	-.008	.011
35. V11: Happiness	.038	.002	.004	.039	.002	.025	-.774	-.014	.002	-.003	-.006
36. V82: Freedom & Control	-.051	-.076	.040	-.049	-.030	.067	-.639	.039	.000	-.092	.082
37. V69: Neighbors: Different Race	.000	.009	.042	-.004	.020	.033	-.026	.863	-.040	-.004	.030
38. V73: Neighbors: Immigrants	-.016	.019	.041	-.029	.013	.028	-.015	.861	-.039	.011	.022
39. V90: Job: Good Hours	.046	.102	-.015	-.004	.007	.007	.033	.027	-.723	-.018	-.035
40. V92: Job: Generous Holidays	.007	.190	-.007	.018	.044	.032	.008	.086	-.664	-.149	-.010
41. V87: Job: Not Too Much Pressure	.040	.220	.034	.015	-.064	.022	-.046	.065	-.571	-.174	-.003
42. V86: Job: Good Pay	-.003	.040	-.024	-.039	.105	-.006	-.020	.010	-.564	.192	.039
43. V88: Good Job Security	.056	.104	.025	.021	-.064	.038	-.051	.020	-.533	-.335	.039
44. V126: Fight in War	.007	.081	-.025	.122	-.047	.033	.049	.002	.078	.624	-.061
45. V148: Confidence: The Armed Forces	.237	.009	.152	.394	-.004	.114	.035	.068	.025	.514	-.090
46. V109: Child Needs Mother & Father	.027	-.003	.055	.019	.005	.188	.008	.038	-.001	.005	.663
47. V110: Women Need Children	.038	-.023	.071	.016	.095	.109	-.126	.080	.021	-.079	.668
Eigenvalue:	7.36	3.34	2.72	2.45	1.86	1.66	1.50	1.38	1.22	1.20	1.10
Alpha:	.910	.731	.764	.708	.579	.813	.556	.703	.672	.408	.365

Appendix C: Question Wording, Variable Coding, and Scale Construction

I. Religiosity (Scale) = ([v196/9] +v197
+v191+v195+[v186/4]+[v185/6]+v192+[v147/3]+v194)/9

1. V196 HOW IMPORTANT IS GOD IN YOUR LIFE

How important is God in your life? Please use this scale to indicate – 10 means very important and 1 means not at all important.

> 1 (0)[31] Not at all
> 2 (1)
> 3 (2)
> 4 (3)
> 5 (4)
> 6 (5)
> 7 (6)
> 8 (7)
> 9 (8)
> 10 (9) Very

2. V197 COMFORT AND STRENGTH FROM RELIGION

Do you find that you get comfort and strength from religion?

> 0 No
> 1 Yes

3. V191 BELIEVE IN GOD

Which, if any, of the following do you believe in? Believe in God.

> 0 No
> 1 Yes

4. V195 BELIEVE IN HEAVEN

Which, if any, of the following do you believe in? Believe in heaven.

> 0 No
> 1 Yes

5. V186 RELIGION IMPORTANT

For each of the following aspects, indicate how important it is in your life: religion.

> 1 (3) Very important
> 2 (2) Rather important
> 3 (1) Not very important
> 4 (0) Not at all important

---

[31] Values in parentheses represent variable recoding where different from the original.

6. V185 HOW OFTEN DO YOU ATTEND RELIGIOUS SERVICES
Apart from weddings, funerals and christenings, about how often do you attend religious services these days?

1 (6) More than once a week
2 (5) Once a week
3 (4) Once month
4 (3) Only on special holy days/Christmas/Easter days
5 (3) Other specific holy days
6 (2) Once a year
7 (1) Less often
8 (0) Never, practically never

7. V192 BELIEVE IN LIFE AFTER DEATH
Which, if any, of the following do you believe in? Believe in life after death.

0 No
1 Yes

8. V147 CONFIDENCE: CHURCHES
I am going to name a number of organisations. For each one, could you tell me how much confidence you have in them: is it a great deal of confidence, quite a lot of confidence, not very much confidence or none at all? The churches.

1 (3) A great deal
2 (2) Quite a lot
3 (1) Not very much
4 (0) None at all

9. V194 BELIEVE IN HELL
Which, if any, of the following do you believe in? Believe in hell.

0 No
1 Yes

II. Work Motivations (Scale):
A. Fulfillment = (V91+V94+V93+V96+V95+V89)
B. Comfort = (V90+V92+V87+V86+V88)

Here are some more aspects of a job that people say are important. Please look at them and tell me which ones you personally think are important in a job.

Mentioned 1 | Not Mentioned 2 (0)
Personal Fulfillment:

10. V91 An opportunity to use initiative

11. **V94** A responsible job

12. **V93** A job in which you feel you achieve something

13. **V96** A job that meets one's abilities

14. **V95** A job that is interesting

15. **V89** A job respected by people in general

Economic Comfort:

39. **V90** Good hours

40. **V92** Generous holidays

41. **V87** Not too much pressure

42. **V86** Good pay

43. **V88** Good job security

III. Protest Potential (Scale) $= (v136+v137+v135+v138+v134)/5$
Now I'd like you to look at this card. I'm going to read out some different forms of political action that people can take, and I'd like you to tell me, for each one, whether you have actually done any of these things, whether you might do it, or would never under any circumstances do it:

Have Done 1 | Might Do 2(1) | Would Never 3(0)

16. **V136** Attending lawful demonstrations

17. **V137** Joining unofficial strikes

18. **V135** Joining in boycotts

19. **V138** Occupying buildings or factories

20. **V134** Signing a petition

IV. Moral Permissiveness (Scale) $= (v211+v210+v212+v208+v213)/5$
Please tell me for each of the following statements whether you think it can always be justified, never be justified, or something in between:

1(0) 2(1) 3(2) 4(3) 5(4) 6(5) 7(6) 8(7) 9(8) 10(9)

Never   **Always**
Justifiable   **Justifiable**

29. **V211** Divorce

30. **V210** Abortion

31. **V212** Euthanasia

32. **V208** Homosexuality

33. **V213** Suicide

V. Single Items:
A. Left–Right Self-Identification
V139 In political matters, people talk of "the left" and "the right." How would you place your views on this scale, generally speaking?

1(0) 2(1) 3(2) 4(3) 5(4) 6(5) 7(6) 8(7) 9(8) 10(9)

Left   **Right**

B. Economic Egalitarianism
V141 How would you place your views on this scale? 1 means you agree completely with the statement on the left; 10 means you agree completely with the statement on the right; and if your views fall somewhere in between, you can choose any number in between.

| Incomes should be made more equal | We need larger income differences as incentives for individual effort |

(0) 2(1) 3(2) 4(3) 5(4) 6(5) 7(6) 8(7) 9(8) 10(9)

3

On Different Planets

News Media in the United States and Europe

Donald Morrison

Whenever a problem of sufficient magnitude and complexity presents itself, a standard twenty-first century response among policy makers is to blame the media. And why not? The press is clearly pervasive, supposedly influential, seemingly unaccountable, and, best of all, singularly inept at defending itself against attack. So when assigning responsibility for the current transatlantic divide, the news media present a tempting target. Have they quietly and ruthlessly been sowing the seeds of mistrust between Europe and the United States? Do they have an interest in fanning the embers of transatlantic anger, perhaps to build circulation or indulge the jingoism of some moss-backed proprietor? Have they been conspiring, from opposite sides of the ocean, to cook up this nasty, newsworthy conflict?

The short answer is possibly yes, to a limited degree, but not enough to matter. The news media, as we shall see, are too diverse and feeble to impose their will on the rest of us. Other questions seem more pertinent: Why do Americans and Europeans appear to hold such widely differing versions of what is happening in the world? Is the press to blame? There is no short answer to these questions. The long, complicated explanation has much to do with the war in Iraq. This is no surprise. But well before the United States arrived in Baghdad, there were factors driving U.S. and European opinion apart. To understand them, it is useful to examine the history of the press, which developed in differing ways on either side of the Atlantic and continues to bear the marks of this bifurcated gestation. In addition, a number of structural and economic changes in the media industry have been propelling the U.S. press and its European counterpart in different directions. These two major factors – history and commerce – have combined to give Americans and Europeans dissimilar models of journalism, which in turn have helped foster differing views of the world. Interestingly, new economic forces have lately been pushing the news media toward an odd kind of transatlantic convergence that may, just possibly, help diminish the problem they have caused.

Common Roots

First, let us review some history. In the beginning, America's press did not differ much from Europe's. The modern newspaper originated in the early seventeenth century in Europe, where it remained subject to government censorship and licensing. As newspapers proliferated in Europe, so did the idea of press freedom. John Milton argued for it in *Areopagitica* in 1644, and the chaos surrounding the English Civil War allowed newspapers to editorialize with unprecedented vigor. Licensing was ended in 1695, and the idea that the press has a right to criticize government took root. That notion was further propelled in the eighteenth century by the values of the Enlightenment, which held that human reason could be used to combat ignorance, superstition, and despotism.

The first American newspapers contained mostly news lifted from the European press. A survey of nineteen hundred items printed in Benjamin Franklin's *Pennsylvania Gazette* from 1728 to 1765 found that only thirty-four touched on local politics.[1] As the colonists' grievances against Britain deepened, however, publications began playing a more assertive role in the struggle for independence. After the Revolutionary War, press freedom was enshrined in the First Amendment to the U.S. Constitution.

At that point, American publications were generally less advanced in typography and writing quality than their European equivalents. This pattern endured well into the nineteenth century: Europe innovated, America adopted. That was certainly the case when it came to political coverage. Like their counterparts in Europe, U.S. papers reflected the views of their owners, which were often political parties. In Thomas Jefferson's day, for example, the only sources of printed news in New York City were a handful of newspapers that sold for the then rather stiff price of six cents a copy. Each was attached to a political party and followed a partisan agenda.

That model began to change in the 1830s. The introduction of the rotary press and the rise of the more egalitarian, Jacksonian brand of democracy heralded the dawn in the United States of mass-circulation penny newspapers, so-called because they undersold their partisan rivals by a nickel. The penny papers relied not on party patronage but on sales and advertising for their revenues. They were written in a lively style, reporting on crime,

---

[1] Michael Schudson, *Media Studies Journal*, Spring–Summer 1998.

scandal, and other largely nonpolitical topics. Between 1860 and 1880, the number of American newspapers more than doubled to seven thousand, and the largest ones were outselling their counterparts in Europe.[2]

As advertising and mass circulation transformed U.S. newspapers into successful commercial enterprises, they started to be seen less as vehicles of political opinion and more as sources of information. The rise of wire services, which distributed the same story to papers of different political stripes, also militated against partisanship. So did the new reverence with which facts were being treated in the late nineteenth century, thanks to the growing prestige of science and, in literature, the popularity of realism. In 1870, by one estimate, only 11 percent of urban American dailies were "independent" of any political party; by the 1920s, that number had leapt to 62 percent.[3]

This new veneration for facts was also connected to an American innovation in journalistic tradecraft: the late nineteenth century development of the "inverted pyramid" style of news writing, in which information is presented in order of importance, not chronologically as before. Journalists began to think of themselves as experts in the subjects they covered, with their own professional standards. The world's first school of journalism opened at the University of Missouri in 1904. (Europe didn't get one for another two decades, and such institutions remained a rarity there until the 1960s.) The American Society of Newspaper Editors' 1923 "Canons of Journalism" held that "News reports should be free from opinion or bias of any kind."[4] Such a goal was impossible, perhaps, but there was no similar declaration in Europe at the time – and American journalists were determined to give it a try.

The forces of reason, science, and commerce that loosened the grip of partisanship on the U.S. press also worked their magic in Europe, though later and less visibly. While the penny press was flourishing in the United States, censorship and taxes retarded the growth of independent newspapers in Europe. In Britain, the rise of late Victorian mercantile society and the spread of literacy among the working class finally gave the British press the prosperity it needed to resist government (and party) domination. Newspaper independence in France was more limited, starting with an 1820 requirement that anyone who wanted to launch a newspaper had to put up a large financial deposit – clearly to ensure that only trusted members of the elite

---

[2] Mitchell Stevens, "History of Newspapers," *Colliers Encyclopedia*, 1994.
[3] Matthew Gentzkow et al., "The Rise of the Fourth Estate," paper presented at the 2001 National Bureau of Economic Research Conference on "Corruption and Reform," available at http://kuznets.fas.harvard.edu/~goldin/papers/GGG_CR.pdf.
[4] The entire text of the Canons is available online at http://www.iit.edu/departments/csep/codes/coe/American%20Society%20of%20Newspaper%20Editors%2023.html.

could publish; the restriction was not removed until 1881. In Germany, advertising itself was a state monopoly until after the upheavals of 1848. Once that source of revenue was freed from the government's grip, German newspapers flourished.

Advertising has long been generally less important for the press in Europe than in the United States. The total advertising "spend" on daily newspapers in the United States is an estimated $50 billion a year; in the European Union, despite a slightly larger population, the figure is less than half as much.[5] European readers provide the bulk of revenues, along with, in some cases, government subsidies for newsprint. That relative underreliance on pleasing advertisers has helped perpetuate partisanship and ideology in the European press. European publishers just have to concentrate on the people who mainly agree with them. After decades of such partisanship, many Europeans have come to think that a newspaper by definition should have a clear political or ideological line. Americans still prefer their news organizations to maintain at least an appearance of balance and nonpartisanship.

When radio and television were introduced in the twentieth century, they developed in markedly different ways on either side of the Atlantic – as commercial enterprises in the United States, and as government-controlled entities in Europe. Those dissimilar paths have had implications for news coverage. As private businesses, American broadcast operations have had a measure of independence from government influence – although their own dependence on advertising has fostered an inoffensive blandness and, increasingly, a tendency to blur the line between news and entertainment. Like publishers, broadcasters were eager to reach as large an audience as possible. For that reason, they were reluctant to alienate any sector of the public through displays of partisanship or ideology. The three major U.S. network evening newscasts, for instance, have been virtually indistinguishable in content and tone since their beginnings in the 1960s. In France, Germany, Italy, and elsewhere in Europe, by contrast, major TV channels have long been owned by, linked to, or nakedly supportive of their governments. In Italy, for instance, Silvio Berlusconi was rarely criticized on television when he was prime minister, from 2001 to 2006. It is no mystery why this was the case: He controlled all three government channels by virtue of his office, and, as the country's leading media baron, he also controlled nearly all of the private ones.

For most of the post–World War II era, those differences in ownership and revenue streams have had few serious implications for the transatlantic

---

5 World Association of Newspapers, *World Press Trends 2000* (Paris: World Association of Newspapers, 2000).

relationship. News coverage has tended to reflect the shared eighteenth century values of reason and respect for science, as well as the post–World War II consensus about the importance of peace, democracy, and free markets. "Much of the history of the 20th century can be told through the rubric of the U.S.-European relationship," press critic Eric Alterman wrote in *The Nation* in 2005. "Two world wars, the Cold War, most of what is considered high culture in the United States and much of our popular culture, including our best cinema and works of literature, are unthinkable without Europe's example and influence."[6]

Accordingly, major political, economic, and social developments were reported on both sides of the Atlantic in roughly similar ways. A reader or a television viewer in Boston or Butte got pretty much the same version of the world as someone in London or Lisbon. The transatlantic alliance and its press were on the same side of most major issues and events, from the establishment of the great multilateral institutions of the postwar era to the prosecution of Axis war criminals. A broad consensus developed on the reporting of news about one another's countries: Putting things into a context that will make them more comprehensible for local readers was acceptable; leaving out or seriously downplaying essential information was not. Thus, Europeans could get a reasonably balanced account of, say, the U.S. civil rights movement in their press, and Americans could follow the attempts by European countries to deal with postwar waves of immigration. One reason for this consensus was that both the United States and Europe found themselves on the same side of the Cold War. True, there were transatlantic tiffs over U.S. support for anticommunist forces in the developing world or over the deployment of American missiles in Europe. But such differences paled in comparison to the yawning divide between East and West, Soviet-style communism and capitalist democracy.

Things Fall Apart

That consensus has broken down in the past decade. The immediate cause, of course, is the Iraq War. But a number of other controversial U.S. moves prepared the way: the failure to support such international agreements as the Kyoto Protocol on greenhouse gases, the Nuclear Test Ban Treaty, the Nonproliferation Treaty, the international agreements on landmines and small arms, as well as the establishment of an international criminal

[6] Eric Alterman, "USA Oui! Bush No!," *The Nation*, February 10, 2003.

court. Europeans were uncomfortable with U.S. efforts to undercut the United Nations in the run-up to the Iraq War, and also with the treatment of detainees at Guantanamo and Abu Ghraib. In France, where I live, the daily *Le Monde* asked authors, academics, and diplomats to contribute a series of commentaries on the Iraq War in 2003. After twenty-six out of twenty-seven contributors wrote articles opposing the conflict, the series was discontinued; the editors explained that they could not find any eminent personages who supported the war. Said Robert Solé, a *Le Monde* editor, "It took Iraq to unify the country in a way that even France's victory in the [1998 soccer] World Cup could not."[7]

A year after the invasion of Iraq, a poll by the Pew Research Center for the People and the Press found U.S. and European views differed vastly. Whereas 60 percent of Americans still thought the war was a good idea (the number later fell), only tiny minorities in European countries agreed. Moreover, there was broad agreement in nearly all of the countries polled – except the United States – that the war in Iraq hurt, rather than helped, the fight against terrorism. One of the largest gaps uncovered in the poll had little to do with Iraq and much to do with what was once an article of faith on both sides of the Atlantic: whether people in the United States have a better life than those in Europe. Americans overwhelmingly believed this to be the case – 88 percent, in fact, compared to just 14 percent of Germans, 24 percent of the French, and 41 percent of the British.[8]

One reason for this divide was that Europeans and Americans were being given differing versions of reality. In the months before the war, the European press was far less likely to report without qualification U.S. assertions about Iraqi weapons of mass destruction than the U.S. press was. President George W. Bush, in a March 2003 news conference, made thirteen references linking terrorism and Iraq without being challenged by the ninety-four reporters present.[9] Perhaps as a result of such willingness to accept administration assertions, as many as 60 percent of Americans in various polls that year said they believed that Iraq was at least partly responsible for the 9/11 attacks. That alleged linkage was almost never discussed in Europe, where even Bush's closest ally, British Prime Minister Tony Blair, did not subscribe to it. Pollsters in Europe apparently never asked about it, nor did they or Europeans

---

[7] Robert Solé, "Tous en choeur," *Le Monde*, February 22, 2003.
[8] Pew Research Center for the People and the Press, "A Year after Iraq War Mistrust of America in Europe Ever Higher, Muslim Anger Persists," Survey Report, March 14, 2004.
[9] Stephan Russ-Mohl, "President Bush's Lapdogs," *European Journalism Observatory*, February 2004.

generally see any reason to do so. Even after Bush finally disavowed the link in 2005, roughly a third of Americans continued to believe in it, perhaps because Vice President Dick Cheney and other officials kept insisting that it existed – and the U.S. press continued to give their remarks wide attention.

Coverage of the war itself has diverged as well. It was Britain's BBC, for instance, not any U.S. news organization, that broke the story of how the U.S. military essentially staged the widely publicized 2003 rescue of injured soldier Jessica Lynch from an Iraqi hospital. American news outlets did not pick up the story for another month, and then mostly to quote official U.S. denials. Similar examples abound – from the "Downing Street Memos" indicating that the United States intended to invade Iraq whether weapons of mass destruction existed there or not, to Bush's reported suggestion that allied forces bomb the Baghdad headquarters of the al-Jazeera news service. European journalists have been considerably more willing to challenge the assertions of the U.S. government than their American counterparts have. The U.S. press, especially cable television news, wrote *New York Times* columnist Paul Krugman shortly after hostilities, "seems to be reporting about a different planet than the one covered by foreign media."[10]

Much of that disparity can be attributed to the fever of patriotism that often grips a country's press in time of war. British coverage of the 1982 Falklands conflict, for instance, was broadly favorable to the British side and slow to delve into disturbing developments, such as the controversial sinking of the Argentine cruiser *General Belgrano*. (The *Sun*'s headline that day was "Gotcha!") But even after the Iraq invasion, American publications still tend to quote the statements of U.S. military spokespeople as fact. On May 9, 2005, to cite a typical example, most of the largest U.S. newspapers said, without adding "claimed" or "reported" or any other qualification, that American forces had killed about one hundred Iraqi and foreign fighters near the Syrian border – even though no reporters had been present to verify the incident. Anyone who remembers the inflated "body counts" of the Vietnam era may wonder whether much has changed.

Similarly, in the first few years after the fall of Baghdad, European news organizations generally focused on the chaos of the occupation, the misdeeds of U.S. troops, the civilian casualties, the religious-ethnic divisions, and other topics that Americans heard about less often. A 2004 estimate by Johns Hopkins University researchers, for instance, that close to 100,000 civilians had died as a result of hostilities in Iraq received more attention in Europe than in the United States, where coverage focused mostly on U.S. refutations

---

[10] Paul Krugman, "Behind the Great Divide," *New York Times*, February 18, 2003.

of the number.[11] Much the same thing happened in 2006, when a new Johns Hopkins study raised the figure to 650,000. And after graphic pictures of U.S. and Iraqi casualties virtually disappeared from U.S. media, they could still be found in Europe.

The transatlantic differences in story selection and emphasis, especially in the past few years, are evident. Take May 5, 2005, a typical enough day. In most national British dailies, Tony Blair was campaigning for reelection amid disclosures that he had disregarded legal advice that attacking Iraq would be illegal, that he knew Iraq did not possess weapons of mass destruction, and that the United States had no detailed plan for the war's aftermath. Relatively little about Blair's Iraq troubles appeared that day in the *New York Times*, *Washington Post*, *Boston Globe*, or *Los Angeles Times*, in *Time* or *Newsweek*, or on the major TV networks, whose election coverage instead emphasized Blair's likelihood of victory and his widespread popularity in the United States. (He won the election, but chose to retire early in his mandate.)

On an entirely different topic that day, the mildly conservative *Financial Times* (*FT*) front-paged a story about the U.S. decision to revive the discontinued thirty-year Treasury Bond – a move that the paper said, somewhat acidly, "highlights the degree to which America's fiscal position has deteriorated since 2001," which it noted was the year George W. Bush took office. By contrast, the *FT*'s U.S. counterpart, the *Wall Street Journal*, buried the story inside, as did the *New York Times*. Meanwhile, the *Washington Post* and *Los Angeles Times* evidently didn't cover the subject at all.

Earlier, hardly any U.S. news organization devoted much attention to the fact that France in 2004 joined China in military exercises directed at Taiwan, or to Pakistani President Pervez Musharraf's 2005 failure to keep his promise to resign as army chief. France's *Le Figaro* on May 6, 2005, had a lengthy report about increased American pressure on Tunisia to adopt democratic reforms or face unspecified consequences; I could find no story on this topic in the United States longer than a paragraph. Meanwhile, stories about Africa could be read in Europe almost daily, but apart from the humanitarian crisis in Darfur, the U.S. press had virtually forgotten that continent.

So What?

The U.S. press appears to be producing a public virtually oblivious to the outside world. A 1997 poll showed that only 40 percent of Americans were

---

[11] The original *Lancet* article, published first online on October 24, 2004, can be seen at http://image.thelancet.com/extras/04cmt384web.pdf.

aware that the British colony of Hong Kong was about to be returned to China, but 79 percent knew boxer Mike Tyson had recently bitten the ear off an opponent.[12] In a 1999 survey for the Luce Foundation of twelve hundred Americans, most could not answer simple questions about Asia correctly. In a 2005 survey for the Interscholastic Studies Institute, fewer than half of the fourteen thousand U.S. college students polled could accurately describe NATO, Saddam Hussein, or even World War II. Such polls are relatively rare in Europe, but a 1994 survey did show that 19 percent of respondents from Britain, Canada, France, Germany, and Italy could not answer any of a list of questions on foreign affairs, compared to 37 percent of Americans.[13]

One reason for such apparent nearsightedness is that Americans are exposed to relatively little foreign news. The Newspaper Advertising Bureau estimated in 2001 that foreign stories accounted for 2 percent or less of the average daily paper's "news hole," down from 10 percent in 1971.[14] Shortly before 9/11, the major TV network newscasts often had no international stories at all, though a generation ago foreign reports constituted an average of 45 percent of the newscasts.[15]

Why the decline? The waning of the Cold War and the 1991 breakup of the Soviet Union clearly took foreign news off the front burner for many Americans. So too did the end of the Vietnam War and the spread of the "Western consensus" favoring democracy and free markets. For the first time in decades, Americans had relatively few foreign problems to worry about, few overt enemies to keep track of. The elements of conflict and tension that animate many news stories were simply lacking. Americans, or so conventional journalistic wisdom went, simply were not interested in foreign news.

Yet there is evidence they are interested. The Pew Research Center in 1996 asked Americans what kinds of stories they regularly followed. Fifteen percent said international news – only one percentage point behind Washington politics, and two ahead of celebrity news. That number went up after 9/11 and the start of the Iraq War. When Pew asked a similar question in 2004, 39 percent of Americans said they followed international news closely, more than twice as many as followed national political news. The *Los Angeles*

---

[12] Andrew Kohut, "More News Is Not Necessarily Good News," *New York Times*, July 11, 2004.

[13] Pius Kamau, "Americans' Ignorance of Foreign News Appalling," *Denver Post*, August 23, 2006.

[14] Michael Parks, "The Future of Foreign Coverage," World Press Institute, available online at http://www.worldpressinstitute.org/parks.htm.

[15] Ibid.

Times has long conducted daily tracking polls on readers' preferences. After 9/11, foreign news moved up from the twelfth most interesting subject to number two, behind only local news. Sports, by comparison, remained at number twenty.

The problem is that foreign news, with the exception of Iraq, is not being covered. The reason for that is money. In a 2002 survey of 218 newspaper editors by the market research firm Morris and Associates, 53 percent cited "high costs" as the major obstacle to better international coverage. Maintaining a correspondent overseas can cost more than $250,000 a year, including housing, home leave, and other expenses. As a result, many U.S. news organizations have sharply reduced the number of Americans holding these jobs and replaced them with locals, who usually cost less but may not have the same professional skills or ability to put things in context for Americans. Other employers have simply cut their overseas headcounts. *Time* reduced its foreign correspondent corps from 33 to 24 in the 1990s, and ABC News halved the number of its foreign bureaus to seven. The Project on the State of the American Newspaper found in 2000 that there were only 282 full-time correspondents working abroad for all the nation's daily newspapers. Two-thirds of those worked for four major papers (the *Wall Street Journal, New York Times, Los Angeles Times,* and *Washington Post*), which meant that the other fifteen hundred or so U.S. dailies had fewer than one hundred correspondents among them. Perhaps that is why the 9/11 attacks seemed to take Americans so much by surprise.

European figures and studies are difficult to come by – the continent lacks the infrastructure of journalism schools and media researchers that flourish in the United States – but the European press clearly devotes more attention to international news than its U.S. counterpart does. *Le Figaro,* for instance, has at least four, mostly advertising-free broadsheet pages of foreign news a day, more than nearly any U.S. paper except perhaps the *New York Times.* It is much the same at *Le Monde,* which also has a freestanding monthly supplement of international articles, *Le Monde Diplomatique.* Even the European editions of *Time* and *Newsweek* contain vastly more foreign news than their U.S. versions, and both feature international subjects on their covers in Europe more than twice as often as in the United States.

Accordingly, Europeans had been reading in their mainstream press for years about Osama bin Laden, the rise of fundamentalist Islam, and the extent of Arab anger at U.S. policy in the Middle East. Many Americans remain puzzled by the low standing their country enjoys in the Muslim world. They do not think it has much to do with U.S. policy in the Palestinian–Israeli conflict, despite findings by the Pew pollsters and others that it very much does. Europeans, however, tend to have fewer illusions; their press devotes considerable space to U.S. Middle East policy and its unpopularity in the Arab world. The same is true of the failings of U.S. policy in Iraq and the war on terror. A June 2006 Pew Center poll found that between 90 percent and 98 percent of respondents in four European countries had heard of the U.S. abuses at Abu Ghraib and Guantanamo compared to only 76 percent of Americans.

It would be nice to report that U.S. media provincialism has evaporated for good after 9/11, but it has not. True, the major news organizations have enlarged their reporting presence in Iraq – the *New York Times* in 2005 had more than fifty employees in Baghdad – but not, for the most part, elsewhere in the world. CNN, for instance, closed its bureau in Paris and greatly cut back staffing at its Asian headquarters in Hong Kong after 9/11. *Time* announced it would pull out of Paris, Seoul, and Shanghai. And although Iraq continues to dominate the foreign coverage of U.S. news organizations, they are unable to provide an entirely accurate picture of life in Iraq. For lack of security, Western reporters have been largely confined to their hotels and dependent on official sources. Elsewhere, on America's front pages and TV screens, life is returning to its normal pattern of Washington politics and celebrity scandal. The Project for Excellence in Journalism examined sixteen newspapers in various circulation categories in late 2003 and found that foreign news accounted for 21 percent of front-page stories – the same share as in 1997, and *down* from 27 percent in 1977, when the Cold War was still on.[16] In the 2002 survey of editors by Morris and Associates, about 95 percent of respondents said reader interest in foreign news increased after 9/11, and 78 percent said the amount of space devoted to foreign news had increased. But 64 percent expected readers to lose interest and 58 percent predicted that foreign news space would shrink to previous levels. Interestingly, only 43 percent of editors thought they were doing an "excellent" or "good" job of satisfying reader interest in international news.

Different Folks

Why does the European press seem so critical of the United States these days? Rather than just blaming Bush and the war in Iraq, it is instructive to cite the enduring strain of anti-Americanism that Europe has nursed for decades. Anti-Americanism is usually more pronounced on the political left, but it's also a staple of the right. It flourished in Europe throughout the twentieth

---

[16] Project for Excellence in Journalism, "State of the News Media," 2004, available online at http://www.journalism.org.

century, as personified by Charles Maurras, a right-wing French journalist and politician (1868–1959) who launched the nationalist L'Action Française political movement. Maurras denounced the United States as an unmitigated hell of greed, ruthless capitalism, and brutal disregard for human dignity, as well as a rootless society disconnected from principle or tradition.

Those views are reflected today in Europe's antiglobalization movement and even in the "slow food" movement, which was launched in Italy in the 1990s as a reaction to the growth of the fast-food industry. You can even see anti-Americanism in an entertaining 2004 documentary film about the wine industry, *Mondovino*, whose many targets include the triumph of marketing over craft, as well as the alleged homogenization of worldwide wine styles fostered by American-influenced producers. Indeed, when it comes to wine, Europe takes no prisoners. Try to find a California cabernet in a Paris or Rome wine shop. It's easier to get a Bordeaux or a Barolo in any midsized American city.

Besides, the political and cultural center in Europe has long appeared to be firmly to the left. Most of Europe's biggest countries have in recent years been run by leftist or center-left governments. Conservative parties in Europe are distinctly moderate, supporting abortion rights, gay rights, affirmative action, the European "social model," and other positions that would make American conservatives blanch. Even in European countries that have long been governed by the center-right – Britain, Italy, and, yes, France – public opinion remains solidly against the Iraq War and highly disapproving of Bush. While eleven American states were banning same-sex marriages in 2004, Spain began allowing them, and an Italian official was forced to withdraw from almost certain nomination as the European Union's human rights commissioner because of his view that homosexuality is a sin. A 2004 Gallup poll found that 55 percent of Britons hold the rather forgiving notion that gays are born that way, compared to only 37 percent of Americans.[17]

Indeed, the European press routinely treats matters dealing with sexuality in a way that many Americans would find shocking. During the 2005 British election campaign, for instance, the *Sun* newspaper asked Tony Blair and his wife Cherie about their sex life:

Q: What, five times a night?
Tony Blair: At least. I can do it more depending on how I feel.
Q: Are you up to it?
Cherie Blair: He always is!

---

[17] Josephine Mazzuca, "Origins of Homosexuality? Britons, Canadians say 'Nature,'" *Gallup Poll on Demand*, November 2, 2004.

The exchange was picked up by other British news outlets. Blair's office never saw a need to dispute it.[18] It is difficult to imagine a similar exchange with a U.S. politician.

Stories favorable to the American right are hard to come by in the European press, which seems baffled by U.S. religious fundamentalism and sexual prudery. Still, Britain's *Economist* and *Spectator* magazines, as well as the tabloid *Sun* and the broadsheet *Times* and *Sunday Times* (the latter three all owned by conservative media mogul Rupert Murdoch), have been admiring of U.S. policy and particularly its economic dynamism. In Italy, many of the publications and broadcast outlets controlled by former prime minister Berlusconi have been mostly pro-U.S. and friendly to the Bush administration. Yet European publications, by and large, even some of those linked to conservative parties and proprietors, have been more critical of the United States than many allegedly leftist American publications. Britain's *Financial Times* is a good example, as is France's *Le Figaro*. Both are center-right, except perhaps for their coverage of U.S. policy. *Le Figaro*, for instance, dismissed a 2003 trip to the United States by President Jacques Chirac to mend fences with the Bush administration as "appeasement."[19]

Contrary to what some Americans believe, the rupture in U.S.–European thinking cannot easily be directly attributed to recent changes in the U.S. psyche, or even to 9/11. Like most of their readers and viewers, most European news organizations continue to make a distinction between Americans and their government. Immediately after 9/11, Europe erupted in spontaneous, pro-American vigils and prayer services. German President Gerhard Schröder described the continent's mood as one of "unconditional solidarity." *Le Monde* ran a banner headline declaring "*Nous sommes tous Americains.*" Support for the U.S. military action in Afghanistan was high. And even today, if you travel in Europe, it is likely that you will be treated cordially and that people will tell you endlessly that they like Americans and were disconsolate over the 9/11 attacks – and that they can't understand why the United States didn't grasp their extended hand of friendship. As *Le Monde* put it in 2002, "Nothing could be worse, in the uncertain period that began on September 11, than to identify the American people as a whole, and the American press, with the policies followed by the White House."[20]

---

[18] *The Sun*, May 4, 2005. An entertaining summary is available online at http://www.guardian.co.uk/diary/story/0,3604,1476672,00.html.

[19] Pierre Rousselin, "L'editorial: L'apaisement," *Le Figaro*, September 23, 2003.

[20] As quoted by Adam Gopnik, "The Times, V. O.," *New Yorker*, April 22–29, 2002.

The 2004 Pew poll found that in Britain, Germany, and Russia, views of Americans remained highly favorable. Even a majority of French – 53 percent – had a positive opinion of Americans, though the figure was down from 71 percent two years earlier. A study in the September 2005 *Harvard Business Review* reported that opposition to U.S. foreign policy around the world had not translated into a rejection by consumers of U.S. brands.[21]

Different Strokes

One problem in making comparisons between U.S. and European news coverage is that the two sides have different conceptions of journalism and journalists. Not only do European readers and viewers expect their news outlets to follow recognizable political lines, but they also consider European journalists to be intellectuals, not mere reporters. That's apparent in any number of leading European dailies, where a major news event will be swaddled in analysis. My favorite example is France's *Le Monde*, which has for years been a sea of dense and serious essays on the Middle East, nuclear proliferation, and arcane disputes in French academia. Writing in the *New Yorker* magazine about *Le Monde*'s 2002 decision to begin running a twelve-page weekly section of stories from the *New York Times* – in English – Adam Gopnik neatly summed up the difference between the two national styles of journalism:

The *Times*, surrounded by the French pages, looked virtuous and sincere, and even a little wide-eyed, like a Henry James hero entering a Paris hotel. Where the pages of *Le Monde* were, as always, devoted to standing conventional wisdom on its head, so that all the blood just pools there while the writer waves his feet in the air, the *Times* stood up and told it straight. (Even when the *Times* was being philosophical, it looked innocent. Might America be an empire? one writer wondered. *Le Monde*'s readers settled that question in their own minds long ago.) The "news" stories in the French paper tended to flit by the news on the way to a Higher Theory, but the American paper was as fact-filled as a science project; you almost expected to see a blue ribbon pinned to it.[22]

Likewise, many German dailies are gray deserts of comment and Higher Theory unrelieved by news reporting, let alone illustrations. (A 1994 study

---

[21] Douglas B. Holt et al., "How Global Brands Compete," *Harvard Business Review*, September 2004.
[22] Gopnik, "The Times, V. O."

of 350 German newspapers found that readers generally preferred them to be serious and to avoid flashy design.[23]) Germany does have its racy tabloids, of course, as do Spain, Italy, and other European countries. But serious journalists with good university degrees tend not to frequent their premises. The difference may have something to do with the education system in many European countries. In France's elite academies, typically there is less emphasis on science and other manifestations of the real world and more on reasoning ability, intellectual gymnastics, and, especially, theory. Former U.S. secretary of state Madeline Albright famously recalled a meeting with one of her French counterparts to discuss some new initiative in the Middle East. "That's all very well in practice, Madame," declared the Frenchman, "but how will it work in theory?"[24]

European journalists generally believe that providing context and meaning is a more useful exercise than just reporting dry facts. When George W. Bush visited Russia and a number of surrounding countries in May 2005, most U.S. news accounts of his stop in the Republic of Georgia began with a "lead" paragraph saying little more than that Bush was welcomed by an enthusiastic crowd of 250,000 in Tblisi, the capital. *Le Figaro* reporter Laure Mandeville, however, had a more typically European opening paragraph: "The fact that the Moscow stop was sandwiched between the visits to Latvia and Georgia underlines Bush's double strategy in the region: maintaining a frank and direct dialogue with Moscow while the American diplomatic steamroller pursues its policy of 'democratic encirclement' of Russia."[25] Mandeville, like many European journalists, would argue that his approach was more informative than an "objective" first paragraph about the Bush stop; an American journalist might say Mandeville was swerving from reportage into commentary.

Indeed, U.S. journalists are sometimes slaves to an "objectivity" that obscures meaning as often as it illuminates it. Too often, American objectivity means simply quoting somebody with an opposing view, regardless of its validity. Michael Doyle, foreign editor of Britain's daily *Independent*, summed up the European scorn for this approach during a 2004 dialogue organized by the *Columbia Journalism Review*: "The loudest demands for

---

[23] "Comment: The Soft News Deficit," National Radio Mediawatch (mediawatch.co.nz), August 12, 2001.

[24] As told to the author by a former U.S. diplomat. Intriguingly, similar quotes turn up in the literature of international affairs, involving other regions and issues, but the speaker is invariably a French diplomat.

[25] Laure Mandeville, "Bush en Géorgie ...," *Le Figaro*, May 9, 2005.

objectivity are made by groups or lobbies who want to ensure that they get equal time in any story." He denounced "an all-encompassing and spurious right of reply designed to protect reporters and their news organizations from powerful interests and their own governments."[26]

The American press has in recent years come under fire from a number of sides over the issue of objectivity. Most of the pressure is from the U.S. political right, which has become especially effective at denouncing the mainstream press for various shortcomings – often through partisan web logs (blogs) and occasionally via threatened advertiser boycotts. The right complains that major news organizations use the pretense of objectivity to conceal a bias against conservative positions – a critique that would have pleased (mostly left-wing) French deconstructionists such as Ronald Barthes and Jacques Derrida. A number of high-profile media blunders – such as a hotly disputed 2004 report by the CBS show *60 Minutes* questioning details of George W. Bush's military career – have provided abundant ammunition for critics. Grumbled syndicated columnist E. J. Dionne, Jr.:

Conservative academics have long attacked "postmodernist" philosophies for questioning whether "truth" exists at all and claiming that what we take as "truths" are merely "narratives" woven around some ideological predisposition. Today's conservative activists have become the new postmodernists. They shift attention away from the truth or falsity of specific facts and allegations – and move the discussion to the motives of the journalists and media organizations putting them forward.[27]

Meanwhile, various newsroom polls indicate that U.S. reporters are more likely to vote Democratic than Republican, and that most U.S. journalists acknowledge the problem of keeping personal beliefs and biases out of their copy – although they insist that they are able to do so. "Objectivity, or the pursuit of it, separates us from the unbridled partisanship found in much of the European press," wrote Brent Cunningham in the *Columbia Journalism Review*. He did, however, quote a number of critics of American-style objectivity, among them author Joan Didion:

The genuflection toward "fairness" is a familiar newsroom piety, in practice the excuse for a good deal of autopilot reporting and lazy thinking.... What "fairness" has often come to mean is a scrupulous passivity, an agreement to cover the story not as it is occurring but as it is presented, which is to say as it is manufactured.[28]

[26] "Brits vs. Yanks: Who Does Journalism Right," *Columbia Journalism Review*, May/June 2004.

[27] E. J. Dionne, Jr., "Assault on the Media," quoted from *Washington Post*, May 27, 2005.

[28] Brent Cunningham, "Toward a New Ideal," *Columbia Journalism Review*, July/August 2003.

Indeed, by focusing on presenting "both sides" of a story, even when one side's case is far less substantial, the U.S. press creates the impression that truth cannot be ascertained, even when it can. Coverage of the debate over climate change is a case in point. Even when the global scientific community shifted toward accepting the phenomenon as a fact, U.S. news organizations felt the need to give considerable weight to dissenting viewpoints – a punctiliousness that their European counterparts had long ago abandoned on that subject.

Another problem with the objectivity model is that it promotes the impression that all news involves conflict, even when little or none exists. A 2005 study by the Project for Excellence in Journalism found that stories emphasizing conflict were at least 50 percent more likely to get onto a U.S. newspaper's front page than those stressing cooperation.[29] That bias toward confrontation may boost circulation and ratings, but it can also undermine respect for democratic processes by focusing on partisan strife and ignoring the arguably more common cases of compromise and collaboration.

The fuss over objectivity has crowded out debate over more substantive complaints: that the press is too concerned about circulation and ratings to report anything except the blandest and most trivial of events or, as cited previously, cases of meaningless conflict; and that such commercial considerations are blurring the line between news and entertainment. There is some anecdotal evidence for those observations. Television, as well as print, devotes increasing space to the personal, financial, and pharmacological problems of sports and entertainment celebrities. Celebrity magazines constitute one of the most robust segments of the publishing industry, and newspapers have expanded their gossip and entertainment pages at the expense of more serious coverage. One reason for that shift is an assumption that readers increasingly demand it. Another is that editors find such trivial, nonpolitical subjects less likely to provoke left- and especially right-wing complaints. In the words of Michael Doyle, "The mainstream American press is often spineless in the face of government bullying, terrified of getting on the wrong side of public opinion. . . ."[30]

Thinking Small

No wonder the repute of the U.S. press is sinking. A 2005 Pew Center poll found that 45 percent of Americans believe only a fraction of what they

---

[29] Project for Excellence in Journalism (journalism.org), "State of the News Media," March 2005.

[30] Cunningham, "Toward a New Ideal."

read in their daily newspapers, compared to 16 percent who were similarly skeptical two decades ago.[31] The National Opinion Research Center, which conducts periodic measures of public confidence in thirteen American institutions, found that all have generally retained a good measure of public respect – except the press, in which confidence has fallen sharply since 1990.[32] Such surveys are rarely conducted in Europe, where press credibility is not a salient issue and media consumers are generally aware of a particular news outlet's political line.

Partisanship has been on the rise in the United States, to the alarm of many American journalists. More than ever, media consumers have been selecting their news sources according to their political predilections. Media self-selection is, of course, not entirely new. Maybe you have heard this one:

The *Wall Street Journal* is read by the people who run the country.

The *Washington Post* is read by people who think they run the country.

The *New York Times* is read by people who think they should run the country.

The *Los Angeles Times* is read by people who wouldn't mind running the country if they didn't have to leave Southern California.

The *Boston Globe* is read by people whose parents used to run the country – and did a much better job of it, thank you very much.

The *Miami Herald* is read by people who are running another country but need the baseball scores.

None of these is read by the guy who actually *is* running the country. He doesn't read newspapers.

This trend toward self-selection – which somewhat resembles the partisanship of European newspapers – is being propelled by structural changes in the news industry. In general, mass media are being replaced by narrow media. Consider television. A generation ago, the bulk of American households tuned in to one of the (then) three major network evening newscasts: the *CBS Evening News*, the *NBC Nightly News*, and *ABC World News Tonight*. On a good night, the shows together got as much as 75 percent of the entire viewing audience, or a total of 50 million to 60 million people.[33] Thus, it could be argued that the nation was getting pretty much the same news at the same time.

With the rise of cable television, the number of available channels has proliferated from a half-dozen in the 1960s to as many as one thousand, most of them catering to far smaller audiences than the three traditional

[31] Pew Research Center for the People and the Press, *Trends 2005*.
[32] National Opinion Research Center, *General Social Survey* (Chicago: University of Chicago, 2004).
[33] Project for Excellence in Journalism, "State of the News Media," 2004.

networks. These narrower markets are more efficient for some advertisers, who can reach precisely the consumers they need. The three network news shows still exist, but their share of the audience is today only half what it was a generation ago.[34] A 2002 Gallup poll showed that 43 percent of Americans get their news from cable TV, double the percentage in 1995.[35] And cable, with its smaller audiences (less than 3 million at any moment for Fox News Channel and CNN combined, compared to 9 million, still, for *each* of the network newscasts),[36] can profitably target narrower segments of the market. Fox, for instance, attracts a politically conservative audience; CNN's viewers are more likely to be politically moderate or leftist.

Similarly, in U.S. radio, the development of the long-neglected FM band in the 1970s meant that the big metropolitan "Top 40" radio stations, which aimed for the largest audiences possible, were replaced by stations with more specialized formats targeting narrower segments of the market. Again, advertisers preferred the more focused markets. Talk radio, which had been around since the 1960s, became an increasingly popular format, accounting for about 10 percent of all stations by the 1990s. The repeal of the federal "fairness doctrine" in 1987 encouraged the growth of partisan, sometimes deliberately inflammatory talk shows. Conservatives have been especially successful with this format: A recent survey for *Talkers*, a radio industry magazine, found that 3,349 stations broadcast national conservative programs, while only 250 carry liberal shows. The 2002 Gallup poll showed that 22 percent of Americans get most of their news from talk radio, nearly double the figure in 1995.

But perhaps the most dramatic example of the increasingly fractionalized media market is the rise of the Internet as a source of information. In a 2004 Gallup poll, 20 percent of Americans said they obtain their news every day from the Internet, up from 15 percent two years earlier.[37] For young people, the figure is no doubt higher. The Internet's flexibility allows consumers to find the news and views they want and avoid exposure to things that aren't of interest to them. The rise of blogs has been amply reported, as has their intensely partisan nature and the challenges they pose for the mainstream media.

The Pew Research Center in 2005 found that Americans were increasingly choosing news sources that conform to their political biases. Thus,

[34] Ibid.
[35] "How Americans Get Their News," *Gallup Poll On Demand*, December 20, 2002.
[36] Project for Excellence in Journalism, "State of the News Media," 2005.
[37] "How Americans Get Their News," *Gallup Poll On Demand*, December 18, 2004.

Republicans typically watched the Fox News Channel, whereas Democrats favored CNN and National Public Radio. Among conservative commentator Rush Limbaugh's 14.5 million weekly listeners, Pew found, 77 percent were conservative and 7 percent liberal. By contrast, the audience for public television's *NewsHour with Jim Lehrer* was 22 percent conservative and 27 percent liberal. (Overall, 36 percent of Americans called themselves conservatives and 18 percent liberal, with the rest, as in all the preceding cases, describing themselves as moderates.[38]) And Internet users, of course, choose their blogs to suit their biases. Consumers of partisan media evidently don't trust anything else: The 2004 Pew survey found that only 14 percent of Republicans believe all or most of the *New York Times*, less than half the percentage of Democrats.

That trend could have important consequences. If viewers get news that only reinforces their worldview, the current fissures in U.S. politics and society, as well as in the transatlantic relationship, may widen – and Americans' knowledge of the outside world may shrivel. "If liberals and conservatives migrate to rival media camps," warned *Newsweek*'s Robert J. Samuelson, "both camps may ultimately submit to the same narrow logic: like-minded editors and reporters increasingly feed like-minded customers stories that reinforce their world view."[39] The disadvantages are obvious. "The risk is that people will turn inward," Pew Center director Andrew Kohut wrote in the *New York Times*. "They're going to be exposed to fewer things that may challenge their points of view. And it would make sense that this is not an especially good thing for a democracy."[40]

Indeed, back in the golden age of the network evening newscasts, Americans had a common context for debating the issues of the day. They may have disagreed on the Vietnam War, for instance, but television brought the same war into all their living rooms, with the same images seen by everybody. That common reality is less likely today. With everyone getting a different version of the news, it may become more difficult for the country to enjoy the same shared values or to mobilize for the same purposes. Jürgen Habermas insisted that clear communication was essential for democratic societies to function. But what if people talk only to their own, self-selected, ideological tribes? Alexis de Tocqueville recognized the importance for democracy of

[38] Pew Research Center for the People and the Press, *Trends 2005* (Washington: Pew Center, 2005).

[39] Robert J. Samuelson, "Picking Sides for the News," *Newsweek*, June 28, 2004.

[40] Kohut, "More News."

reaching a large audience. "The effect of a newspaper is not only to suggest the same purpose to a great number of persons, but to furnish means for executing in common the designs which they may have singly conceived," he wrote in *Democracy in America*. "If there were no newspapers, there would be no common activity."[41]

This vanishing sense of community in the United States has drawn frequent commentary. Robert Putnam, in his 2000 book *Bowling Alone: The Collapse and Revival of American Community*, charted the long decline of civic and neighborhood ties in the United States. Researchers from the University of Arizona and Duke University found in 2004 that Americans had markedly fewer close friends than they did two decades earlier.[42] The political right, with its commitment to individualism and its suspicion of government, was handed an opportunity to put those views into practice with the arrival of George W. Bush. The relative tax burden on the wealthy was lightened, the social safety net was curtailed, and government regulation was trimmed in the name of economic growth.

The contrast with Europe is clear. There, social safety nets have long been more elaborate, and in recent years governments have largely declined to make significant reductions in them, despite mounting costs. Politicians, regardless of party or ideology, rarely attack the idea of government, as their conservative counterparts in the United States do regularly. Economic growth is prized in Europe, but generally not at the expense of social protections. Income distribution remains stable. Tax rates remain high (85 percent in France's top bracket, although a proposal has been made to lower that percentage). Civic participation rates are difficult to compare to those in the United States, as are Putnam-style findings about bowling leagues and the like. But it is true that voting turnout is generally higher in Europe than in the United States. Moreover, public discourse in Europe is saturated with a concept virtually unknown in the United States: "solidarity," the notion that citizens share responsibility for each others' well-being. France even calls its tax on wealth a "solidarity" levy.

The aftermath of Hurricane Katrina in the United States is a good illustration of the difference. Europeans (along with most Americans) were horrified at the slow and ineffectual response of federal, state, and local governments,

---

[41] Alexis De Tocqueville, *Democracy in America*, translated by Henry Reeves (New York: Adlard and Saunders, 1838). Reprint, The Lawbook Exchange, 2003. An online version is available at http://xroads.virginia.edu/~Hyper/DETOC/ch2_06.htm.

[42] Lynn Smith-Lovin and Miller McPherson, "Social Isolation in America," *American Sociological Review*, June 2006.

a failing that would have been nearly unthinkable in Europe. (In France, government ministers lost their jobs over feeble responses to a 2003 heat wave.) Much of the European and other international press commentary centered on the absence of "solidarity" in the United States. Veteran America-watcher Janadas Devan expressed the European reaction succinctly, although he was writing in the Singapore *Straits Times*: "It is not only government that doesn't show up when government is starved of resources and leached of all its meaning. Community doesn't show up either, sacrifice doesn't show up, pulling together doesn't show up, 'we're all in this together' doesn't show up."[43]

What role does the press play in the divergence of attitudes in Europe and the United States? Researchers since Paul Lazarsfeld in the 1940s have found that the media's ability to influence public opinion is far less than commonly believed. (Peer groups seem to be more important.) The problem comes when important information is not made public, as noted earlier. In such cases, the effects can be dramatic, at least in the short term and on the margins. It is likely that the gulf between Europe and the United States would not have widened so much over the Iraq War if the U.S. press had reported widely that, early in the conflict, France offered to train Iraqi police and that Germany even volunteered to send troops to fight; for various reasons, the United States refused France's offer and did not even respond to Germany's. The German snub was big news in Germany, where it no doubt helped inflame opinion against the Bush administration and the war; in the United States, it passed virtually unreported.

Likewise, massive media coverage can have an impact on public opinion. After U.S. news organizations focused intently on the aftermath of Hurricane Katrina, the president's approval ratings plunged. When the Bush administration in 2006 unveiled a new initiative to curb illegal immigration, that topic suddenly went from its usual position near the bottom of pollsters' lists of issues of greatest concern to American voters and headed almost to the top. After the Bush reforms encountered political opposition and were quietly put on the back burner, immigration slid down toward its usual position on the lists. Then, when Congress took up immigration reform in 2007, the issue started climbing again.

The question is whether the differences between U.S. and European coverage have helped move the two sides further apart. The answer, in general,

---

[43] Janadas Devan, cited in Thomas Friedman, "Singapore and Katrina," *New York Times*, September 14, 2005.

is yes. Inflammatory, divisive stories – an alleged rise in French anti-Semitism (despite a few high-profile cases, the number of incidents was declining at the time), the fuss over "freedom fries" – have since the Iraq War been played up in both places, as we have noted; stories focusing on mutual interests and amity involving trade, peacekeeping, and all sorts of other important subjects have been played down. But that failing may be a short-term aberration involving a host of issues that can all be traced to a specific point of disagreement, the Iraq War.

Convergence of Sorts

In recent years, it has been clear that the U.S. media scene is in some sense becoming more like – guess what? – Europe's. America in the early twenty-first century seemed to be moving toward a more ideological, European-style press. Indeed, some commentators saw the U.S. press returning to its own, intensely partisan roots of the early nineteenth century. Readers certainly knew where their news sources stood in those days. But, perhaps because people rarely heard opposing viewpoints and regularly had their biases reinforced, the period was a nightmare of divisiveness, conflict, and intemperance, a miasma of slavery, corruption, and sectional strife. "Our nostalgia about our country, which each succeeding generation tends to believe is only now going to the dogs, leads us to forget what a fractious, bare-knuckles bunch we have been," wrote *Newsday*'s Noel Holston. "During an 1858 debate in the U.S. House over whether Kansas would be admitted to the Union as a free or slave state, for example, two members traded insults, then went for each other's throats. More than 50 of their esteemed colleagues joined the melee, punching, kicking and gouging on the floor while the Speaker of the House helplessly banged his gavel."[44] On the whole, such an atmosphere is not a pleasant prospect. The European model seems more attractive, with readers knowing where news outlets stand but debate falling within the usual bounds of civility.

As the Iraq War staggers on and the Bush administration heads into its last years, the U.S. press has begun to shake off some of its somnolence and acquire a European-style pointedness. With Democrats in control of Congress, news organizations could use congressional hearings as a news "peg" to examine the war's conduct, the alleged politicization of the Justice Department, various regulatory lapses, and other failings of the

---

[44] Noel Holston, "Putting a Spin on the News," *Newsday,* August 15, 2004.

administration. Even conservative talk-radio hosts were beginning to ques-tion the administration's competence and efficacy.[45]

Meanwhile, the administration has begun to alter some of the policies that have alienated Europe. The United States has begun working closely with Europe and the United Nations on problems like Iran's and North Korea's nuclear programs, as well as China's and Russia's human rights records and trade policies. Al Gore and a spate of ominous scientific reports have revived the topic of climate change in the United States, to the delight of many Europeans. The dramatic 2005–6 rise in the price of oil has had a similar effect on once-divisive energy-related issues. Even the president began talking about renewable energy as a priority. Meanwhile, Europeans were starting to confront the costs of their expensive retirement systems, much as Bush proposed an overhaul of social security. The issue of immigration was proving to be just as painful in Europe, with its large Muslim minorities, as it was in the United States. Circumstance and mutual interest seem to be pushing the United States and Europe back toward each other. That is only natural. As advanced democracies, the two do after all have a lot of problems in common. The June 2006 Pew Center poll, for instance, showed that Americans and Europeans shared roughly the same relatively high levels of concern over Iran's nuclear ambitions and the rise of Hamas as a threat to Israel.

The prospects for the press are less encouraging, although the debates over objectivity and bias may subside somewhat. Mainstream news outlets in the United States are increasingly sensitive to their political leanings, real or alleged. Some are making a better effort to identify the ideological pro-clivities of the sources quoted in news stories. At the *New York Times*, a committee examining how the paper can restore its credibility (damaged by the inventions of reporter Jason Blair and by the paper's timid coverage of the weapons-of-mass-destruction issue) recently recommended a further separation of news and comment in its pages.[46] A few outlets are hiring commentators with clearly delineated ideological affiliations in an attempt to placate critics and broaden their appeal. The *Times*, for instance, added two conservative regular columnists to its Op-Ed page and relegated liberal firebrand Maureen Dowd to less prominent exposure. The *Washington Post* hired a conservative "red state" blogger for its website, though the man soon withdrew amid allegations of plagiarism. If the critics of objectivity have their way, such clearly ideological hiring and labeling will accelerate,

---

[45] Jim Rutenberg, *New York Times*, October 17, 2006.
[46] The entire report is available online at http://www.nytco.com/pdf/siegal-report050205.pdf.

allowing readers and viewers to know what they're getting into. That might help ease the distrust many Americans have for their press.

Although mass advertising has declined as a moderating influence on partisanship now that audiences are ever-narrower, overall U.S. ad spending was in fact growing – by 3 percent in 2005, and four times faster on the Internet, where a moderating influence is perhaps needed most.[47] Witness the rise of bloggers and blog-aggregators who supported themselves with ads dispatched from the servers of Google and Yahoo. Although Matt Drudge may not become the Walter Lippman of blogging just because his website has grown into an advertising vehicle, it may make him think a bit harder about his reputation for accuracy. Indeed, the growth of the blogging industry has fostered calls from within its ranks for better journalistic standards, codes of ethics, and the other trappings of respectability that print reporters adopted nearly a century ago.

Looking Forward

The European and the U.S. media are starting to become more alike in other respects as well. Cable television has been growing in Europe, and digital cable – which promises hundreds of new channels – is if anything further advanced than in the United States. Internet usage is soaring, and broadband penetration is higher in some European countries than in the United States. Talk radio is on the rise. At the same time, the "mainstream" media are on the decline, as newspaper advertising has migrated to the Internet and a new breed of free newspapers distributed largely in public transportation systems has invaded many cities. Newspaper circulation has fallen 3 percent in Europe since 1995, and 5 percent in the United States.[48] Mainstream media on both sides of the Atlantic face the same challenge of persuading a rising generation of nonreaders to get into the newspaper habit. These young people have alarmingly low rates of news consumption, and they tend to get their information from entertainment vehicles such as Comedy Central's *The Daily Show*, Britain's comedy-quiz program *Have I Got News for You*, and France's satirical puppet show *Les Guignols d'Info*.

Those new realities mean that the mainstream media in both Europe and the United States may concentrate less on improving their news coverage and more on maximizing audiences and advertising revenues. That could

---

[47] "2005 Spending Rose 4.2%," *Mediaweek*, March 15, 2006.
[48] World Association of Newspapers, *World Press Trends 2004*.

entail softening their ideological lines and trying to please as many peo-ple as possible – although perhaps on multiple "platforms," such as print, web sites, streaming audio, and sender rewriting scheme (SRS)/really simple syndication (RSS) feeds. For the last three of those (that is, those involving the Internet), advertising is by far the major online revenue stream. And, as we have seen, advertising can have a moderating effect on news cover-age. Media organizations are businesses, after all. Perhaps for that reason, Rupert Murdoch's right-wing *New York Post* became openly supportive of the right's arch-villainess, Senator Hillary Clinton. Murdoch evidently sensed which way the wind was blowing: Clinton was then New York's most pop-ular politician, even among *Post* readers, and the leading 2008 Democratic presidential candidate.

A recent Pew study of media habits found that Americans have less trou-ble than widely assumed in distinguishing fact from opinion, a finding that should reassure those worried by the increasing politicization of the press.[49] Other Pew surveys have shown that Americans remain interested in inter-national news, as previously noted, that they generally support multilateral institutions such as the U.N., and that they want the United States to coop-erate with its allies, European and otherwise.[50] The problem, then, may be not so much the polarization of the U.S. press as a growing blandness – a process that has also been under way in Europe.

Consider the problem facing newspapers, which was pretty much the same challenge facing broadcast news as well. As noted, circulation was declining at a slow but steady rate in both Europe and the United States. Advertis-ing is fleeing to the Internet. Combined ad revenues for Google and Yahoo in 2006 outstripped those of the entire newspaper industry.[51] Nonetheless, newspapers remained profitable. In 2005, publicly traded American news-paper companies reported operating profit margins of 19.2 percent. That is more than double the average for the Fortune 500 list of the largest U.S. com-panies. (Privately owned newspapers, many of them local monopolies, often have even larger operating margins.) But conventional wisdom in the finan-cial community is that publishing is a slow-growing "mature" industry. So to keep their share prices from plunging, managers of publicly traded newspa-per chains have come under pressure to raise their margins even higher. And because some of the least distinguished newspapers have the highest profit

---

[49] Pew Research Center for the People and the Press, *Survey Reports*, June 26, 2005.
[50] Chicago Council on Foreign Relations, *Leaders and the Public*, 2002.
[51] "The Online Ad Attack," *Economist*, April 30, 2005.

margins (they generally spend less on news coverage and have virtually no local competition), the financial community demands that all newspapers approximate those lofty margins. Otherwise, investors punish the laggards by avoiding their shares.

The traditional method to raise margins in a mature industry is to cut costs, typically by shrinking editorial spending. Trying to improve margins by expanding editorial coverage is rarely considered; the payoff would be long-term, and managers of public companies need to show results every quarter. The Project for Excellence in Journalism reported in 2006 that U.S. news-rooms had lost 3,500 professionals since 2000, a shrinkage of 7 percent.[52] The figure was expected to increase in 2006 because of a wave of newly announced layoffs. Many of these followed mergers, such as the takeover of the respected Knight-Ridder chain by its more profitable, less journalistically distinguished rival McClatchy.

That cost-cutting mania, by reducing news coverage, has the perverse effect of making papers even less useful and attractive to readers. The Project studied two thousand stories that appeared in a sampling of fifty-seven major newspapers, TV and radio stations, and Internet sites on a single, randomly chosen day, May 11, 2005. It found that most of the stories were near-identical versions picked up from wire services or other syndicated sources. On that day, the study found, Google offered access within two clicks to fourteen thousand stories, but in reality they involved just twenty-four news events. The study also found that blogs and other Internet sites contained virtually no original reporting. "It's probably glib and even naive to say simply that more platforms equal more choices," said Tom Rosensteil, the Project's director. "The content has to come from somewhere, and as older news-gathering media decline, some of the strengths they offer in monitoring the powerful and verifying the facts may be weakening as well."[53]

News outlets owned by publicly traded companies are often more focused on profits than on public service. They are also less likely to court controversy through investigative reporting or vigorous editorializing. They are more susceptible to intimidation by politicians and organized pressure groups. There were admirable exceptions, of course. The *New York Times* (which printed the Pentagon Papers in 1971 and uncovered the government's war-rantless wiretap operation in 2006) and the *Washington Post* (of Water-gate fame) are both owned by public companies. And the Knight-Ridder

[52] Project for Excellence in Journalism, *State of the News Media*, March 2006.
[53] Ibid.

chain's Washington bureau was the first to report skeptically about the Bush administration's claims of weapons of mass destruction in Iraq before the war. Yet after Knight-Ridder's takeover by McClatchy, its Washington bureau was merged with the acquiring company's less vigorous operation. Twenty-five years ago, about fifty corporations owned most of the media outlets in the United States. By 2006, that number had fallen to no more than a dozen.[54]

The situation is similar in Europe. Diversity of ownership is declining in many countries, as media conglomerates gobble up ever more properties. A 2002 study by Deutsche Bank Media Research of ten European countries found that the three biggest publishers in each one controlled anywhere from 35 percent of the market (France) to 88 percent (the Netherlands). Crossborder mergers – such as Britain's Pearson combining its TV operations with Luxembourg's CLT and Germany's Bertelsmann, or France's Vivendi purchasing America's Universal – are on the rise. To halt the continuing decline in readership, European newspapers are introducing more entertainment and "lifestyle" features – which can be produced more cheaply than news pages and are thought to draw young readers – and subtly softening their political lines. Editorial staffs and "news holes" are being pared in an attempt to boost margins. France's financially troubled daily *Libération*, for instance, has shed nearly one-third of its editorial staff since 2005.

The trend toward consumer self-selection may moderate once those outlets become blander and less ideological. Discussions I held with several dozen students at Paris' Institut des Médias in 2005 and 2006 indicated that hardly any of them saw much difference between *Le Figaro* and *Le Monde*, which for a previous generation were at the opposite ends of the political spectrum (the students did, however, prefer *Le Figaro* for its entertainment coverage). And the kind of aggressive reporting that undermines political elites may fade as well. The outlets themselves may prefer to avoid controversy in an attempt to enhance audiences and advertising revenue. Although newspaper ownership was once seen as a route to political influence – ask Berlusconi, Murdoch, and generations of European press lords – today it is seen increasingly as yet another profitable if rather stodgy business.

So the American and European media, which helped widen the transatlantic divide by providing their respective audiences with differing views of each other's countries, may not play such a divisive role in the future. Instead, the two media models will likely converge toward an inoffensive, nonpartisan

54 Molly Ivins, "So Papers Are Dying? Who Says?" *Fort Worth Star-Telegram*, March 26, 2006.

blandness. Profitability may increase, but newsgathering resources will shrink. Rather than getting distorted news of each other, Europeans and Americans will not get much news at all. The effect of that change on transatlantic amity may well be positive. The prospects for maintaining an informed citizenry, on both sides of the ocean, are considerably less encouraging.

4

One Ring to Bind Them All

American Power and Neoliberal Capitalism

Mark Blyth

In 2007, the United States government will spend more on its armed forces than all other countries combined. This fact, plus U.S. operations in Afghanistan and Iraq, tensions with Iran, and the "war on terror," all make it easy to forget that American power is *not* based solely on its military might. At a time when pundits and policy makers alike speak of the "unipolar moment" or a new age of "empire," it should make us pause to consider what such power is *also* based upon.

Unlike the dark lord Sauron of *The Lord of the Rings*, the United States does not rule the world through the cruelty of a great army of Orcs. Like most successful great powers, military power is only part of the story. But like the dark lord Sauron, to stretch the analogy to its fullest, the power of the United States rests not merely on military might, but on "binding" men together with a conception of, if not what is "right," then at least what is desirable. As the political scientist Joseph Nye argues, as well as applying force, a state can "obtain desired outcomes in world politics because other countries want to follow it, admiring its values, emulating its example, aspiring to its level of prosperity and openness."[1]

Consider, by way of contrast, the late Chairman Mao's statement that "power comes from the barrel of a gun." This is undeniable. But what Nye is suggesting is that power also resides in the ability to make others want what you want so that you don't have to stick a gun in their face in the first place. This has been, I argue, the more subtle, but just as vital, basis of American power: getting other states to want what you want.

---

[1] Joseph Nye, "Hard and Soft Power in a Global Information Age," in Mark Leonard, ed., *Reordering the World: The Long-Term Implications of September 11th* (London: Foreign Policy Centre, 2002), pp. 4–5, available online at http://fpc.org.uk/fsblob/36.pdf, accessed December 12, 2006.

In this chapter, I discuss how developing and deploying ideas about "the way the economic world works" has facilitated American power, enabling it to shape other states' conceptions of their self-interest – that is, convincing other advanced industrial states through the ideas that the United States promotes, as well as the institutions that the United States sets up and the outcomes they deliver, that what the United States wants is good for them too. None of this suggests that "material" factors such as the postwar strategic balance or the sheer size of the U.S. economy do not matter. Rather, this chapter focuses on a less remarked upon aspect of U.S. power: the attractiveness of U.S. ideas.

The ideas that made the United States strong from the 1940s until the 1980s – multilateralism, consultative diplomacy, and an expansionary and redistributionary macroeconomic policy – have given way today to a new set of ideas based around unilateralism, indicative diplomacy, and a restrictive and regressive macroeconomic policy. Key to this transformation post-1975 has been the rise of so-called neoliberal economic ideas as the touchstone of "sound" economic governance. The adoption of these ideas by the U.S. governing elite has led U.S. policy down a path that sees the supply side of the economy as dominant, wages as a cost to be minimized, and government as the cause of, rather than the solution to, economic problems. Being the proverbial three hundred pound gorilla in the room, the embrace of these ideas by the United States has had massive consequences for Europe, as Steven Teles and Daniel Kenney will show in the next chapter of this book.

As the U.S. business press frequently puts it, Europe's bloated welfare states are no longer viable in this new "globalized" environment. High tax states must lose to low tax states; redistributionary states must give way to "competition" states; and labor protections must give way to "flexibility." In short, European states must accept "the way the world now works" according to the United States, and accept the policies these new ideas demand. Given the ferocity with which such claims were trumpeted during the 1980s and 1990s, many observers saw European states as inevitably falling into an increasingly pernicious race to the bottom, with widening inequality the cost to be paid. To paraphrase Margaret Thatcher, "there [was] no alternative," or as Lord Sauron would have it, neoliberalism was the new "One-Ring that binds them all."

Indeed, during the 1980s and 1990s it seemed that European states were following the United States in liberalizing their economies. Large-scale privatizations of public assets and institutional reforms unthinkable a generation ago were undertaken across all of Europe, culminating in the European Monetary Union. Once again it seemed that what the United States wanted,

Europe wanted too. After all, if these new ideas delivered the prosperity they promised, who would not want to be bound by the new "One-Ring"?

Things are often not what they seem, however, and once European governments became aware of the very real political and economic costs of "wanting what the United States now wants," they balked, and the power of the new "One-Ring" began to fail. This has resulted in a growing divergence between the type of political economy many European governments still want (equalitarian and compensatory) versus that now sought by the United States (inegalitarian and nonaccommodating); and such divergence constitutes part of why the United States and Europe are growing apart today.

To make this case, the first part of this chapter sketches out the ideas that underpinned U.S. power between 1945 and 1975. This order was based on a specific version of "the way the economic world works" born in the Great Depression. The global acceptance of these ideas made American power in this period extremely robust since it successfully portrayed the particular interests of the United States as being the general interest of Europe. The next part of this chapter details why some groups in the United States found this order to be not in their best interests, and discusses how they overturned it, as detailed by Teles and Kenney (in Chapter 5), using neoliberal ideas. I then discuss how these ideas came to Europe, and detail the transformations they wrought during the 1980s and the 1990s.

The next part of the chapter argues that although the construction of common interests by the United States was possible in both periods, the neoliberal ideas underlying the current order make for a much more fragile compact – one that many European governments are unwilling to join. To substantiate these claims, comparisons are made between the United States and Europe in the areas of economic performance, welfare policies, and inequality. We find that there is indeed increasing divergence between the United States and Europe in terms of economic policies and outcomes, and I question the extent to which Europe is really "going neoliberal."

Although European leaders were willing to embrace the first compact given the positive-sum nature of the outcomes they offered, the more that the economic and social costs generated by the current order became apparent, the less they were willing to adhere to the second neoliberal compact. Consequently, what we increasingly see is European governments "talking a good game" regarding neoliberal policies while in fact doing something quite different in practice. If U.S. strength were based merely on brute force, this incongruence would be of little consequence, but it is not. To return to the dark lord Sauron, deprived of the ability to bind men together with a common conception of "what we all want," what could be termed "Mao's revenge" may begin to affect U.S. interests – that is, if you can't make someone want what you want, you may have to stick a gun in their face.[2] The costs of doing so, however, may ultimately prove to be very high indeed.

Economic Ideas and the Foundations of American Power

From Interference to Intervention

The basis of American power lies in the military victories of World War II. Yet acknowledging the importance of these military victories is just one aspect of a full understanding of how the United States was able to shape the post-war world. What was also critical was the conception of what government should do in the economy, both locally and globally, *after* the war. Basically, government intervention into the economy became respectable. Building on the successes of the New Deal period, those planning for the postwar world sought to build, as political scientist John Ruggie has described it, a new form of capitalism that combined the welfare-enhancing aspects of free trade with domestic institutions designed to avoid the instability and unemployment characteristic of the 1930s.[3]

The need for such a new form of capitalism was as much political as it was economic. On the economic front, postwar planners believed that the reason fascism came to power in Europe in the 1930s was that when the world economy deflated in the Great Depression, the costs of deflation (falling prices) were borne for over a decade mainly by labor in the form of declining wages and higher unemployment. This was allowed to occur since, according to the economic ideas of the 1920s and 1930s, deflation was a series of shocks to the global economy that would ride themselves out through the adjustment of wages and prices, if the price mechanism was allowed to operate without the well-meaning but ultimately harmful interference of government. If there was unemployment, it had to be the result of labor bargaining for too high a wage; to restore balance, wages had to fall to match prices. Cushioning adjustment would simply pile on the pain and delay the inevitable.

---

[2] This is not to say that coercion doesn't work – it does – but it also suffers diminishing returns.

[3] Ruggie termed this an "embedded" liberalism, in contrast to the "classical" liberalism of the previous prewar era, where trade in things that produced jobs was encouraged, but financial speculation that did not was ruled out. See John Gerald Ruggie, "International Regimes, Transactions, and Change: Embedded Liberalism in the Post-war Economic Order," *International Organization* vol. 36, no. 2, Spring 1982, pp. 379–415.

There were unfortunately two problems with such a view. First, if it was correct, adjustment costs were still shouldered by labor, and what the 1930s seemed to show was that labor, wherever it was located, did not respond well to precipitous drops in the real wage.[4] Second, such a theory simply could not explain why between 1924 and 1931 millions of people across the world seemed to decide that the prevailing wage in their job was too low and that an extended unpaid vacation was in order. Indeed, the poverty and upheaval caused by the Great Depression made the claim that unemployment was voluntary seem quite absurd. As far as the postwar world was concerned, then, a simple return to the status quo ante, where the external financial balance automatically governed internal wages, prices, and employment levels, was not going to suffice.

Rethinking the Way the World Works

In terms of governing ideas, the critical lesson learned from the Great Depression was that unemployment persisted not because people were unwilling to work at the prevailing wage, but because there was no work to be had; unemployment could be involuntary. These new ideas stressed that the reason economic depressions were so difficult to get out of was that investors were depressed – in a very specific sense. The new idea was that although investors and investment (the supply side of the economy) ultimately create jobs and growth, investors tended to have rather short-sighted expectations regarding the future.[5] If investors think that the past three months were bad, and the three months before that were bad, then regardless of the preceding twenty months of bliss, they will probably think that the next three months will also be bad. The result is that, quite rationally but perversely, individual investors are unwilling to invest, with the consequence that economic activity as a whole declines, despite this being the very outcome that everyone wants to avoid.

To cap it all off, if the distribution of income and wealth is highly unequal (as it was in most countries during the 1930s), then investors do not need to invest to survive given the disproportionate amount of income and wealth they already hold. Labor, on the other hand, cannot have wages without investment, and without wages fascism and communism lay just around the corner. Seen in this way, something had to be done to give a shock

---

4 See Karl Polanyi, *The Great Transformation: The Political and Economic Origins of Our Time* (Boston: Beacon Press, 1944), passim.
5 See John Maynard Keynes, *The General Theory of Employment, Interest and Money* (New York: Harcourt Brace, 1964), chapters 10–12.

to the system and stimulate investment. That something was government. These new ideas proposed that boosting demand through spending would raise consumption, signaling to investors that prices were rising, thereby encouraging investment: Interference became intervention.[6]

Some investors, suspicious of the government, argued that this was government trickery, since any spending now would be paid for in the form of higher interest rates (or taxes) in the future due to the government squandering available investment; or it would ruin business confidence, the very thing that government was trying to encourage. However, if investors' expectations were indeed "front-loaded," then raising prices through government spending would create a situation where investors *could* make money. All investors would then be faced with a choice: Hold out in principled opposition to government policy, or make money (since clearly someone else could), thus expanding the economy and reversing the self-fulfilling dynamic of investor expectations through the raising of prices.[7]

Changing the Way the World Works – and Augmenting American Power

Investors chose the latter option, and after 1945 government took on a role hitherto unprecedented: the active steering of the economy, both domestically *and* internationally. In addition to the New Deal institutions, the United States designed the new international order of the period: the Bretton Woods exchange rate system (designed to stabilize world trade by fixing exchange rates), the International Monetary Fund (designed to help states avoid internal deflations by providing financing for balance of payment problems), and the International Bank for Reconstruction and Development (encouraging state-led development outside the developed world). Despite domestic opposition to such "socialistic" policies, the political costs of not pursuing them seemed simply too high given the experience of the 1930s.[8] And there was another good reason for doing so: the credible alternative posed by the Soviet Union.

Although it is hard to imagine today, the USSR was widely seen in the postwar era as a viable alternative road to prosperity. With large (and popular) communist parties in many European states, especially France and Italy,

---

[6] Mark Blyth, *Great Transformations: Economic Ideas and Institutional Change in the Twentieth Century* (Cambridge: Cambridge University Press 2002), chapters 3, 4.

[7] This is why Friedman's argument that Keynes needs to "fool" people into investing is mistaken. One can know it's a government trick, but you can still make money out of it. So if you go for it, are you being fooled or simply selling out?

[8] Eric Helleiner, *States and the Reemergence of Global Finance* (Ithaca: Cornell University Press, 1994).

capitalizing on the wartime success of the USSR, and the fear of a return to mass unemployment after the war, both American and European political elites saw the need to stabilize Europe. Although the Marshall Plan may be the most famous example of this commitment, equally important was the U.S. response to the Soviet alternative. Containment was one part of the strategy, but another part was the construction of redistributionary welfare states throughout Europe, all supported by the Bretton Woods order.

In this period of common interests and positive sum politics, where one state's growth was not seen as another state's loss, Western Europe voluntarily aligned itself with an American-designed form of capitalism that guarded the real wage of labor, sponsored interclass mobility through publicly funded education, and, crucially, taught Western European leaders of all political stripes that it was good to be bound to the "One Ring" of the United States. After all, nothing succeeds like success, and in this period Western European incomes in many cases tripled in less than twenty years. Such ideas and the policies they necessitated clearly served American interests, but did so in such a way as to make Western European political elites' interests parallel to those of the United States. There was no need to stick a gun in somebody's face.

Does Anyone Have a Problem with This?

Upsetting the Orthodox

Figuring out the answer to this question is hardly rocket science. Under the prior model of "the way the world works," investors and entrepreneurs were the heroes. As liberal theorists from Adam Smith onward argued, savings led to investment, which led to wages to buy the products made by the workers themselves, which led to profits reinvested in the firm. In short, investment led to income, which led to investment – a virtuous circle. But in the 1930s, the virtuous circle broke down and the new ideas previously discussed came to prominence. But what is not often noted in discussions of the rise of these new ideas was the distributionary politics that they necessarily enshrined.

As discussed previously, these new ideas deemed that the key to encouraging investment was rising prices, and saw the government as being able to raise prices via spending. But in the long run such a position suggests something quite political: that consumption drives investment, not the opposite. Under these new ideas, the demand side, not the supply side, is seen as dominant. In such a world, consumers become heroes – not investors – and in making this change, political power becomes redistributed.

In this world, consumers' demands determine investors' supply schedules. So if one wanted to improve the economy, who should get the tax cut?

Not the investor, but those most likely to consume – labor. No longer is Adam Smith's "parsimonious Scot" the hero. Now the heroes are millions of "average Joes" whose joint consumption decisions determine the supply of investment. This fact, plus mass democracy (another post-1945 invention for most of the developed world), threatened to lead to what John Maynard Keynes called "the euthanasia of the rentier" – the end of the world in which investors ruled the roost. That such groups recoiled at such ideas is hardly a surprise.

Taxing Times Ahead

Although investors were not euthanized under the new regime, they certainly had to share the wealth a little more. Economists Claudia Goldin and Robert A. Margo call this period "The Great Compression."[9] After the Great Depression, the wage structure of the United States compressed considerably. The differentials between workers at the top and bottom of the income scale narrowed, while the real wages of all groups (who received wages) increased. *This had never happened before.* This redistribution of income and wealth was further aided by the new institutions of the postwar world that acted as a tax on investors' earnings by making some practices either more difficult, or in some cases, downright illegal – financial speculation, for example. Similarly, a policy of cheap money and reflationary countercyclical fiscal policies aided those at the bottom of the income distribution far more than those at the top. And to pay for all this, investors as a class actually had to pay more in taxes, with the tax burden proportionately shifting towards upper-income earners *for the first time in history.*[10] Taking the top 1 percent of U.S. households as the core of the investor class, this group's marketable wealth declined from 44 percent of the gross domestic product (GDP) in 1930 to around 20 percent by 1970. In the United Kingdom, the redistribution was just as drastic, with the top 1 percent's net worth declining from 55 percent in 1930 to 28 percent in 1970. In Sweden, it fell from 38 percent to 18 percent over the same period.[11]

Clearly, something had to be done about this. It was bad enough to go from being the heroes of the system to being seen as the shortsighted adjuncts of the consumption decisions of the *profane vulgar*. But when this new system

---

[9] Claudia Goldin and Robert A. Margo, "The Great Compression: The Wage Structure in the United States at Mid-Century," National Bureau of Economic Research (NBER) Working Paper 3817, August 1991.

[10] See, among other sources, Edward N. Wolff, *Top Heavy: A Study of Increasing Inequality in of Wealth in America* (New York: Century Fund Press 1995).

[11] Ibid., pp. 22–3.

actually redistributed income and wealth from the top to the bottom, those who benefited from it had to be convinced that despite all this growth and income going their way, such a system was actually not really in their best interests. Yet thirty-plus years of higher taxes and bigger government had produced *more wealth* for the bottom four-fifths of the income distribution in the United States than at any other time in history. Clearly, if there were going to be some new ideas that would make the majority of people believe that this system was not in their interest, they would have to be very creative, and also have more than a bit of luck on their side.

The Return to Orthodoxy

The upsetting victory of these ideas was not uncontested; there were hold-outs. Seen during the 1950s and 1960s as little more than old-fashioned conservatives confined to the so-called Freshwater schools of Chicago, Carnegie Mellon, and Wisconsin, these intellectual stalwarts of the old order bided their time, offering alternative ideas to the status quo. They waited, preparing to take the offensive when the opportunity presented itself. As Teles and Kenney put it, "taking advantage [of a] window of opportunity . . . turns largely on the transmission of ideas."[12] As if realizing this, the poster child of this movement, Milton Friedman, once argued that the point of his work was

to keep options open until circumstances make change necessary. There is enormous inertia – a tyranny of the status quo – in private and especially governmental arrangements. Only a crisis – actual or perceived – produces real change. When that crisis occurs, the actions that are taken depend on the ideas that are lying around. That, I believe, is our basic function: to develop alternatives to existing policies, to keep them alive and available until the politically impossible becomes politically inevitable.[13]

Friedman's contributions to neoliberal economics were legion, but one stands out for its elegance (it seemed to fit the facts) and its timing (it did so at the right time). Beginning in the late 1960s, Friedman began to question something that the "new economists" (the pro-government economists of the 1960s) such as James Tobin and Paul Samuelson had popularized: the Phillips curve.[14]

[12] Steven Teles and Daniel Kenney, "Spreading the Word: The Diffusion of American Conservatism in Europe and Beyond," chapter 5 in this book.
[13] Milton Friedman and Rose Friedman, *Capitalism and Freedom* (Chicago: University of Chicago Press, 1982/1962), p. vii.
[14] A. W. Phillips. "The Relation between Unemployment and the Rate of Change of Money Wages in the United Kingdom, 1861–1957," *Economica*, vol. 25, no. 100, November 1958, pp. 283–99.

The idea behind the Phillips curve was that there existed a trade-off between the rate of change in wages and the general level of prices (more prosaically, unemployment versus inflation). This curve seemed to offer policy makers a menu of choice between the two outcomes, trading one off against the other, which was nice; but it also had some rather unsettling distributional implications. For example, if the party that benefited most from these new ideas (that which represented the majority of the income distribution, the Democrats) preferred to trade off a little more inflation against a little more unemployment, then to the extent that inflation is a tax on time-deferred investment incomes, that tax would be paid by the Republican Party's most powerful constituency – the investor class. Friedman helped to portray this as a disaster waiting to happen, not just for the investor class, but for everyone.

Neoliberal Lesson #1: Activism Is Harmful to Your Health
To turn this particular redistribution into a general disaster, Friedman made four assumptions that today form (with some modification; two were added later) the core of contemporary neoliberal thinking:

1. There is a "natural" rate of unemployment beyond which the economy cannot be pushed.
2. Job seekers and investors have "adaptive" rather than shortsighted expectations.
3. In the long run, there is no trade-off between employment and inflation.
4. Unemployment is voluntary.[15]

These assumptions enabled Friedman to tell the following story.

Imagine you live in an economy with a level of unemployment that is seen as "too high" and a government that wants to do something about it. According to the Phillips curve, it can do so by spending money to increase prices, signaling investment, and tightening labor markets, all of which would be reflected in higher wages that would encourage the unemployed to return to work (since their current unemployment is voluntary – assumption 4). This would trigger still higher prices, as the Phillips curve predicted, which would bring forth new growth. The problem, Friedman insisted, was that this

---

[15] For an accessible summary, see Milton Friedman, "Inflation and Unemployment: The New Dimensions of Politics," in Milton Friedman, *Monetarist Economics* (London: Institute of Economic Affairs, 1991); idem, "The Role of Monetary Policy," *American Economic Review*, vol. 58, no. 1, March 1968, pp. 1–17.

trade-off between unemployment and inflation is an illusion, since workers had "adaptive" and not shortsighted expectations (assumption 2).

Unemployed workers would take the new job at the seemingly higher wage, only to discover that prices have also risen. Therefore, although their money wage had increased, their real wage (money wage minus the price level) would not have risen at all. Workers would then withdraw their labor (assumption 4) such that unemployment returns to its "natural rate" (assumption 1). If the government tries to do this again, it does so from a higher baseline of inflation (assumption 2), and once the price increases filter through the economy, workers again withdraw their labor and unemployment rises, and all that the state is left with is higher and higher inflation and the same rate of unemployment (assumption 1). The take-home message is clear: Government causes inflation – not greater employment.

Despite resting upon some rather heroic assumptions, the timing of this argument was perfect. Coming on the heels of Vietnam War expenditures, the 1960s' welfare expansion, rising deficits, and the November 1973 oil shock, the Phillips curve broke down with unemployment and inflation rising together to produce "Stagflation." Although this phenomenon was actually quite explicable in terms of Keynesian ideas, Friedman's ideas gained much currency and, as detailed by Teles and Kenney in Chapter 5, were promoted with vigor by business-funded think tanks and Republican policy makers. It also spawned a political variant of the same lineage that was even more damning.

Neoliberal Lesson #2: You Can't Trust the Government with Your Money

If there were more workers/consumers than capitalists/investors, then Democratic Party administrations, those that nominally served the worker/consumer constituency, could effectively lock in their electoral advantage. By meshing the electoral cycle to the business cycle, such governments, it was argued, could cynically manipulate the economy to boom when an election was coming and bust once it was won. But given that the unemployment/inflation trade-off that such manipulation would be based on was unstable (as shown by Friedman), rather than just soaking the rich, such behavior would produce lower growth and higher inflation for all. So even if you were in the constituency of the "many," in the end you would get hurt too.[16]

---

[16] The classic contributions to this literature are William D. Nordhaus, "The Political Business Cycle," *Review of Economic Studies*, vol. 42, no. 2, April 1975, pp. 169–90; C. Duncan MacRae, "A Political Model of the Business Cycle," *Journal of Political Economy*, vol. 85,

Like Friedman's version of events, this "political business cycle" theory saw government not as the stabilizer of the economy, but as the cause of inflation, recession, and unemployment. Governments were now seen as cynically causing inflation to enhance their electoral prospects, while federal bureaucrats were seen to expand their budgets relentlessly to swallow more and more of national product and investment. Such ideas found particular resonance in the context of large budget deficits and swollen tax receipts due to inflationary "bracket creep" during the economic slowdown of the mid-1970s. The tide was turning.

Neoliberal Lesson #3: Government Is Pointless – or Toxic – or Both

Two more ideas were important for the full development of neoliberal thinking. First of all, why assume that people have adaptive expectations? If being wrong is expensive, then we would expect people to invest in being correct. We know people in fact do this because if we assume that markets are efficient (assumption 5), then consistently wrong choices (and thus choosers) would be eliminated from the market. Therefore, those agents in the market at any given point must be those people who use the available information efficiently since they are not dead yet. Such agents must have "rational," not adaptive, expectations (assumption 6).[17]

If this is the case, and these agents know that in the past the government has expressed a preference for lower unemployment, then they can reasonably expect the government to spend money to lower unemployment. But if spending now means either higher interest rates or higher taxes later on, then such "rational" investors will alter their budgets to compensate before the policy comes into effect, thereby nullifying the effect on real variables. In other words, policy becomes futile. However, knowing that investors would do this, the government could try and spend unexpectedly, in an effort to get around the anticipated reactions of investors. Doing so would interfere with the otherwise efficient price signals of markets, thus causing confusion and thereby bringing about a recession. Government was therefore toxic, or pointless, or both.

The final nail in the coffin of the new economics was supply-side tax theory, a reinvention and reinstatement of the classical view that investment

---

no. 2, April 1977, pp. 239–63; Assar Lindbeck, "Stabilization Policy in Open Economies with Endogenous Politicians," *American Economic Review*, vol. 66, no. 2, May 1976, pp. 1–19.

[17] For a nontechnical introduction, see Mark H. Willes, "Rational Expectations as a Counterrevolution," in Daniel Bell and Irving Kristol, eds., *The Crisis in Economic Theory* (New York: Basic Books, 1981).

drives income, and not the other way around.[18] This "supply-side revolution" was also very effective bribery. As Americans have shown in the past two decades, when faced with a choice between a tax cut and "any other policy," the tax cut wins every time, despite the redistribution being rather obviously skewed toward the top earners. Add all this together, and fund it with lavish press campaigns, television programs, and research grants to sympathetic economists, and the result was to turn the world (neo-) liberal again.

America and Europe, Skin-Deep Neoliberalism, and the Waning of American Power

As Goes America? The U.K. Goes Neoliberal

Prior to Ronald Reagan implementing many of these ideas in 1981 and 1982, thereby causing a deep recession that decimated those U.S. industries traditionally aligned with the Democratic Party, such ideas had another champion, Margaret Thatcher. Coming to power in 1979, one early act of Thatcher's chancellor of the exchequer, Nigel Lawson, was to abolish U.K. exchange controls, remnants of the Bretton Woods system. The collapse of the Bretton Woods system of fixed exchange rates from 1971 to 1973 presented private financial interests in the United States and the United Kingdom with the opportunity to make billions by picking up the new market in currency risk. The abolition of exchange controls opened up London to such flows and abandoned any buffer between domestic and world prices.[19] Such a policy change served two goals. First, it rewarded investors by opening up new markets. Second, it weakened the bargaining power of domestic labor by, once again, making wages adjust to external prices.

Building on this, the Thatcher government embarked upon a Friedmanesque policy of targeting the money supply to reduce inflation, which had the effect of precipitously raising real interest rates, but did so with a less obvious mechanism. This policy constricted the economy, caused massive unemployment, and, combined with a series of legislative assaults on trade unions, further weakened the bargaining power of labor. It also increased further the value of paper assets by lowering inflation and further boosting the profitability of the financial sector.

---

[18] For an excellent discussion of supply-side and rational expectations theories, see Paul Krugman, *Peddling Prosperity: Economic Sense and Nonsense in the Age of Diminished Expectations* (New York: W. W. Norton, 1994), pp. 82–103.

[19] See Nigel Lawson, *The View From No. 11: Memoirs of a Tory Radical* (London: Corgi Books, 1993), pp. 38–43.

Having succeeded in these tasks, the British government next pursued a series of privatizations that included the further deregulation of finance, thereby encouraging the growth of the service sector and unorganized white-collar labor. Capping all this off were supply-side tax cuts that redistributed even more wealth back to investors.[20] The United Kingdom and the United States, by embracing neoliberal ideas, both as a critique of existing institutions and as a guide for their replacement, reorganized their economies in such a way as to redistribute from bottom to top, weaken the power of labor, and delegitimate state interventionism. This was neoliberalism in practice.

As Goes America? Europe Goes Neoliberal

Such policies, emanating from two of the largest economies in the world, had effects elsewhere. With the end of fixed exchange rates and abolition of exchange controls by the two largest financial centers, an era of global capital flows began that shifted the cost of adjustment back onto domestic labor everywhere. From the point of view of other European states, when the United States and the United Kingdom opened up their markets, deregulated finance, and encouraged inward flows of capital, the costs of maintaining controls became ever more expensive. It became rational for the remaining states to abolish controls and bandwagon with the liberalizing states (and get some of the action) rather than hold out against the tide. What turned many European states in this direction was what happened to France in the early 1980s.[21]

Coming to power in 1981, the Socialist government of François Mitterrand attempted to reflate its way out of the recession that had spread from the United States and Britain to continental Europe. Relying on methods of nationalization, controls, and fiscal stimulus, at a time when everyone else was deflating, Mitterrand's policies produced massive capital flight out of the franc, which seemed to prove that controls did not work, and a massive appreciation of interest rates that caused the economy to slow even further. After a year of holding out, the French government executed a famous policy U-Turn and gave up trying to control the franc, the domestic rate of interest, and aggregate demand. Having "learned" from this, even Sweden, that paragon of social democracy, saw the writing on the wall and in 1987

---

[20] For an overview of the Thatcher period, see Andrew Gamble, *The Free Economy and the Strong State*, 2nd edition (Durham: Duke University Press, 1994).

[21] See the sections on France and its U-turn in Peter A. Hall, *Governing the Economy: The Politics of State Intervention in Britain and France* (Cambridge: Cambridge University Press, 1988); Kathleen McNamara, *The Currency of Ideas* (Ithaca: Cornell University Press, 1998).

deregulated its domestic credit markets and abolished exchange controls shortly thereafter.

By the time that the Berlin Wall came down, it seemed that there was indeed "no alternative." This was confirmed further in the 1990s, when right-wing governments lost power and putatively left-wing parties were returned throughout Europe with large majorities. However, as the cases of Tony Blair, Gerhard Schröder, Wim Kok, and Romano Prodi demonstrated, redistribution, higher taxes, and demand-side economics were conspicuous by their absence. In their place these "left" governments created independent central banks and currency unions. To update Richard Nixon, it seems that "we are all neoliberals now." Appearances, however, can be deceptive. As the costs of pursuing such policies have become more obvious over time, the less European states are willing to bear them. Europe increasingly "talks a good game" about deep neoliberal reform, but in fact does something quite different in practice.

Comparing Europe and the United States

To make the case that the appearance and reality of a neoliberal Europe are actually quite different things, we must first have a benchmark as to what a neoliberal state looks like. Appropriately, the United States suffices. Having began the period as the most liberal of developed states, it embraced neoliberalism with gusto and underwent a more profound transformation than any other country except the United Kingdom. A quick examination of what happened to the United States since 1980 in terms of macroeconomic policy, welfare policies, and inequality serves as the basis for our contrast with contemporary Europe.

In contrast to what occurred in the United States during the Great Compression, during the 1980s, 37 percent of the total income gains of that decade went to the top 1 percent of households. Meanwhile, the bottom 80 percent of the distribution received only 24 percent of the gains.[22] During the 1990s, these trends continued despite redistributionary programs such as the Earned Income Tax Credit. In 2004, 37 million Americans lived below the poverty line, up from below 25 million in 1973, and despite the growth in real GDP since the 1970s, the poverty rate has remained virtually unchanged.[23] This is a complete reversal of the patterns of the previous thirty years.

[22] Wolff, *Top Heavy*, p. 7.
[23] Carmen DeNavas Walt et al., *Income, Poverty and Health Insurance Coverage in the United States 2004* (Washington: U.S. Census Bureau, 2004), p. 16.

The figures for wealth are even more illustrative than the figures for income. From 1945 to 1976, the share of marketable wealth controlled by the top 1 percent of households fell by 10 percent. Between 1983 and 1989, it rose by 39 percent. Nearly everyone else, the bottom 80 percent of the income distribution, saw their wealth holdings fall by nearly a fifth over the same period. By 1989, the top 1 percent of households owned 48 percent of total marketable wealth (stock, bonds, and real estate).[24] To use a summary measure of inequality, the Gini coefficient, which gauges between 0 (perfect equality) and 1 (perfect inequality), the United States went from a Gini of 0.301 in 1979 to a Gini of 0.372 in 1997, a 24 percent increase.[25] Among developed states, only the United Kingdom bests the United States in achieving a greater growth in inequality over the same period.[26]

Such outcomes are not simply the result of partisan tax policies. The overall macroeconomic framework developed since the 1980s aided in this upward redistribution. Beginning in 1978, the Federal Reserve pushed up interest rates in an effort to control inflation. By the 1980s, interest rates reached double figures, which had two effects. First of all, it provided a bonanza for bond holders, who received unprecedented returns on their investments. Second, it caused a massive contraction of the nonfinancial economy and created unemployment in traditionally highly paid jobs, thus lowering the real wage, weakening labor, and increasing corporate profits.

On top of these changes, not only are more Americans poor and without adequate health care and fewer benefits, more of them are working, and they are working longer hours too. "In 1960 employed Americans worked 35 hours a year less than their counterparts in the Netherlands, but by 2000 were on the job 342 hours more."[27] More broadly, "Liberal countries [the United States and the U.K.] experienced ten years of declining hours into the 1980s . . . [but] . . . by 2000 liberal regime hours per working age person were 13 percent more than the social democratic countries [Denmark, Norway, and Sweden], and 30 percent more than the Christian Democratic countries [France, Germany, and Italy]."[28]

[24] Wolff, *Top Heavy*, p. 10.
[25] Data are available in extensive and summary form at the Luxembourg Income Study (LIS) website: http://www.lisproject.org. Summary country Ginis are available online at http://www.lisproject.org/keyfigures/ineqtable.htm.
[26] Ibid.
[27] Brian Burgoon and Phineas Baxandall, "Three Worlds of Working Time: The Partisan Politics of Work Hours in Industrialized Countries," *Politics and Society* vol. 32, no. 4, December 2004, p. 443.
[28] Ibid., p. 452.

It is worth noting that a high employment participation rate and long working hours are often noted as being a good outcome. This is strange, however, when one considers that according to (even neoliberal) economic theory, the richer a country gets, the less it is supposed to work. This is called the labor/leisure trade-off, which the United States seems determined to ignore. This might also explain why U.S. productivity is held to be so much better than that of Europe – Americans simply work longer. But does that make the United States more efficient, hence making neoliberal outcomes unavoidable? We often hear that it does, or at least that the United States is more productive than the rest of the world, and that Europe needs to catch up. However, in actual fact, this may not be the case either.

Taking 1992 as a baseline year (index 100) and comparing the classic productivity measure – output per employed person in manufacturing – the United States posts impressive productivity figures, from an index of 100 to 192.3 in 2005. Countries that beat this include that social democratic laggard Sweden (261.0), with the rest of Europe averaging about 30 to 40 percentage points behind the United States.[29] However, as noted previously, if U.S. workers work on average 30 percent more than French workers, then the fact that the French productivity index is approximately 30 points lower than the United States' figure (163.8 compared to 192.3 in 2005) indicates that French workers are just as productive as their U.S. counterparts – it's just that they actually do trade off leisure against labor. This is a political choice, not an economic failing.

In sum, neoliberalism in the United States has meant an upward redistribution of wealth, increased labor market "flexibility" (growth in low-paid jobs without benefits and with rapid turnover), and longer hours. The end result has been a profound alteration of the political economy of the United States. The question is, have we seen changes of such magnitude in Europe? Has Europe really "gone neoliberal"?

Europe and the Politics of "Skin Deep" Neoliberalism
Let us take each of the previously discussed areas – macroeconomic policy, welfare policies, and inequality – and judge the degree to which Europe has indeed "gone neoliberal." Macroeconomic policy may be the place where the greatest convergence has taken place, with a common concern for stability being pronounced since the 1980s. But the key to consider here is, what is Europe in this context? Although West Virginia and California are

---

[29] U.S. Department of Labor, Bureau of Labor Statistics, available online at ftp://ftp.bls.gov/pub/special.requests/ForeignLabor/prodsuppt02.txt, accessed May 29, 2007.

vastly different places, they at least have common currencies, fiscal policies, monetary policies, and national governments. Despite the Euro, the states of Europe do not share such commonalities. As political scientist Jonathan Hopkin puts it:

[I]n much of the policy debate, the non-English speaking advanced industrial countries tend to be lumped together as market-averse welfare states, with sluggish growth and high unemployment brought about by well-meaning but wrongheaded equality-focused systems of social protection. Sweden's generous social benefits, Italy's state pension liabilities, Germany's restricted shopping hours, and France's insistence on "national champions" are mixed together in the same Eurosclerotic bag. This "continental corporatist" model is then contrasted with the "Anglo-American" market-based model: a "capitalist culture-clash" in which the latter is usually tipped as the winner.[30]

But is this Europe a plausible entity to compare with the United States? Consider that modern Europe contains oil-rich Norwegians, poor Italian peasants, and unemployable postcommunist East Germans. The United Kingdom was deregulating its financial sector at the same time as Spain and Ireland were shedding agricultural labor. It is little wonder, then, that neoliberal ideas would be adopted to varying degrees throughout Europe. Certainly, some states embraced neoliberalism with gusto, the United Kingdom being chief among them, but it was already liberal from the start.[31] Such "neoliberalization" may be only skin deep, however.

Income inequality figures are illustrative in this regard. Whereas the United States and the United Kingdom have seen large increases in income inequality, much of Europe has not. France, for example, actually reduced inequality from a Gini of 0.298 to 0.293 from 1979 to 1994. Germany likewise reduced its Gini from 0.271 to 0.264 between 1973 and 2000, as did the Netherlands, which went from 0.260 to 0.248 between 1983 and 1999. Even Ireland, often lumped in with the neoliberal states in many studies and which had a high degree of inequality to begin with, decreased inequality from 0.328 to 0.323 between 1987 and 2000.[32] To be sure, inequality has increased in some countries, but for a variety of country-specific reasons. If one of the main corollaries of neoliberalism is increased income inequality, then there are, at the very least, some interesting (and large) exceptions out there.

[30] Jonathan Hopkin and Mark Blyth, "Equality versus Efficiency? Structural Reform, Inequality, and Economic Performance in Western Europe," unpublished manuscript, 2005, p. 6.

[31] This supports Teles and Kenney's finding that the adoption of libertarian (neoliberal) ideas in the developed world has ultimately been rather uneven at best.

[32] Data are available online at http://www.lisproject.org/keyfigures/ineqtable.htm.

Wealth inequality tells a similar story. Despite an enormous increase in wealth inequality occurring in the United States, redistribution has not been as dramatic in Europe. Rather than seeing an abrupt reversal in the downward trend of wealth concentration beginning in the late 1970s, the top 1 percent of households in the United Kingdom today continue to hold less, rather than more, of total marketable wealth. Although there was an upward redistribution, it did not all go to the very top.[33] The story is similar in France.[34] And although wealth inequality has increased in countries such as Sweden, it has done so from such a low baseline that such states are still far more equalitarian today than the United States was at the end of the 1970s. Despite twenty years of neoliberalism, the concentration of wealth in the United States looks like prewar Europe, whereas contemporary Europe looks more like the postwar United States.[35] Indeed, focusing on Sweden is especially illustrative of "talking the talk while not walking the walk," as a quick look at what has actually happened there over the past fifteen years reveals.

Exceptions Don't Prove Rules: Sweden's Neoliberal Moment

When Swedish real GDP declined by 5 percent and unemployment reached 12 percent between 1990 and 1993, analysts were quick to proclaim the end of the "Swedish model." And when the Swedish Social Democratic Party (SAP) returned to power in 1994, far from repudiating the avowedly "neoliberal" policy stances of the prior liberal government, the SAP sought to further such policies in the areas of pensions, labor markets, social welfare provision, and macroeconomic policy. Neoliberalism, it seemed, was very much alive and well in Sweden in the early 1990s.

Weakened public finances in the mid-1990s led to reductions in public employment, and the government began a program of deregulation and privatization that eventually encompassed postal services, telecommunications, domestic aviation, electricity, and the rail network. Further microeconomic reforms aimed at increasing flexibility and part-time work were made throughout the decade. Macroeconomically, the neoliberal objective of price stability rather than full employment was enshrined as the number one goal of economic policy, while the Riksbank acted as the guardian of the currency without regard to domestic economic conditions. The state similarly tied its hands by adopting a target of a 2 percent budget surplus to be achieved over the business cycle while reducing marginal tax rates. These reforms suggest

---

[33] Wolff, *Top Heavy*, p. 22.
[34] Ibid.
[35] This is a paraphrase from Wolff, *Top Heavy*, p. 24.

a profound neoliberalization of the Swedish political economy. Indeed, the results of these reforms on Swedish business, and the overall macroeconomy, have been dramatic, but not at all neoliberal.

From 1993 to 2000, "industrial production rose by about 60 percent, equivalent to annual growth of about seven percent."[36] The services sector grew from 48 to 60 percent of the economy from 1990 to 2000, and as noted previously, Sweden more than doubled its labor productivity over the decade 1997–2007 to an index value of 261.0.[37] Moreover, unit labor costs in Swedish manufacturing from 1992–2005 plummeted by nearly 50 percent in real terms over the same decade (from 100 to 53.5) in comparison with the United States decline of a mere 13 percent over the same period (from 100 to 87).[38] Given these transformations, one must conclude that the Swedish model, and the equality associated with it, has gone out the window. Yet to conclude this would be a mistake.

First of all, as noted previously, in comparison with the United States and the United Kingdom, Sweden's Gini coefficient has hardly moved in the past three decades. Second, the adoption of neoliberal reforms in countries such as Sweden is in fact much more complicated than the simple "reform -> inequality" equation would allow. Regarding pensions and unemployment benefits, although changes were made overall, "the generosity of Swedish social security was on average the same in 1998 as in 1980."[39] In fact, "the unemployment benefit was [even] more generous [than formerly]."[40] Spending on private health and retirement certainly has increased, as has means-tested benefits, which implies more markets and less equality. However, this too is misleading, since the proportion of the population covered by such benefits has actually increased, largely due to immigration.[41] Finally, although taxes were cut in the early 1990s, they were raised again in the latter half of the decade when the regressive nature of such changes became apparent.[42] Once Sweden recovered from the collapse of the early 1990s

---

[36] Swedish Institute, "Fact Sheets on Sweden, FS 1 ab Qad," May 2001, p. 2.

[37] U.S. Department of Labor, Bureau of Labor Statistics, available online at ftp://ftp.bls.gov/pub/special.requests/ForeignLabor/prodsuppto2.txt, accessed April 27, 2006.

[38] U.S. Department of Labor, Bureau of Labor Statistics, available online at ftp://ftp.bls.gov/pub/special.requests/ForeignLabor/prodsuppt10.txt, accessed May 29, 2007.

[39] Anders Lindbom, "Dismantling the Social Democratic Welfare Model: Has the Swedish Welfare State Lost its Defining Characteristics?" *Scandinavian Political Studies*, vol. 26, no. 2, 2003, p. 178.

[40] Ibid.

[41] Ibid., p. 182.

[42] Sven Steinmo, "Bucking the Trend? The Welfare State and the Global Economy: The Swedish Case Up Close," *New Political Economy*, vol. 8, no. 1, March 2003, pp. 31–48.

and began to run a budget surplus in 1998, as well as paying down the national debt, the government increased spending on child support and other benefits. As Prime Minister Goran Persson said, "healthcare, social services and schooling come before tax cuts,"[43] and indeed they did, consistently. In sum, although there has certainly been economic reform in Sweden, it is simply not the case that such transformations lead inevitably down the same path as the United States. Despite seemingly neoliberal measures being implemented from the early 1990s on, Sweden remains a social democracy with a large public sector, generous social benefits, public services, and low levels of inequality. But perhaps Sweden is both lucky and unrepresentative. After all, aren't the Germans and the French, much larger European economies, doing terribly in comparison with the United States and the United Kingdom? Hasn't globalization simply left these states with no alternative but to go neoliberal? Is the world not, as Thomas Friedman put it, flat?

The World Is Not Flat: Globalization and the Myth of European Sclerosis

As Thomas Friedman and others have argued, the changes previously detailed are the result of structural and "globalizing" forces beyond the control of any one state. As a consequence, the world is "flat," and unless states adopt neoliberal policies, they will become mired in low growth and unemployment, as evidenced by the larger continental economies, especially Germany and France. Ideas don't matter; economic forces manifest in "the unstoppable freedom and technology train" do.[44]

Although appealing, such a logic, popular though it is, is actually quite overwhelmed by the available evidence. Such an analysis suffers two key failings. First of all, the timing is off. That is, although global forces may be strong today in 2006, they were not when such claims were being made the most, in the 1980s and 1990s. Quite simply, the numbers don't back up the story, even today. The quantitative effect of such forces leads us to a rather curious "tail wagging the dog" scenario. Second, although France and especially Germany do have real economic problems, such problems are self-inflicted wounds that have little to do with not adhering to neoliberal ideas. Indeed, it can be shown that when Germany has adhered to such ideas, the result has been to worsen its economic problems.

---

43 Quoted in Keesings Record of World Events, available online at http://keesings.gvpi.net/ keesings/lpext.dll/KRWE/krwe-23594/krwe-24472/krwe-24706/krwe-24798/krwe-24799, accessed August 17, 2004.
44 Thomas Friedman, *The World Is Flat* (New York: Farrar, Straus, Reese, and Giroux, 2005).

The issue of timing is important since if the claim is that "globalization made me do it" historically, then the quantitative data simply do not support the argument. One such claim is that competition from East Asia lowered costs and so impacted European labor markets during the 1980s that mass unemployment was the result since strong unions would not allow the necessary wage reductions to compensate. However, as Robert Wade has shown, exports from East Asia to the United States and Europe in the period 1980 to 1990 peaked at 5.5 percent of *world* trade, which is a case of the tail wagging the dog.[45]

In the early 1990s, a similar claim was made by presidential candidate Bill Clinton during the 1992 election that "the new global economy" had changed everything, despite the fact that the United States was then, and still is, apart from Japan, the least globalized economy in the world. Taking a standard measure of an economy's openness – that is, one that measures how much consumption GDP is generated by imports and exports – the U.S. openness figures are 20.75 for 1980, 20.54 for 1990, and 25.44 for 2006, a mere 6 percent increase over twenty years.[46] Moreover, to show what part of the U.S. economy is globalized, one has to divide these numbers in half to ascertain the sectors of the economy competing with imports. Do this, and once again the tail wags the dog, with just over 10 percent of the U.S. economy in 1990 (or 12 percent today) dictating the other 80 percent or so.

The same story is true of Europe, which has under the auspices of the EU been steadily *deglobalizing* its trade with the rest of the world while trading more internally. As Vivien Schmidt has shown, the argument that European states must compete for footloose global foreign direct investment (FDI) or suffer the consequences is likewise well short on the available evidence. In 1998, Germany's inward FDI as a percentage of GDP was 0.9 percent. France's figure was 2 percent. Indeed, both states exported more capital than they imported –2.8 percent and 2 percent of GDP, respectively.[47] Again, the tail was wagging the dog.

Turning to the second objection, Germany and France in particular do have very real problems with unemployment and slow growth, but this has very little to do with flexibility of labor markets and a lot to do with internal

---

[45] Robert Wade, "Globalization and Its Limits: Reports of the Death of the National Economy Are Greatly Exaggerated," in Suzanne Berger and Ronald Dore, eds., *National Diversity and Global Capitalism* (Ithaca: Cornell University Press, 1996), p. 69.

[46] Penn world tables; openness current prices, historical data, available at http://pwt.econ. upenn.edu/php_site/pwt62/pwt62_form.php, accessed December 12, 2006.

[47] Vivien Schmidt, *The Futures of European Capitalism* (Oxford: Oxford University Press, 2002), table 3.3, p. 120.

policy choices. Take the case of Germany, the unemployment showcase of Europe. From the mid-1990s until today, its unemployment performance was certainly worse than that of the United States, but it had also just bought, at a hopelessly inflated price, a redundant country of 17 million people (East Germany). It then integrated these workers into the West German economy on preferential terms, mortgaging the costs of doing so all over the rest of Europe via high interest rates that flattened continental growth.[48]

Add into this the further contractions caused by Germany's adherence to the sado-monetarist Economic and Monetary Union (EMU) convergence criteria, the establishment of a central bank for all of Europe determined to fight an inflation that died fifteen years previously, then cap it off with a restrictionary "Stability and Growth pact," and these policies will produce low growth.[49] Now compound this further with the world's most successful exporters shedding labor at an alarming rate in the context of sustained low domestic growth, and unemployment will result.[50] Indeed, when neoliberal reforms were made in the German labor market, unemployment went up, not down, on four successive occasions under the so-called Hartz reforms.[51]

Germany is not Europe, however, and should not be confused with it. Not only have the Scandinavian countries all posted solid growth performances over the past several years, but many of the new accession states have done likewise. Even states replete with supposedly sclerotic institutions, such as Spain, have posted impressive growth rates. Moreover, there are recent signs that Germany has indeed turned the corner, proving that despite its "wrongheaded" policy choices, the world is neither flat nor is it necessarily neoliberal.[52] Nor does the recent election of Nicolas Sarkozy in France signal the triumph of American ideas. Although the election of Sarkozy was seen by many observers outside of France as a move to make France more "Anglo," it is interesting to note how Sarkozy won. Ségolène Royal, the Socialist Party

---

[48] See http://www.bundesbank.de/statistik/statistik_zeitreihen.en.php?func=row&tr=suo113, accessed December 12, 2006.

[49] Known by some inside the European Commission (such as Prodi) as the "stupidity pact."

[50] See http://search.ft.com/searchArticle?page=3&queryText=german+exporters&y=0 &javascriptEnabled=true&id=060518008194&x=0, accessed December 12, 2006.

[51] See Federal Statistical Office of Germany, available online at http://www.destatis. de/indicators/e/arb210ae.htm, accessed May 29, 2007. The decrease in German unemployment from 12.1 percent in January 2006 to 9.5 percent in April 2007 is to be applauded. The extent to which it is attributable to Chinese demand for German exports rather than labor market reforms is open at this point.

[52] See Bertrand Benoit, "The Sick Man of Europe Is Now a Picture of Health," *Financial Times*, December 11, 2006. Available online at http://www.ft.com/cms/s/3ab6ff88-88bc-11db-b485-0000779e2340.html, accessed December 12, 2006.

candidate, won a majority of the nineteen-to-fifty-nine-year-old vote. What won Sarkozy the election, however, was the support he received from the sixty- and seventy-year-old voters (61 percent and 68 percent, respectively). Interestingly, these are exactly those people who will be institutionally protected from exactly those reforms that the younger voters voted against. Moreover, that Sarkozy, a classic French rightist, really wants to turn France into "Les Rosbifs" remains to be seen.[53] America's ideas about the way the economic world works are no longer, it seems, the same as Europe's. States still have room to make choices, and when they do, the result is an inevitable growing apart.

Conclusions: Growing Apart and the Diminution of American Power

I argued at the beginning of this chapter that power comes from getting someone else to want what you want, as well as from forcing them to do so by the barrel of a gun. In the period 1945 to 1975, the United States constructed "the way the world works" in a manner that led to positive-sum outcomes for both the United States and Europe. Indeed, because of this beneficent macroeconomic framework, European mass publics were able to enjoy a transformation of their life chances within a single generation. However, an important part of American society never cared much for this settlement and set about undermining it at the first possible opportunity. The fact that it took these dissenters twenty years and millions of dollars spreading alternative economic ideas speaks to the power of the ideas generating this order.

It also speaks to what such ideas enabled America to do. By improving the life chances of the vast majority of its population, the American project found it easy to persuade European elites to sign on to it. Alliances were built on "common interests" that were instantiated in real gains for all sections of society. Support for this order, and thus for America, was strong. This is why the United States was able to count on its allies in Europe, by and large, pulling in the same direction. To get things done, one did not need to separate "ungrateful old Europe" from the "bribable new Europe." And when those allies disagreed – for example, over Vietnam – the "ties that bound" were strong enough to withstand such strains.

The new order constructed in the 1970s and 1980s clearly had some admirers in Europe, chief among them being the United Kingdom. And in that respect, the devotion to the United States (and the anti-Europeanism)

---

[53] See http://news.independent.co.uk/europe/article2521658.ece, accessed June 13, 2007.

shown by both Thatcher and Blair should perhaps be less surprising. Indeed, in the context of the recession of the early 1980s and the prolonged slump of the 1990s (for some states in Europe), the ideas of neoliberalism as "the only way" gained much credence among European elites. The problem was the outcomes that this policy shift produced. When these became clear, much of Europe balked.

Given their common history, European mass publics are simply not willing to tolerate policies that produce the type of economic outcomes characteristic of the contemporary United States. Equality is not simply a value, it is deemed a political necessity in an environment where instability and inequality have in the past caused untold strife. As scholars as diverse as John Ruggie and Robert Kagan have noted, Europe's all-too-recent history of economic instability and political polarization has made inequality something to be abhorred, not something to be celebrated as an "incentive" for individual effort.[54] This is why in Europe, when micro- and macroeconomic reforms are made, they are made with built-in compensatory payments. When they are not built in, such reforms are challenged. This is not to argue that all Americans want inequality and all Europeans want higher taxes. But it is to claim that such policies are far more sustainable in the United States than they are in Europe. This suggests a growing division between countries over the very type of society deemed desirable. It is worth noting that in French political discourse, for example, the words *mondialisation* (globalization) and *Americanisation* are held as synonyms. Yet if globalization is Americanization, then "being American" is something that many Europeans no longer want. This is something profoundly new for the relationship between Europe and America.

As political scientist Riccardo Pelizzo has shown, in opinion poll after opinion poll, European mass publics want more, not fewer, government-produced goods. When European parties' political offers fail to match voters demands, parties see their votes drop.[55] Neoliberalism has been tried in Europe, its "pure form" has been seen in the United States, and it is not widely embraced, as the failure of the European constitution and the blowback over economic rule making by the EU Commission clearly show. Sauron's ring circa 1945–75 might have been powerful, but his new adornment has proven to be less binding.

---

[54] John Gerald Ruggie, "International Regimes"; Robert Kagan, *Of Paradise and Power: America and Europe in the New World Order* (New York: Knopf, 2003).

[55] Riccardo Pelizzo, "Cartel Parties and Cartel Party Systems," unpublished Ph.D. dissertation, Department of Political Science, Johns Hopkins University, 2003.

This is one of the many ways that Europe and the United States have increasingly grown apart. Europeans view "neoliberalism American-style" as not being in their best interests, and no amount of claims that neoliberalism, or globalization, is inevitable can make it so. As the struggles over the implementation of the Hartz labor market reforms in Germany from 2002 to 2005 and the French labor market reforms of 2006 clearly show, European mass publics simply do not accept that "neoliberalism is good for you." Lacking such common interests, as the United States goes further down a path to a society that Europe increasingly neither wants nor understands, which includes aspects of religion, guns, criminal justice, and foreign policy, as well as economics, growing apart is inevitable. But why should Americans care? I argue that the United States should care since much of what the United States got out of its binding to Europe, it risks losing now.

Due to these policies and the outcomes they produce, the United States increasingly relies upon unilateral action, military strength, and indicative diplomacy to get its way. As such, it cannot necessarily count on Europe to support the United States in its foreign and domestic policy goals given that the other "ties that bind" no longer bind quite as well. If Europe is discussed at all in American policy circles, it tends to be seen as a bunch of "cheese-eating surrender monkeys" who tax themselves to death, who are drowning in a sea of joblessness, and who simply need to be "more like us."[56] Yet where is economic weakness really to be found when you consider the following?

With a few exceptional years in the late 1990s notwithstanding, the United States has been running massive trade and budget deficits for over thirty years. It has also been consuming far beyond its ability to pay for the past twenty. The costs of such policies are huge interest repayments and an almost negative savings rate. To pay for this, the United States needs to maintain above-average growth and import approximately $2.2 billion in other peoples' savings per day to pay its bills. Add on to this military expenditures larger than half the members of the UN's budgets and a debt "ceiling" of $9 trillion, and it is not clear that this model is actually the sustainable one, particularly with the levels of inequality that it generates.

Such sentiment is already commonplace. As a consequence of its insatiable demand for imports, China and other East Asian states hold over a U.S. $1 trillion in their foreign exchange holdings. Yet the value of that debt

---

[56] For a particularly good example of this phenomenon, see John Tierny, "Who Moved My Fromage," originally published in the opinion section of the *New York Times*, March 28, 2006, available online at http://www.denverpost.com/opinion/ci_3648311.

is declining. The dollar fell against the Euro by over 30 percent (2003–7). Meanwhile, the U.S. response to this is to tell China to revalue its exchange rate, which is a little like a crack addict asking the dealer to raise the price so that he can get off drugs.

In the former era (1945–75), when the goals of the United States and Europe were congruent, other solutions were possible. Coordinated reflations and depreciations would have been seen as in the general interest of all states, rather than as special pleading by the United States (even if the United States would have been the primary beneficiary). Disciplinary mechanisms such as the World Trade Organization's Disputes Committee would have been used as a last resort rather than a first resort. And a rumor that the South Korean Central Bank was considering dumping its dollars for Euros in February 2005 would not have caused a panic on the exchanges. In the current era, in a "lean-and-mean," go-it-alone world, such solutions are no longer viable. In a neoliberal world, you can't count on your friends.

The take-home lesson is this: When you have all the other countries on your side because they want what you want, you can do (almost) anything you like at very low cost. However, when the version of "the way the world works" that you are promoting no longer fits the ambitions of your main allies, and there are credible exit options, power can no longer be generated in this way. Like electricity from oil, U.S. power is simply going to cost more to produce. As Iraq clearly shows, when the "One-Ring" of common economic ideas fails, it is not clear that military power alone can suffice if the economic base supporting it is itself less than convincing.

This is why neoliberal ideas and policies have made the United States and Europe grow further apart. When seen on a broader canvas, such policies may have weakened rather than strengthened the United States domestically. They have certainly made its allies rethink what they themselves want. The grand bargain between labor and the state and business that underlay the "Great Compression" is, by political necessity, alive and well in Europe. In the United States, it is as dead as a dodo. And here lies the problem: With two separate visions of society, economy, and politics emerging, the very idea of the United States and Europe constituting "the West" is under strain. Abraham Lincoln once noted that "a house divided against itself cannot stand." Although the United States and Europe may not come to blows, when each side spurns the other's version of "who we are and what we do," growing apart becomes inevitable.

5

Spreading the Word

The Diffusion of American Conservatism in Europe and Beyond

Steven Teles and Daniel A. Kenney

For decades, conservatives were frustrated by what they believed were international networks of leftist experts who preached and implemented schemes for government expansion. These ideas, "vetted" by authoritative sources, came to dominate the policy alternatives available to national policy makers.[1] Because alternatives were filtered through advocates of an expanded state role, conservatives concluded that policy processes across the Western world – and beyond – were hard-wired for expansion. To reverse this bias, free-market actors with substantial resources and a "missionary spirit" sought to inject their ideas into the domestic politics of other states through investing in indigenous ideological allies' efforts at organization building and a global network to knit them together.[2] By providing seed financing, these international network entrepreneurs hoped to overcome the risk of organizing around ideas that lack strong national roots or well-established, indigenous support networks.

More broadly, these agents have sought to create international social capital by connecting domestic actors to international networks that can provide relationships, organizational templates, sources of funding, examples of reform strategies, and evidence of their ideas' viability. By constructing a web of international social capital and by spurring the creation of organizations within nation-states that then can link to that web, conservative organizational entrepreneurs have reduced the costs of diffusing ideas across national borders. As their network increases in strength, agents at the

[1] The concepts come from John Kingdon, *Ideas, Alternative and Public Policies* (Boston: Little, Brown, 1982).
[2] A related discussion of this can be found in Diane Stone, "Non-Governmental Policy Transfer: The Strategies of Independent Policy Institutes," *Governance*, vol. 13, no. 1, 2000, pp. 45–62.

nation-state level have more leverage to bring their state's behavior in line with their ideological goals.

Although the global libertarian network could draw on powerful ideas, ideas alone do not necessarily translate into organizational presence and policy influence. As Jack Walker observed in explaining the explosion of citizens' groups in the 1960s and 1970s in the United States, translating diffuse interests into durable organizations – a task that requires overcoming significant free-rider problems and otherwise crippling startup costs – requires the presence of an actor willing to subsidize groups in their germinal stage. What was true of the groups that Walker studied applies even more strongly to the challenge of forging international social capital: "Their potential membership is extremely large and, in most cases, unknown to one another. There is no ready-made community waiting to be organized, no readily available sources of money, and often not even a clearly articulated common interest in creating an organization."[3] Overcoming these obstacles requires the existence of skilled and well-resourced patrons who can provide potential organizational entrepreneurs with startup financing, expertise, models of successful action, and networks to other sources of support. These patrons are especially important when, as was the case in most countries beyond the United States and Great Britain, domestic allies are scarce, sources of funding all but nonexistent, and the ideas of libertarians severely marginalized. There is little reason to expect, under such conditions, that libertarian organizations could get past the inevitably difficult startup stage without connecting to international patrons and networks.

In contrast to many accounts of conservative organizational mobilization, however, ours is anything but a story of "diabolical competence." Serious constraints on the expansion and efficacy of the conservative policy network – both at the organizational and policy levels – faced the patrons who sought to nurture these international networks. At the organizational level, indigenous conservative policy entrepreneurs faced disinterest or even hostility from the business community, a thorny regulatory/tax environment, powerful competition from more embedded sources of expertise, or a policy-making system that gave them few options of access. At the policy level, such organizations have often discovered that although the environment for

---

[3] Jack L. Walker, "The Origins and Maintenance of Interest Groups in America," *American Political Science Review*, vol. 77, 1983, pp. 390–406, 398. Beth Leech and Frank Baumgartner underscore the importance of patrons and highlight Walker's study of interest groups. Beth L. Leech and Frank R. Baumgartner, *Basic Interests: The Importance of Groups in Politics and Political Science* (Princeton: Princeton University Press, 1998), pp. 74–5.

organization and agenda setting is permissive, the structure of inherited commitments and political institutions renders effective translation of ideas into politically viable policy instruments impractical. These constraints suggest that it is possible for *ideas* to become globalized without a corresponding shift in policy *outcomes*.[4] No matter how successful an ideological network may be at injecting a set of ideas into a particular political environment, there are durable, albeit variable, limits on their capacity to reshape the fundamental political incentives that motivate elected officials to protect existing, often popular, policies.

Our chapter adopts this insight to explain the recent history of Anglo-American conservative efforts to export their ideas across the globe, and to suggest some limitations on that project. First, we briefly examine the conservative coalition in the United States, and explain why libertarians have been more active in spreading their brand of conservatism than have other coalition partners such as social conservatives. Second, we describe the origins of the Anglo-American libertarian strategy for "spreading the word," paying particular attention to why it has taken the form of policy institutes rather than partisan politics. Third, we describe how these organizations operate and how they are connected to, shaped by, and supported through the Anglo-American network. Fourth, we explain the national constraints on the effectiveness of free-market think tanks as a strategy for producing convergence around libertarian ends. Finally, we analyze the failures of the flat tax and social security privatization in the Organization for Economic Cooperation and Development (OECD), and their relative success in central and eastern Europe, as examples of the opportunities and limitations on the free-market network. We conclude by speculating as to the future of the global Anglo-American libertarian social movement, both organizationally and as a mechanism for diffusing free-market–oriented policies.

Who Evangelizes? Why Libertarianism Spreads and Social Conservatism Does Not

In addressing where and why the diffusion of American conservative ideas happens, it is critical to note that the conservative coalition in the United States does not travel well. Business has been largely absent from the effort

---

[4] Torben Iversen, "The Dynamics of Welfare State Expansion: Trade Openness, Deindustrialization, and Partisan Politics," in Paul Pierson, ed., *The New Politics of the Welfare State* (New York: Oxford University Press, 2003), pp. 45–79; Paul Pierson, "Coping with Permanent Austerity: Welfare State Restructuring in Affluent Democracies," in Pierson, *New Politics*, pp. 410–514.

to spread American conservative ideas globally, except as an occasional and often hesitant source of funds. Libertarians and religious conservatives have most actively ministered to those unchurched in conservatism beyond our borders, attempting to bring other nations closer to their version of America.

The American conservative coalition, especially the strong alliance between American Catholic conservatives and evangelicals, has found it difficult to reassert itself on foreign soil. Catholic conservatives (such as Michael Novak, Richard John Neuhaus, and Avery Cardinal Dulles) are actively involved in global Church politics, and have made special efforts to convince Rome of the consistency between American-style capitalism and Church doctrine.[5] But for the most part, they have not taken a missionary posture. Given the state of the Catholic Church in the United States, in fact, they have had to spend most of their time defending Church doctrine to skeptical Americans. So, Catholic conservative activism has been largely circumscribed within the institutional contours of the Church rather than operating through autonomous organizations dominated or led by Americans.

Protestant evangelicals are another story. Without an international institutional structure like the Catholic Church, evangelicals have largely replicated the entrepreneurial approach to seeking souls abroad that has characterized their work in America. In terms of attracting converts, this decentralized strategy has been unquestionably successful. For example, in Latin America, Protestants (especially Pentecostals) have ballooned in the last half-century from almost no presence to one-tenth of the population, and the intensity of their religious practice also appears greater than that of Catholics.[6] Indeed, this pattern is roughly what one would expect on the basis of Steven Pfaff's chapter: The weakening dynamism of the Catholic Church caused by its close links with the state has created a market opportunity for new entrants. This upsurge in Protestantism would seem to provide an opening for American conservative evangelicals to inject their ideas, even if indirectly, into the politics of the developing world.

American evangelicals have been very active missionaries, but their efficacy in transmitting socially conservative political ideas outside the United States appears decidedly marginal. Whereas orthodox Catholics and Christian evangelicals in the United States have largely concluded that their conflict with secularists and liberal Christians trumps their competition with one

---

[5] Michael Novak, *The Catholic Ethic and the Spirit of Capitalism* (New York: Free Press, 1993).
[6] Philip Jenkins, *The Next Christendom: The Coming of Global Christianity* (Oxford: Oxford University Press, 2002), p. 61.

another, in the developing world competition between these two branches of Christianity remains fierce, and in places even violent. This limits the capacity of the religiously orthodox to exercise the kind of combined influence that American religious conservatives have had. What is more, evangelicals in the developing world do not have the sort of structural characteristics that make them very attractive candidates for receiving and spreading American ideas. In his exhaustive study of evangelicals and politics in Latin America, Paul Freston concludes that

> Usually, Third World evangelicalism does not have strong institutions; it is often composed disproportionately of the poor in poor countries, so its cultural and educational resources are limited. It is divided into many churches, making it impossible to establish a normative "social doctrine." It operates a model of cooperative pluralism, in competition for members and resources, which does not encourage reflection or costly stances on ethical principle. It often has no international contacts, cutting it off from the history of Christian reflection on politics.[7]

Freston has found no clear, coherent political ideology among evangelicals, noting that the political positions taken by different evangelical movements seem to be more motivated by a desire to protect their religious practice than to use the public sphere to enact a theologically informed program of reform.

So while American evangelicals have taken a keen interest in fostering the development of their brethren in the developing world, their ability to genuinely guide these movements toward being effective carriers of American Christian conservative ideas has been limited. As Freston concluded, "In most cases, the returns for the American organizers are minimized by the already-established operational agenda of their would-be Latin protégés."[8] Evangelicals in the developing world have devoted their missionary work to the poorest of the poor, those furthest from the levers of political power and most likely to use what power they have simply to preserve their own organizational integrity. When their position in society becomes less tenuous, their ability to compete for followers less controversial, and their flock more educated, developing-world evangelicals may acquire a deeper interest in the ideas of their fellow believers in America. Until then, the conditions for effective influence appear severely handicapped.

All forms of religious orthodoxy appear to have had much more success in the developing world than in Europe, where religion has increasingly become

---

[7] Paul Freston, *Evangelicals and Politics in Asia, Africa and Latin America* (Cambridge: Cambridge University Press, 2001), p. 291.
[8] Ibid., p. 289.

a minority taste. Studies of religious participation show that the United States increasingly resembles Mexico, South Africa, and the Philippines more than it does Britain, Hungary, or the Netherlands.[9] As a result, in most of Western Europe, the religiously orthodox wing of the conservative movement faces societies that, beyond being simply unchurched, appear actively hostile to religion. By contrast, much of the developing world remains open to the religious spirit, and it is here where evangelicals have focused much of their energy and where they have experienced their greatest – sometimes explosive – growth. Slowly, this growth in believers is translating into political influence, providing American religious conservatives at least some opportunities for influence. It may also be that the increasing immigration of Pentecostals and other evangelicals from Latin America has itself had the effect of changing American religious conservatives, eating away at some of their political insularity. If there is any place where the forces of globalization (in this case, population movements) are causing a measure of convergence, it is here – between the United States and the developing world.

Because of the collapse of the religious spirit in Europe, American social conservatives have almost no indigenous roots to build upon and face a political culture that is either hostile or uncomprehending. This has led religious conservatives to focus most of their evangelical energy in the developing world, where their potential converts resemble the American fundamentalists of seventy-five years ago – generally poor and powerless. This distance from power and lack of resources makes them unlikely agents for policy diffusion. Working independently of religious conservatives, it has fallen to the libertarian wing of the American conservative movement to bring the ideas of the movement to the rest of the world. It is to their strategies that we now turn.

The Origins of a Convergence Strategy

The "convergence project" of American conservatives has been left to evangelicals for libertarianism, not Christianity. In this section, we address two basic questions: What strategy have the libertarians adopted to spread their faith beyond its Anglo-American core? And why did it seem like the most effective, or perhaps the most appropriate, strategy to adopt?

---

[9] Pippa Norris and Ronald Ingelhart, *Sacred and Secular: Religion and Politics World Wide* (New York: Cambridge University Press, 2004), chapter 3, p. 24. Accessed online at http://ksghome.harvard.edu/~pnorris/Books/Books.htm.

Spreading free-market think tanks throughout the world is not the only strategy that libertarians have attempted. Universities have also served as vehicles for propagating free-market ideas beyond the Anglo-American sphere. Perhaps the most notorious effort to inject free-market thought beyond our borders was the University of Chicago Economics Department's project in Chile. Using funding from the Ford Foundation and the United States Agency for International Development (then called the International Cooperation Association), the Chicago Economics Department trained dozens of Chilean students, and those students reshaped the economics faculty of the Universidad Catolica de Chile. In so doing, they created a libertarian outpost in a country with almost no such tradition. When Augusto Pinochet came to power in 1973, he brought with him these economists, known as the "Chicago Boys," placing them in senior positions in his government. They became agents for the transformation of the Chilean economy and Chilean society more broadly. The original Chicago project, which was designed to counter the ideas of Raul Prebisch and the *dependencia* school as well as to serve as an experiment in "human capital," became part and parcel of an authoritarian-libertarian revolution.[10]

Friedrich Hayek and the Mont Pelerin Society met in Chile in 1978, implicitly putting their seal of approval on the Pinochet revolution. But this imposition of libertarian economics by force has been the exception, not the rule. The rule dates back to just after World War II, with Hayek. Although Hayek's role in shaping libertarian ideas across the globe is well recognized, his strategy for rendering them politically viable proved an equally powerful influence on the strategy of the movement's organizational entrepreneurs.

Hayek's clearest statement of how to make libertarianism politically viable is found in his 1949 essay, "The Intellectuals and Socialism."[11] Hayek argued that the primary role intellectuals played in politics was to shape the larger climate of public opinion. This does not mean that Hayek held to a populist theory of political change. In fact, his understanding was all but dismissive of the importance of ordinary politicians and political processes: "What to the contemporary observer appears as the battle of conflicting interests has indeed often been decided long before in a clash of ideas confined to narrow circles."[12] He argued that socialism succeeded because its supporters "have always directed their main effort towards gaining the support of this *elite,*

---

[10] The full story is grippingly told in Juan Gabriel Valdes, *Pinochet's Economists: The Chicago School in Chile* (Cambridge: Cambridge University Press, 1995).

[11] Friedrich von Hayek, "The Intellectuals and Socialism," *University of Chicago Law Review,* vol. 16, no. 3, 1949, pp. 417–33.

[12] Ibid., p. 1.

while the more conservative groups have acted, as regularly but unsuccessfully, on a more naïve view of mass democracy and have usually vainly tried directly to reach and to persuade the individual voter."[13] Recruiting and training a cadre of elites, whose writings and debates would have the power to refashion public discourse incrementally, was more important than influencing short-term electoral politics, and less likely to be coopted by what Milton Friedman later called "the tyranny of the status quo."[14]

Two consequences for action flowed from these assumptions. First, ordinary politics was subordinate to intellectual debates held among "second-hand dealers in ideas," the intellectuals who shaped the larger climate of ideas among the elite. The most powerful force in society was the "conventional wisdom," or what Mark Blyth in his chapter calls "how things actually work" – the taken-for-granted assumptions upon which elite actors based their decision making. Second, there was no point seeking to undermine socialism through the electoral process, since elections in an unchanged climate of opinion would at best lead to right-wing governments enacting socialist measures. Hayek held to a "Fabian" theory of politics: Undermining socialism would come by gradually changing the ideas held by society's dominant classes, with political parties eventually following suit. Effective political action, therefore, required changing ideas rather than governing coalitions. Finally, Hayek pointed out that for libertarians in particular countries to be effective, "An integrated structure of liberal thought is required and its application to the problems of different countries needs to be worked out. This will only be possible by a meeting of minds within a large group."[15]

Hayek was directly involved in creating the first part of the network, to produce a "meeting of minds," and acted as an inspiration for the second. In late 1946, Hayek proposed the creation of what became the Mont Pelerin Society, arguing that

While in each country those who think actively on these questions are comparatively few, combined they represent a considerable force and I have been struck by the similarity of the aims and of the conclusions reached by many of the isolated men in different parts of the world. It seems certain that by closer cooperation their work would benefit and gain greatly in effectiveness.[16]

---

[13] Ibid., p. 2.

[14] Milton Friedman and Rose Friedman, *The Tyranny of the Status Quo* (New York: Harcourt, 1984).

[15] Hayek, "The Intellectuals and Socialism," p. 5.

[16] Ronald M. Hartwell, *A History of the Mont Pelerin Society* (Indianapolis: Liberty Fund, 1995), p. 31.

By 1948, Hayek had moved to the University of Chicago, and took with him the focus of his global institution-building work. From the start, Hayek wanted the Society to be a network more than an organization, implanting a suspicion of hierarchy that would later characterize the relationships within the global free-market think tank network. Hayek believed that "the fruits of the activity of the Society must show themselves in the productions of the individual members and that the contacts which the meetings provide and the exchange of opinions between members which the mere existence of a list provides should remain the main function of the group."[17] Mont Pelerin would be a network connecting the libertarian elite across borders.

Even more important than the Mont Pelerin Society was the creation of an international network of free-market think tanks. Although this was the work of many, pride of place must go to Anthony Fisher, the millionaire British chicken farmer turned organizational entrepreneur. According to his biographer, Fisher got the idea for a free-market think tank directly from Hayek in 1945 at the London School of Economics. This meeting apparently had a deep impact on him, and in 1949 he told the future director of the Institute for Economic Affairs that, "One day when my ship comes in I'd like to create something which will do for the non-Labour parties what the Fabian Society did for Labour."[18] When Fisher's ship did come in, he plowed a good part of his wealth into the creation of the Institute for Economic Affairs in London. Later on, Fisher became so impressed with IEA's success that he spent the better part of three decades helping to create clones of it throughout the world.

In creating a global network of free-market institutions, Fisher believed he was simply replicating what the left had done decades before. "Instead of concentrating efforts through the activities of one or two organizations, the key to success lay in a proliferation of organizations and publications sharing a broadly common outlook and aims. In Anthony's view, there needed to be lots of IEAs, a growing international network of market-oriented individuals and organizations."[19] Fisher helped found the Fraser Institute in Canada in 1975, the Manhattan Institute in 1977, and then others throughout the United States, including the Pacific Research Institute in his adopted home of San Francisco. Having established a beachhead in the United States, Fisher then founded the Atlas Economic Research Foundation in 1983 to spread the

---

[17] Ibid., p. 90.
[18] Gerald Frost, *Anthony Fisher: Champion of Liberty* (London: Profile, 2002), p. 44.
[19] Ibid., p. 137.

IEA model throughout the world. By connecting these new organizations to a global network, Fisher hoped that, "Each could learn from the others about those techniques which were likely to be most effective in raising funds or in marketing, but most important, organizations could pass the best research and policy ideas from one to the other, and so avoid the need to reinvent the wheel."[20] This decentralized structure permitted an organizational nimbleness and financial competitiveness that comported with Fisher's free-market mission. Measured by the diffusion of free-market organizations, Fisher's project was a success. Figure 5.1 shows the development of Atlas-network think tanks over the last thirty-five years. With only a few exceptions, the birth of these organizations came after Atlas set up shop (although, of course, many other forces explain their genesis).

The link between Hayek's theories of intellectual influence and the strategies of the Atlas-connected think tanks is direct, as its advice to potential think-tank founders makes clear:

Friedrich von Hayek wrote about the important role of journalists, teachers, and other "second-hand dealers in ideas" in his essay, *The Intellectuals and Socialism*. To thrive, ideas must be disseminated and spread by such dealers. Free market think tanks can serve as the intermediary that brings the ideas to the second hand dealers, allowing them to help change the long-term climate of understanding. By focusing on ideas, we can broaden our base of potential support, rather than alienate folks who only relate to political labels.[21]

John Blundell, the head of the IEA, reinforced the same point: "Some programs are designed to target large numbers of people, the grassroots. Atlas institutes tend to focus on the 'grasstops' – the leaders or gatekeepers of ideas. By definition, that is a much smaller constituency."[22] Atlas also advises its affiliated think tanks, much in the Hayekian spirit, to avoid ordinary politics, in order to maximize their capacity for what it considers real, long-term influence:

Because the work of an institute involves national and local policy issues, there is inevitable confusion as to whether the institute is "political," or whether its free market preferences automatically associate it with "conservative" administrations. It is imperative to avoid reinforcing misperceptions by affiliations with political persons,

---

[20] Ibid., p. 157, quoting Linda Whetstone, director of Atlas/UK.

[21] Jo Kwong, "Guidelines and Recommendations for Starting an Institute," Atlas Economic Research Foundation, July 11, 2003, available online at http://www.atlasusa.org/toolkit/starterkit.php?refer=toolkit.

[22] John Blundell, "Fundraising for the Free Society," Institute for Humane Studies Working Paper 87/12, 1988, available at http://www.atlasusa.org/V2/main/page.php?page_id=187.

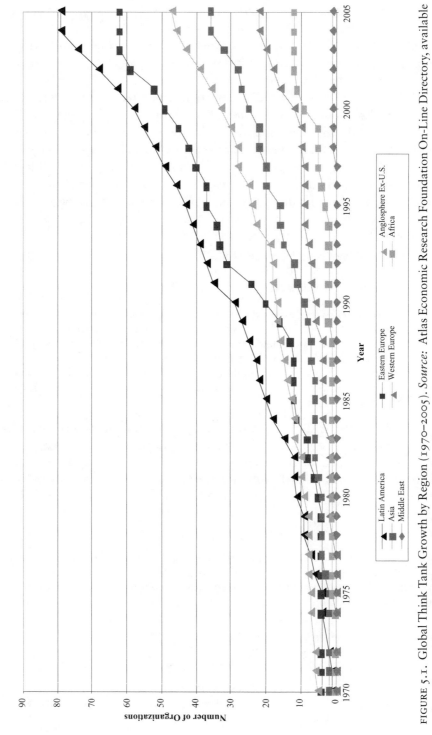

FIGURE 5.1. Global Think Tank Growth by Region (1970–2005). *Source:* Atlas Economic Research Foundation On-Line Directory, available at http://www.atlasusa.org/directory/index.php?refer=directory.

i.e., on the board or among the authors. Potential donors are shy of sponsoring a party-oriented group. Our objective – to find and publish better solutions to problems in hopes of assisting policy decisions – is a totally nonpartisan approach.[23]

This distance from political parties and ordinary interest group politics is essential to understanding how libertarians believe their ideas will spread. The mechanism is not, principally, that they will seize power by getting "their men" elected to office or into positions of party leadership in various countries. In fact, libertarians are equally interested in having their ideas accepted by nonconservative parties as they are by those on the right. Libertarians are universalists, in that they believe their ideas are transpolitical and therefore consistent with a range of political and cultural conditions.

This transpolitical approach to political influence shapes critical aspects of the free-market network's organizational governance. The oldest rule in the Atlas network, and the one that most clearly distinguishes libertarian think tanks from their traditional government- or party-dependent counterparts, is to avoid any direct financial connections with government. Blundell observes that,

Funds from government or quasi-government sources are to be refused. Even if you have no principled objection, such monies will (a) undermine your credibility as a champion of reducing the role of government and (b) deter private sector donors from supporting you. I would go further and also (a) refuse tax funded research/consulting contracts and (b) write into your employee manual that staff who accept such funds in a private capacity (e.g., a lecture or writing fee) are instantly dismissed.[24]

This opposition to government funding is driven by ideological and strategic motivations. The ideological motivations are straightforward, since organizations that believe in a narrowly limited state are understandably hesitant to accept money that government should not be spending. It is the *effect* of shunning government money that is, for our purposes, more interesting.

First, eschewing government funding makes it more difficult for the state to coopt such organizations, which is a real danger in countries with very high government spending. In such a context, accepting government money will almost always be the path of least resistance, even if it means surrendering organizational agenda control. Avoiding government funds forces free-market think tanks to create their own networks and to rely for financial and organizational assistance on the international libertarian network, as well as national networks of their own devising. In essence, to be open to

[23] Ibid.
[24] Ibid.

external influence, free-market think tanks have to insulate themselves from the most tempting internal influence – the state itself. This is not a merely symbolic constraint. The Atlas Foundation makes refusal to accept government funding or formal links to political parties a condition of its support.[25] Further, this constraint is likely to be even more of a hindrance in countries with a limited history of philanthropic support for nonpartisan intellectual activity, and where government, as a consequence, looms large. By shunning government money, free-market think tanks are forced to create networks at the nation-state level, where they may not have existed before, and to depend to a much greater degree on international networks, especially at the startup stage. In this sense, the free-market think-tank movement recognized the dangers of cooptation by the state noted in Pfaff's chapter and have immunized themselves against such co-optation through collective discipline and precommitment.[26]

Although this network is global in scope, most of the ideas that flow through it are American in origin or inspiration. Atlas is based in Arlington, Virginia, the home of a large libertarian organizational infrastructure – the George Mason University Law School, the Mercatus Center, the James Buchanan Center for Political Economy, the Institute for Justice, and the Institute of Human Studies, with which Atlas shares its executive vice president, Leonard Liggio. That said, the network certainly does not operate hierarchically, with orders emanating from Arlington to foot soldiers throughout the globe – quite the contrary. The far-flung network operates, as befits followers of Hayek, through "coordination without a coordinator." They are unified through the fidelity of their members to a core set of ideas and animating texts (the repetitiveness with which its members refer to the work of Hayek and Ludwig von Mises, even in their organizations' names, is evidence of this) and through networks centered in the United States. This makes the network highly effective at projecting the ideas of the American

---

[25] E-mail communication with Leonard Liggio. By contrast, the history of think tanks in the United States shows that government grants have almost always been a central source of funding. The most prominent examples of this are Department of Defense support for the RAND Corporation and Hudson Institutes, or the Department of Health and Human Services support of the Brookings and Urban Institutes. James Smith, *The Idea Brokers: Think Tanks and the Rise of the New Policy Elite* (New York: Free Press, 1993). Atlas's current president, Alexander Chaufen, observes that there are a few exceptions to this rule, but they mainly concern think tanks operating in communist countries, where avoidance of state patronage would be almost impossible.

[26] On the idea of "precommitment," see Jon Elster, *Ulysses and the Sirens: Studies in Rationality and Irrationality* (Cambridge: Cambridge University Press, 1979).

libertarians, as well as serving as a platform for them to be "reimported" back into the United States.

Free-Market Think Tanks: What They Do

What kind of organizations are free-market think tanks, and what do they do? In broad terms, the free-market movement shares the characteristics of what Margaret Keck and Kathryn Sikkink have deemed *transnational advocacy networks*. These networks promote "the centrality of values or principled ideas, the belief that individuals can make a difference, the creative use of information, and the employment by nongovernmental actors of sophisticated political strategies in targeting their campaigns."[27] When viewed as parallel segments of "globalized" civil society, free-market think tanks are a poor fit with the traditional image of think tanks as a cloistered "university without students."[28] This image, often associated with the RAND Corporation, evokes a research-driven environment populated by academics and experts at a substantial remove from day-to-day political battles. By contrast, original, path-breaking research produced by free-market think tanks is the exception rather than the rule. Instead, these organizations are distinguished by three alternative functions: (1) They act as intellectual entrepreneurs by providing a megaphone for ideas produced elsewhere and investigate applications of those ideas to local circumstances; (2) they help to connect and build an indigenous network; (3) and they transmit information and, at times, money across borders.[29] To get a deeper appreciation of how free-market think tanks perform these functions, and the challenges they have faced in doing so, we conducted a number of Internet-based interviews with libertarian think tanks in Europe. The findings, although drawn from an unsystematic sample, are highly suggestive.[30]

---

[27] Margaret Keck and Kathryn Sikkink, *Activists beyond Borders: Advocacy Networks in International Politics* (Ithaca: Cornell University Press, 1998), p. 2.

[28] R. Kent Weaver, "The Changing World of Think Tanks," *PS*, September 1989, pp. 563–78.

[29] Most of these functions are discussed in Stone, "Non-Governmental Policy Transfer."

[30] In May 2005, we distributed an Internet-based survey to 130 free-market think tanks across Western and Eastern Europe, from Glasgow to Montenegro, as well as a small number from Israel. We received thirty-one responses, a meager response rate. The focus on Europe – as opposed to a global survey similar to that presented in Figure 5.1 – was largely a practical decision. We received a credible list of free-market think-tank personnel and e-mails under the condition that the source and individual think tanks would remain anonymous. Future publications in this project will report on the findings of a more systematic survey of think tanks, both free-market and otherwise.

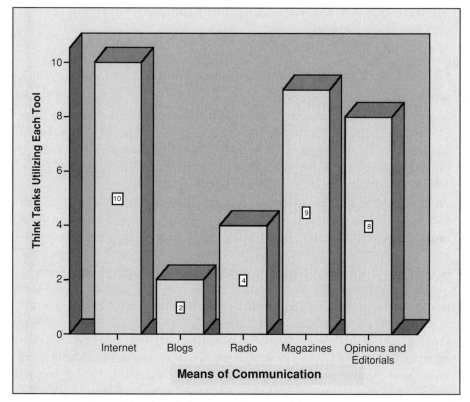

FIGURE 5.2. Most Utilized Tools for Communicating Ideas. *Note:* Respondents were asked to rate each type of communication method on a seven-point scale, from least-utilized to most-utilized. N = 31. *Source:* Free Market Think Tank survey, 2005.

First, these organizations spread ideas across national borders by employing two basic tactics. First, domestic groups introduce ideas in their abstract form, either through literal translation (for example, supporting native-language versions of free-market classics) or by producing books and articles that bring these ideas to a domestic audience. Second, and at a more concrete level, these groups fasten policy ideas conceived elsewhere to ongoing national political debates, connecting them to domestic social and political conditions, national history, culture, and traditions. Although conventional media outlets such as magazines and newspaper opinion pages are employed frequently, free-market think tanks most often utilize the cost-effectiveness and wide reach of the Internet to communicate these fused policy ideas and spread the word (see Figure 5.2).

The latter process involves making the case for free-market principles in particular policy areas, without emphasizing the underlying ideas that animate them, selling them, for instance, as technical solutions to problems that policy makers have had difficulty solving within the framework of existing ideas. For example, respondents from Georgia, the Slovak Republic, and Israel all cited Estonia's experiment with a flat tax as an international precedent for their own reform proposals. The Chilean pension reforms were a consistent source of inspiration, especially for countries in the former Soviet bloc; tax freedom day also received considerable attention across the board. We offer a fuller analysis of the role of think tanks in these two areas in the next section, but it should be noted that all of these ideas originated in the United States – the flat tax at the Hoover Institution, tax freedom day with the Tax Foundation, and pension privatization from a variety of sources, the Cato Institute in particular.[31] Interestingly, other than tax freedom day, these were all ideas that have been failures in the United States. Fifty-two percent of the think tanks we interviewed devote at least half of their publications to international precedents or examples. A substantial percentage of our respondents noted that they drew a number of their ideas from international meetings of free-market organizations. One eastern European respondent observed that "from each meeting we are taking back at least one concrete plan for our next activity." Communication between think tanks is a very common occurrence; 44 percent of our sample communicate with think tanks outside their country at least once a week.[32] The use of this international network as a source of ideas is likely to be especially important for small, underresourced groups without a dense network of domestic allies. In fact, these think tanks frequently provide a forum for free-market (and often American) intellectuals to speak; our sample averaged about five speakers per year, of which roughly two were American.

The second function that free-market think tanks perform is to build an indigenous, national network embedded within a larger, global network. In addition to injecting ideas into local political conversation, they also organize activity around these ideas through meetings, dinners, and debates. These

---

[31] The source of the idea of the flat tax is Robert Hall and Alvin Rubushka, *The Flat Tax* (Palo Alto: Hoover Institution Press, 1985). Information about tax freedom day can be found at http://www.taxfoundation.org. The earliest fully fleshed out pensions privatization proposal was Peter Ferrara, *Social Security: The Inherent Contradiction* (Washington: Cato, 1980).

[32] We explained "communicate" in the questionnaire as follows: "...by communicate, we mean have a meaningful exchange with an identifiable contact person or department in person, by phone, e-mail, or other media."

events help to connect like-minded individuals, creating networks sympathetic to the think tank's ideas, but not directed by them.[33] In addition, the idea entrepreneurs in free-market think tanks help connect policy makers to the producers of ideas. By bringing these two networks closer together, they can both expand the alternatives of which policy makers are aware, as well as provide the producers of ideas a sense of the agenda and constraints of policy makers, allowing them to focus their activity where it might have the greatest impact.

Free-market think tanks' networking function extends to connecting domestic politicians to a wider range of global experts. Although many of these think tanks do not have the resources to perform expert analysis themselves, the global network connects them to those who do. Policy makers usually depend on a small range of "usual suspects" for ideas and expertise, limiting themselves to options with which they are already familiar or that already have domestic political support. Given this, bureaucrats are likely to be powerfully influenced by actors who can reduce the transaction costs of locating new sources of expert knowledge, and who can bring new potential solutions to their attention. By drawing attention to international examples, think tanks can assist policy makers who are sympathetic to their ideas, but are unconvinced that they can adopt them without damaging their political popularity, reputation, or career. Given that coalitional dynamics and political institutions vary significantly across state boundaries, this political engineering function may be the most significant function that free-market think tanks provide: They help to identify methods by which ideas devised elsewhere can be made politically viable for ambitious office holders in very different contexts.

Finally, free-market think tanks provide an international network of people identifiably committed to libertarian ideas, thereby reducing the transaction costs of organization. Their connection to this network and its ideas is, in many cases, as important a part of their identity as their local context. The international network provides them with the confidence to pursue their goals despite their alienation from their local political context: Although they may lack allies within their own nation, they can draw energy from the knowledge that they are a part of a global network of committed believers. Finally, the international network facilitates learning across contexts, by encouraging the diffusion of "success stories" across national borders. This

---

[33] This is similar to the function served in the United States by the Federalist Society. See Steven Teles, *The Rise of the Conservative Legal Movement* (Princeton: Princeton University Press, 2008), chapter 5.

enhances the confidence of local free marketeers (giving them the belief that they are on the "right side of history"), as well as providing examples that show that their ideas are not just persuasive at a theoretical level, but are likely to work at a policy level.

The patterned interaction between think tanks – formally at annual meetings and conferences and informally through frequent telecommunications and e-mail – also serves instrumental aims such as providing connections to sources of funding, many of which have already supported similar organizations in other countries. Furthermore, information sharing also alerts organizations to important precedents rooted in shared ideas and esteem for the value of free-market reforms. Second, beyond the strategic and intellectual resources previously discussed, the network reduces the transaction costs associated with local organizational growth, an essential function given that these think tanks may be an innovation without significant precedents in their national context. In doing so, the network acts to diminish the time it takes a new think tank to develop into a serious player in national politics, which is critical given that its ability to attract resources beyond seed funding is likely to depend on some form of measurable results (such as policies passed and reports produced).[34] Third, the international network provides a ready-made source of individuals willing and able to serve on organization boards, which provide prestige and thus confidence (sometimes misplaced) that potential supporters are not getting behind a fly-by-night organization. Finally, the network may serve an important juridical function: Through the resources that flow through it, centrally placed actors have sufficient leverage to settle conflicts between organizations over political and intellectual "turf." This can help avoid unnecessary duplication of effort and internecine conflicts that distract attention, damage organizational reputations, and deflect energy from influencing the external environment.

The relationship of influence in this network may seem hierarchical, in the sense that much of the startup funding and the core of the network is Anglo-American, as are most of the original ideas. But to see it purely in this way would be to miss a great deal. We have described a burgeoning transnational network in frequent communication, committed to promoting a normative vision that converts principles into workable policies and acts to soften the edges that divide domestic and international politics. Think tanks

---

[34] Requiring measurable outputs – especially in the form of policies – as a funding condition may strike the reader as counterintuitive given Hayek's focus on altering elite debates and gradually adjusting public perceptions about "what really works." Our interviews suggest that funding competitions lean much more toward public writing rather than direct involvement in the policy process.

are, therefore, "carriers" that give energy to the free-market movement and act as necessary agents that deepen the reach of a powerful *transnational* network, one not captured by an academic literature focusing largely on organized labor, human rights, and environmentalism.[35]

Free-Market Think Tanks: National Constraints and Global Opportunities

The effectiveness of these organizations in transferring free-market ideas is not simply a function of the strength of the international network within which they are embedded. Rather, effectiveness comes from a combination of the ease with which think tanks are able to organize, their "fit" with the policy-making process in the country where they are operating, and the resources they are able to leverage outside their home country. This section describes these constraints to lay the foundation for understanding the pattern of think tanks' successes and failures described in the following section, "Driving Policy Change: Developing World Successes, OECD Failures."

What influences the spread of free-market think tanks? Perhaps the most obvious influence is the tax code, which may provide incentives for generating independent ideas, and which identifies the kinds of activities that may be engaged in under a tax-exempt rubric. The effect of the tax code on organizational development is a matter of significant disagreement within the free-market think-tank movement, with many of the participants in our survey (see Figure 5.3) identifying the tax code as an obstacle to their operation, and officials at Atlas arguing that it is important but possible to overcome.

Another important obstacle is a state's organization of interests. According to Peter A. Hall and David Soskice, advanced industrial states can be divided into two clusters of institutional arrangements for organizing interests: liberal market economies (LMEs), such as those found in Great Britain and the United States; and coordinated market economies (CMEs), such as are found in Germany, France, the Czech Republic, and Scandinavia.[36] The latter form of interest organization is most problematic from the point of view of free-market think tanks, as policy and idea generation occurs primarily within powerful bureaucracies, political parties, or research

---

[35] Sanjeev Khagram, James V. Riker, and Kathryn Sikkink, *Restructuring World Politics: Transnational Social Movements, Networks, and Norms* (Minneapolis: University of Minnesota Press, 2001).

[36] Peter A. Hall and David Soskise, *Varieties of Capitalism: The Institutional Foundations of Comparative Advantage* (Oxford: Oxford University Press, 2001).

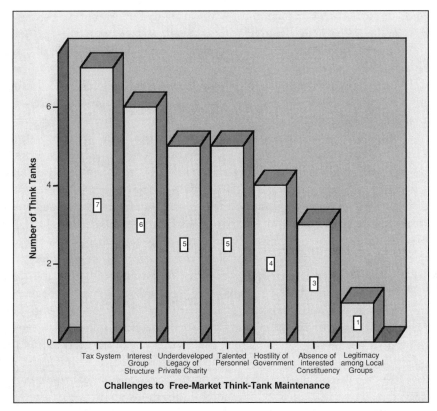

FIGURE 5.3. Most Severe Challenges to Organization Maintenance. *Note:* Respondents were asked to rank these challenges to maintaining their organization. The graph displays the frequencies for obstacles respondents rated the "most challenging" aspect of organizational maintenance. N = 31. *Source:* Free Market Think Tank Survey, 2005.

institutes closely linked to them. In addition, CMEs, especially that of Germany, tend to control the development of civil society through subsidizing group maintenance (a phenomenon that includes religion, as noted in Chapter 1 of this book). As Alexander Chaufen, the president of Atlas, observes of German government policy: "They've collectivized the non-profit world, by giving to each segment of society an allotment of money... [it] makes breaking ranks and going on your own a hard sell."[37] In CMEs, the organization of interests often referred to as corporatism crowds out the demand for expertise by internalizing the market for it, and in so doing, chokes off

[37] Interview with Alexander Chaufen, September 2005.

opportunities (both financial and organizational) for promoting extragovernmental entrepreneurial activity.

Perhaps most striking in our respondents' comments is the role that the (un)availability of talented personnel presents as a challenge to organizational flourishing. Without the firm establishment of a "culture" of think tanks, it is likely to be very difficult to persuade talented minds to throw caution to the wind and join a risky venture in economies with unemployment in the double digits. This is especially true where there are few other such organizations. The failure of a new organization in the American libertarian organizational economy is likely to mean that their staff simply move elsewhere or start organizations of their own, but staff in less developed organizational economies may have no alternative employers. Combined with the perceived hostility of the policy environment to free-market reforms (and thus the probability of futility), these factors all point toward severe difficulties in attracting motivated, high-quality personnel in coordinated market economies.

A final constraint on the effectiveness of organizations within the free-market think-tank network concerns their "legitimacy." For good or ill, the ideas of participants in the policy process are judged as much by who they are as by the evidence that they bring to bear on particular issues.[38] A representative of a Scandinavian think tank told us that one of the most important constraints on its ability to influence the policy process was simply the novelty of the think-tank form: "We have no tradition of political think tanks in Sweden, so we are constantly faced with questions about the nature of a think tank: propaganda or science?" Connected to this, financial pressures may tempt free-market think tanks to accept funding for very specific purposes, or to spend their time doing corporate relations work. In addition, some think tanks have been started by prominent political figures, or have been used as jumping-off points for those with political ambitions. Chaufen observes that these activities appear to have increased in the last few years, especially in Western Europe, and that they threaten the "brand name" of free-market think tanks: "We are still a young industry, and if people think we are second-class political parties, or second-class corporate affairs groups, we are doomed."[39]

Given the general suspicion of libertarian ideas in much of Europe, free-market think tanks often have to downplay their ideological underpinnings.

---

[38] The role of reputations in the marketplace of ideas is explored in Glenn Loury, "Self-Censorship in Public Discourse: A Theory of 'Political Correctness' and Related Phenomena," *Rationality and Society*, October 1994, pp. 428–61.

[39] Interview with Chaufen.

Another respondent observed that, "There is, in Europe, a rejection of the whole idea – which makes it very challenging. You have to emphasize the more practical outcome-based research type work and emphasize less the philosophical side." Finally, there is the negative side of being globally networked, which is the suspicion that a think tank is simply an instrument of foreign influence. Although global networks can often help free-market think tanks get off the ground (through financial assistance, for instance), that same assistance renders its beneficiaries suspect in political cultures where nationalistic appeals continue to be very powerful. Chaufen points, for instance, to the example of Venezuela, where National Endowment for Democracy support of the think tanks SUMATE and CEDICE (the latter a member of the Atlas network) led them to be attacked as tools of the United States. As a consequence, the legitimacy of these think tanks depends on their ability to rapidly develop a base of indigenous support, support that is often difficult to acquire given the structural factors identified earlier. Therefore, continuing dependence on outside sources raises questions about their integrity in the national community. As Chaufen observes, "In Central and Eastern Europe it was a grass-roots effort to create the think tanks, from the bottom up. In Western Europe many of the think tanks rely on corporate money, but I believe it is U.S. money, or multinational money, which disengages the think tank from the local community. [They are] more concerned with the big disputes between the U.S. and Europe, rather than what concerns the local citizens there, in Spain or in France or in Brussels."[40] This points to the essential challenge of free-market think tanks: to maintain their embeddedness in their local community while simultaneously serving as a conduit for ideas from outside it. Think-tank funding sources, broken down by region as shown in Figure 5.4, bear out Chaufen's observations. Only in Western Europe did domestic sources provide a greater average percentage of funding for think tanks in their startup phase than they do currently. This growth in domestic sources suggests that think tanks in eastern Europe have been relatively successful at overcoming the legitimacy gap. Doing so requires that they solve not only organizational challenges, but also overcome the difficulties of policy inheritance.

Driving Policy Change: Developing World Successes, OECD Failures

We identify two policy areas, tax and pension reform, through which to examine the *potential* for think tanks to effect political change. The flat tax

[40] Ibid.

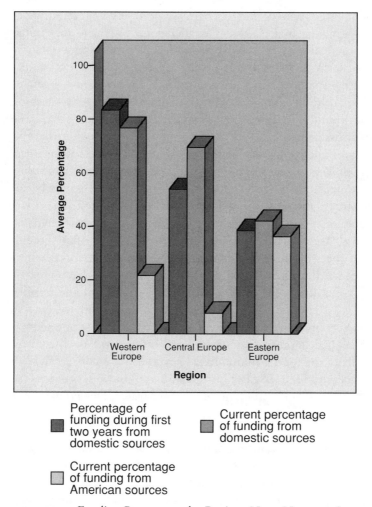

FIGURE 5.4. Funding Percentages by Region. *Note*: N = 31. *Source:* Free Market Think Tank Survey, 2005.

and pension privatization, two of the leading policy instruments advocated by the free-market movement, have witnessed spirited, but not wholesale adoption within the postcommunist world.[41] These same reforms have fared

---

[41] Both the flat tax and pension privatization are fraught concepts. The flat tax applies a uniform rate of taxation, generally speaking, to income, corporations, and, if applicable, value-added or sales tax. Pension privatization, as Paul Starr notes, "is a fuzzy concept that evokes sharp political reactions." Steven R. Smith follows Starr to point out that privatization may mean (1) a move toward private alternatives after a program stops, (2) assumption of private ownership of public assets by a private enterprise or person, (3) the move of private

far worse in the United States and Western Europe, however, thus suggesting the limited potential for these ideas to be "reimported."[42]

Pension Reform

Recasting long-held, intergenerational contracts such as pay-as-you-go (PAYG) pension schemes poses steep challenges to reformers. PAYG schemes, which enjoyed widespread adoption across the industrialized West after World War II, generate powerful constituencies vigilant against even incremental reforms, such as hikes in the retirement age or reformulations of benefit calculations, let alone radical restructuring. Consequently, pension systems in Western Europe and the United States have been resilient despite loud ideological calls for retrenchment in the name of economic growth and the projected insolvency of these defined benefit systems as the elderly population grows.[43]

The introduction of extensive pension reform in Latin America and central and eastern Europe (CEE) thus poses a puzzle for the proposed logic of PAYG durability. Political economy scholarship on programmatic restructuring of pensions posits a long list of mechanisms and factors explaining variation in the legislation of a mandatory, fully funded tier.[44] Committed leadership with a vision of "the promised land," limited institutional veto points, support by international financial institutions such as the World Bank and the International Monetary Fund that act as agents of "blame avoidance" for unpopular policies, and destabilizing periods of "punctured equilibrium" – all provide plausible opportunities for altering the political agenda and building reform coalitions.[45] Taking advantage of these windows of opportunity, however, turns largely on the transmission of ideas.

enterprises into public service provision after regulatory reform, and (4) the "contracting out" of public services to private enterprise. We largely refer to privatization to mean the adoption of reformed pay-as-you-go (PAYG) schemes and the introduction of a mandatory defined contribution, individualized account tier. It's also known as a partially privatized system. Paul Starr, "The Meaning of Privatization," *Yale Law and Policy Review*, no. 6, 1988, pp. 6–41; Steven R. Smith, "Privatization, Devolution, and the Welfare State: Rethinking the Prevailing Wisdom," in Bo Rothstein and Sven Steinmo, eds., *Restructuring the Welfare State: Political Institutions and Policy Change* (London: Palgrave, 2003), pp. 78–101.

42 "The Flat Tax Revolution," *Economist*, April 14, 2005, available online at http://www.economist.com/printedition/displayStory.cfm?Story_ID = 3861190.

43 Paul Pierson, "When Effect Becomes Cause: Policy Feedback and Political Change," *World Politics*, vol. 45, no. 4, 1993, pp. 595–628.

44 Katharina Müller, "The Making of Pension Privatization in Latin America and Eastern Europe," in Robert Holzman, Mitchell Orenstein, and Michal Rutkowski, eds., *Pension Reform in Europe: Process and Progress* (Washington: World Bank Press, 2003), pp. 47–79.

45 Orenstein proposes a three-stage process of implementation of radical pension reform. The stages include the agenda-setting, coalition-building, and implementation stage. We address hypotheses in each stage of the sequence without dwelling on them. Mitchell Orenstein,

By the early 1990s, the World Bank began a vigorous campaign for the restructuring of states' public-private mix of pension financing, especially in the developing world. The traditional PAYG system was, the World Bank maintained, insolvent in the long run. *Averting the Old Age Crisis*, a World Bank policy report that drew on and extended years of scholarly criticism of large public "defined benefit" programs (including criticism from members of the free-market think-tank network), trumpeted a defined contribution scheme as a viable substitute for the impending fiscal crisis of such systems. The 1981 Chilean adoption of individualized accounts along with the dismantling of its publicly financed PAYG scheme provided evidence from the field to support the World Bank's empirical claims about the fiscal and economic viability of the reforms. The swift spread of the "Chilean model" across Latin America has similarly emboldened reformers in CEE. As hinted at previously, however, the implementation phase presents the prickliest political obstacles in the move toward mandatory defined contribution pension schemes.

What explains why some CEE countries reformed and others did not, despite similar policy legacies (see the appendix)? Agnieszka Chlon-Dominczak and Marek Mora surveyed decision-makers and experts in both reforming and nonreforming countries, testing hypotheses taken from the political economy literature. The authors quickly dispensed with claims that emphasize distributional conflicts (old versus young, and rich versus poor), authoritarianism, constitutional differences, ideology, and leadership as sufficient determinants of radical pension reform because they were fixtures in both reforming and nonreforming countries.[46] In CEE states, the role of the World Bank and national experts exerted the greatest degree of influence – more than trade unions and private market institutions as well – according to their survey.[47] In addition, the authors found that the size of the fiscal deficit (or current financial considerations) was a strong determinant of reform. One respondent noted, "the deficit also acts as a driving force to proceed with the planned reforms, and even to take decisions that are not always popular."[48]

"How Politics and Institutions Affect Pension Reform in Three Postcommunist Countries," World Bank Policy Research Paper, 2000, pp. 1–84.

[46] Agnieszka Chlon-Dominczak and Marek Mora, "Commitment and Consensus in Pension Reform," in Holzmann, Orenstein, and Rutkowski, *Pension Reform in Europe: Process and Progress*, pp. 131–57.

[47] Ibid., p. 142. On average, the Ministry of Labor exerted the greatest degree of influence in CEE reforming states.

[48] Ibid., p. 144. Latvian, the former Yugoslavian republic of Macedonian, and Romanian respondents expressed similar considerations.

Building a reform coalition, the authors suggest, depends on including and convincing social partners such as trade unions and tripartite councils of the viability of reform. Critical for our argument, there was general agreement among participants in the reform process, in both reforming and nonre-forming countries, that the diffusion and transmission of ideas – largely Anglo-American – ties together these diverse determinants. It is here that free-market think tanks have their greatest potential for influence, by pro-viding indigenous support for privatization, and for helping policy makers discover how to apply the generic recommendations of international bod-ies. In addition, think tanks help to soften up the climate of opinion prior to the intervention of international organizations, making key actors more receptive to comprehensive change than they might otherwise be. It is this linkage between the prestigious recommendations by external actors and the political engineering by think tanks that we suspect explains the widespread adoption of partial privatization in the CEE, and, to some degree, variations across states.

The link between the agenda status of pension privatization and the role of think-tank political engineering is even clearer in the United States. Start-ing in the early 1980s, libertarians and conservatives at the Heritage Foun-dation, Cato Institute, American Enterprise Institute, and Hoover Institute began to implement a multidecade strategy aimed at undermining the cur-rent structure of America's deeply entrenched social security program. The privatization network attempted to weaken the certainty of receiving social security benefits among the young while simultaneously encouraging the expansion of individualized savings vehicles and familiarizing policy makers with the (purportedly positive) experience of other countries with pension privatization.[49]

This strategy bore fruit when, beginning with his 2000 run for president and continuing into his second term, George W. Bush proved that a Repub-lican candidate could run and win on creating private accounts in social security. Republican strategist Grover Norquist went so far as to predict that they "will be called W accounts.... Fifty years from now, children will learn that Ronald Reagan ended the cold war and George Bush privatized Social Security."[50] However, once Bush tried to put together a detailed pro-posal, the difficulties in financing the transition associated with privatization

[49] Steven Teles and Martha Derthick, "From Third Rail to Presidential Commitment – and Back?" in Brian Glenn and Steven Teles, eds., *Conservatism and American Political Devel-opment*, unpublished manuscript, 2007.

[50] Adam Nagourney. "Putting It Back Together Again," *New York Times*, October 30, 2005.

became clear, and the public and members of Congress became more attentive to the proposal's costs than its purported benefits. The failure of social security privatization initiated a decline in the president's approval that has not yet been reversed.

The failure of the president's privatization gambit points clearly to the limits of think-tank influence. On the one hand, getting privatization on the agenda was a remarkable accomplishment, given the extraordinary entrenchment of social security, the lack of a short-term financing crisis, and its continuing popularity. This success can be largely laid at the feet of libertarian and conservative think tanks, which kept the idea alive for two decades, ensuring that it was vetted when a powerful, sympathetic political carrier for the idea came on the scene. Moving from setting the agenda to policy passage, however, means facing down the stubborn forces of policy inheritance (in the case of social security, the problem of transition costs) and the inherent blame-avoidance dynamics that elected politicians face in altering existing government commitments. These forces are less pressing in developing contexts, such as CEE, and, as a result, actors such as think tanks that are successful in injecting an idea into the policy agenda are less likely to be disappointed when democratic politicians are actually asked to commit to weighing the costs and benefits of ideas such as pension privatization.

The Flat Tax

Perhaps more stunning than the expansive introduction of pension privatization is the substantial number of postcommunist states that have adopted the flat tax. In fact, nine out of twenty-one former Soviet Bloc states have passed tax reform legislation that imposes a uniform rate of taxes on both personal and corporate income without deductions or rate schedules.[51] Tax reform means either simplifying rate schedules and/or broadening the tax base by eliminating incentives such as exemptions, credits, or other preferences that seek to encourage individuals or corporations to participate in "certain socially desirable activities."[52] In the United States, for example, the tax code acts as a partial income maintenance program for low wage earners through the Earned Income Tax Credit (EITC), subsidizes the housing market through mortgage interest deduction, and distributes hundreds of billions of dollars in tax-based subsidies to the middle class and corporations. Similarly, in Europe such tax "preferences" operate as instruments of indirect government policy, subsidizing childcare and low-income housing

---

[51] The proliferation of the flat tax adoption in CEE has not been matched by the scale of literature on the subject, which while small is dominated by law journals.

[52] Smith, "Privatization, Devolution, and the Welfare State," p. 85.

construction.[53] In OECD countries, these subsidies are often closely guarded by well-entrenched interest groups, and the introduction of a flat tax would all but eliminate the capacity of governments to utilize the tax code as an instrument for social policy making. Even more important, despite the fact that OECD tax codes are not as progressive as their marginal rates would make them appear, the flat tax invites attacks on it as making construction workers and CEOs pay the same rate.

These considerations, when combined with the huge mobilization around tax subsidies on the corporate side of the code, have defeated (so far) the flat tax wherever it has appeared in advanced industrial economies. For example, in the 2005 German election, Angela Merkel and her Christian Democrat Union (CDU)/Christian Socialist Union (CSU) appeared just a month before the election to be cruising toward a resounding defeat of the ruling Social Democrats (SDP). Her future finance minister, Paul Kirchof, brought to Merkel's campaign an ambitious flat tax plan that would have slashed income tax rates to 25 percent and eliminated a huge swath of deductions. The flat tax idea appears to have been just the opportunity that the SDP needed to pull itself back into contention. Gerhard Schröder repeatedly hammered the CSU standard-bearer over the campaign's last weeks for proposing the "Merkel minus," because the flat tax would eliminate a raft of middle-class tax subsidies. Instead of the overwhelming success that pundits had predicted just months before, Merkel limped into office as chancellor in a coalition government, the flat tax was never spoken of again in CDU/CSU circles, and Kirchof has gone back to life as a professor of law. In a pattern strongly reminiscent of the American experience with pension privatization, the global free-market network was very successful in injecting the idea of the flat tax into the mainstream of German policy discourse – a feat all the more impressive given that the idea had previously been so obscure that Germans lacked a proper word for it – but was wholly unsuccessful at persuading the public that it was worth the risks of adoption.[54]

But given the abject failures of the flat tax in rich democracies like the United States and Germany, and the limited market experience of postcommunist democracies, why have so many CEE states pursued such a reform path? Unlike pension reform, it is *unremarkable* that postcommunist states seized on tax reform early in the transition to a market economy. Under the fixed price regime of the centrally planned economies, manifestly lopsided tax rates signaled the public (or Politburo's) esteem for particular industrial

53 Ibid., p. 86.
54 Daniel Gross, "Das Flat Tax," *Slate*, September 16, 2005, available online at http://www.slate.com/id/2126386/.

and agricultural segments of the economy rather than serving as a vehicle for revenue extraction.[55] The rates were the by-product of a negotiated settlement between a host of players ranging from central planners and ministers to local governments and works councils. However, transition economies, as Hillary Apel explains, required a tax scheme that negotiated a set of intractable political choices:

... which kinds of taxes would reliably raise budgetary revenue, which tax forms were hardest to evade, which forms would seem distributionally just to a population raised in a paternalistic state and lacking personal experience in honoring tax responsibilities, and which would advance the country's foreign policy goals and international interests.[56]

Spurning these reforms would create distortions in labor and capital markets, dampen growth, and exacerbate already sizable tax shirking. It is therefore not surprising – especially considering the appeal that EU accession offered – that tax reform appeared atop the agendas of CEE governments early in the transition phase, and that most imitated their continental counterparts in fashioning a progressive, if simplified, tax scheme.[57]

[55] Taxes inside the Iron Curtain reflected a series of negotiated contracts rather than preset rates. As Coulter et al. note, "[S]pecial tax schedules for agricultural earnings and for self-employed or non-wage incomes were less a reflection of the need for revenue than a statement of the ideological status of such activities." Fiona Coulter, Christopher Heady, Colin Lawson, and Stephen Smith, "Fiscal Systems in Transition: The Case of the Czech Income Tax," *Europe-Asia Studies*, vol. 47, no. 6, 1995, pp. 1007–23, 1011.

[56] Hillary Appel, "International Imperatives and Tax Reform: Lessons from Postcommunist Europe," *Comparative Politics*, vol. 39, no. 2, 2007, pp. 43–63, 44. While we agree with Appel that international variables – especially the draw of foreign investment – accelerated tax reforms, we find little evidence that EU membership per se drove flat tax reforms in particular. None of the cases that she analyzes has adopted the flat tax, and there is considerable support for the ideational or "priming" role that think tanks supplied within these countries. The implementation process itself adheres closely to what Theda Skocpol calls "competitive emulation." Theda Skocpol, *Diminished Democracy: From Membership to Management in American Civic Life* (Norman: University of Oklahoma Press, 2003). Large, federated voluntary associations in the postbellum United States gradually came to resemble one another in structure and design through a process of borrowing the organizational templates of groups that had themselves sought to mirror the local-state-federal institutional structure of the United States. In this case, tax harmonization and specifically a value-added tax (VAT) quickly became a necessary condition for postcommunist states to join the EU. In all cases the flat tax was an instrument that adopting states selected to strengthen competitiveness and increase tax receipts.

[57] Coulter et al., "Fiscal Systems in Transition," p. 1010; Dena Ringold, "Social Policy in Postcommunist Europe: Legacies and Transition," in Linda J. Cook, Mitchell A. Orenstein, and Marilyn Reuschemeyer, eds., *Left Parties and Social Policy in Postcommunist Europe* (Boulder: Westview Press, 1999), p. 11; Andreas Tzortzis, "Flat-Tax Movement Stirs in Europe," *Christian Science Monitor*, March 8, 2005. Available online at http://www.csmonitor.com/2005/0308/p01s03-woeu.html.

The Baltic states were the first to buck the trend and implement a flat tax regime.[58] Russia, Serbia, Slovakia, Ukraine, Georgia, and Romania followed close behind, introducing a uniform rate on corporate profits and personal income, combined with a threshold or exemption that applies for low-wage incomes up to a certain level. Poland, Hungary, and the Czech Republic, citing competitive pressure from their flat-tax neighbors, are currently debating a similar shift.

A combination of factors helps explain the spread of the flat tax in the CEE. First, CEE tax reformers, in their initial, simplified adoption of progressive taxation, abstained from utilizing the tax code as an indirect instrument of government policy. Evasion was rampant across the former Soviet Bloc in terms of both private income and corporate profits. Simply put, the utility of the tax code for providing incentives for public action rests on the assumption that people are actually *paying* their taxes. The converse is true in states with high degrees of compliance, such as Germany and the United States. Individuals are reluctant to give up current benefits acquired through tax preferences (credits, deductions, exemptions) in exchange for forecasted future growth gains, even if those later gains are expected to pay bigger dividends than current tax preferences do. Hence, one of the leading reasons that a move to the flat tax is so challenging for policy makers with largely compliant taxpayers is that individuals (and, to a lesser extent, businesses) "discount" future earnings against current benefits. Governments in CEE nations, plagued by poor tax compliance, could not use the tax code as an instrument of social policy as easily as their Western cousins. Thus, the powerful constituencies that effectively block reform in countries with high relative rates of compliance and comparatively generous tax preferences remain in their infancy.[59]

Unconstrained by clienteles eager to preserve generous tax benefits, reformers in CEE countries viewed the flat tax as a means of bolstering public finances and attracting capital investment. Rampant tax evasion in the transition economies saddled them with mounting political and fiscal problems. Heightened administrative costs, poor monitoring capability, and threadbare public coffers made foreign capital investors nervous. The flat tax offered to broaden the base and yield greater net revenue, and at least had

---

[58] Purists take exception with Lithuania because, although it taxes wages and income at a flat 33 percent, it imposes a "variety of rates depending on the source of income." See Alvin Rabushka's comment available online at http://www.russianeconomy.org/comments/010305-2.html.

[59] "The Flat-Tax Revolution," *Economist*, April 16, 2005; Robert Shapiro, "The Flat Tax, Flat-Lined," *Slate*, November 26, 2002, available online at http://www.slate.com/id/2074589/.

the potential to reduce widespread evasion by reducing the marginal rate and promoting greater equity. Similarly, improved predictability of the political and economic climate combined with a depressed rate of taxation, reformers speculated, would attract desirable foreign direct investment. These forecasts have largely come true: Flat tax states have witnessed an increase in receipts, compliance, and foreign direct investment. Slovakia, a noted success story, was named the World Bank's economic reformer of the year in 2004. What accounts, then, for the variation in CEE states adopting the flat tax?

Fiscal deficits played a large role in the turn to partial privatization. Did these same deficits also lure policy makers toward the flat tax? European Union accession – and the financial adjustments such as structural deficit targets, budgetary adjustments, and tax restructuring that EU membership demands – is a plausible mechanism driving flat tax adoption, but the correlation between accession and flat tax adoption is fairly weak. In the countries we consider, five postcommunist EU members have adopted the flat tax and five have not. Gerhard Schröder and Jacques Chirac had both vigorously advocated tax harmonization with the Euro-zone economies. Although those bids floundered, the anticipation of such potential reforms – and their upfront budgetary and political costs – could have dissuaded policy makers in EU candidate countries from flat tax adoption. Yet, of the two most recent inductees, Romania adopted the flat tax whereas Bulgaria has not. Second, the timing of the reforms does not correlate with membership candidacy. Although all postcommunist states that have joined the EU implemented the flat tax *prior* to membership, the other five achieved accession without such reforms, and three states – Russia, Georgia, and Ukraine – adopted the flat tax without any hope of EU membership in the short or medium term.[60] Hence we find the case for the EU as a driver of flat tax reform to be weak.

This suggests that the sources of movement toward the flat tax lay elsewhere. On the agenda side of the equation, almost all CEE countries were facing substantial noncompliance with the tax code, a phenomenon that tends to

---

[60] We label the following countries as postcommunist: Albania, Belarus, Bosnia-Herzegovina, Bulgaria, Croatia, the Czech Republic, Estonia, Georgia, Hungary, Latvia, Lithuania, Macedonia, Moldova, Poland, Romania, Russia, Serbia-Montenegro, Slovakia, Slovenia, and Ukraine. We somewhat arbitrarily exclude the Central Asian countries Kazakhstan, Kyrgyzstan, Mongolia, Tajikistan, Turkmenistan, and Uzbekistan. In a two-by-two table, we see that distribution of EU membership and flat tax adoption do not even weakly correlate:

	Flat Tax Adopted	Flat Tax Not Adopted
EU Member	5	5
Not EU Member	4	7

lead to a downward spiral in revenue collection. In addition, noncompliance tends to lead to both the perception and reality of corruption, and with it a tarnished reputation of government among both citizens and outside actors, including corporations considering inward investment. Faced with these two forces on the agenda side, governments in the CEE, regardless of ideology, have been open to policy solutions that promise an increased and more predictable tax yield and an improved state reputation for probity. Given that free-market think tanks are so well organized, considerably more insulated from government in CEE countries than elsewhere on the continent, and effectively linked to sources of expertise in OECD countries, they were well positioned to take advantage of these changes in their countries' agenda stream.

The adoption of the flat tax by a number of CEE countries is not quite the boon for libertarianism that one might imagine. First, although the flat tax may be a successful policy in terms of compliance for CEE states, its effect has been to increase the tax yield, and thus the capacity for government spending, not to reduce it. So although reducing the regulative component of the tax code is a victory for free markets, increasing the capacity of CEE governments to spend is not. Second, given CEE states' comparatively minor reliance on tax subsidies and such mammoth problems with tax compliance, these countries can provide only a very weak example for actors in OECD countries hoping to reimport this idea back to its source, where neither of these factors applies. At best, if economic growth in states that adopt a flat tax continues and compliance improves at a steady clip, these states may serve as plausible precedents in the future.

This variance in political legacies and economic situations point to the limits of think-tank influence. Although they may be very effective at injecting particular solutions into public debate when trends in the agenda stream are moving in their direction, they have only a very limited capacity to transform that agenda into public policy themselves. And when politicians, such as Bush with social security or Merkel and Kirchhof with the flat tax, attempt to jump-start this agenda-setting process, they run the risk of getting ahead of where the public is willing to go. In these cases, it may be that free-market think tanks, by changing the perception of the political viability of critical actors, may lead to excessive risk taking by persuading political actors to go places that prudence would dictate they avoid.

Conclusion: The Future of Efforts to Spread American Conservatism

To the degree that American conservatism has been able to actively produce convergence through international networking, that effort has been dominated by only one wing of the movement, the libertarians. At this point, libertarians have created outposts throughout the world, although there are still places that are "unchurched," and many of their institutions are, if not Potemkin villages, at least too small to have a major impact on their nation's politics. In some cases, the constraints of national politics on the effectiveness of the model of free-market think tanks are so daunting that they will have a major impact only when one of two things happens: (a) there is an endogenously produced shift in the character of the policy-making process, driven by forces unconnected to free-market institutions; or (b) these institutions are able to attain substantial influence over government through their links to increasingly powerful international organizations (as has happened in some cases with human rights organizations, and could happen through the ability of free-market institutions to leverage the similarity of their agendas to that of the EU, World Bank, or WTO). Future gains, in short, are likely to be incremental, for the ability of free-market think tanks to produce policy convergence with the United States are limited by deeply rooted institutional and cultural factors. Convergence in an organizational sense, therefore, is hard enough, given policy and institutional legacies. Translating what organizational convergence there has been into policy convergence is even harder.

The missing pieces of the puzzle, as we hinted earlier in this chapter, are the efforts of social conservatives to spread their ideas beyond America. Libertarians have been effective largely because theirs is a genuinely global movement. Americans have disproportionate influence over this movement, but can count on the existence of at least a small and highly motivated contingent of followers throughout the globe. American social conservatives, on the other hand, have few allies in most advanced countries, where the cultural constraints on social conservatism are quite powerful.[61] Where they are growing in the sense of attracting converts, their allies are still quite poor and politically weak. In that sense, social conservatives in much of the developing world resemble American evangelicals before the 1980s. But like American social conservatives, the religiously orthodox beyond our shores may grow more powerful as they attain greater levels of social mobility.

Where this is the case, social conservatives in the United States may find an increasingly receptive audience for their ideas, and richer opportunities for the sort of networking that libertarians have engaged in so aggressively. And when they do so, they may find that they will have even greater levels of effectiveness than the libertarians have been able to achieve, because they

---

[61] Canada, which we have not discussed in detail here, may be a partial exception.

will be able to combine globally sophisticated networking with a reasonably large mass base. At that point, the interesting question will be whether the religiously orthodox in the developing world choose to network with libertarians, thereby bringing the two parts of the American conservative movement together globally. Or, given the lack of a common enemy (in the form of secular liberalism and its peculiar American institutional manifestations), social conservatives and libertarians may continue to go their own way, with religious conservatives outside of America linking up with movements traditionally associated with the left around issues of human rights, redistribution, and the environment, issues that can all be seen as having a plausibly biblical foundation. These are questions that are highly indeterminate, depending on the development of ideas and the formation of coalitions country by country. The most reasonable prediction is that, as it has in the past, the American conservative coalition will continue to travel under different flags.

Appendix: Pension Reform: Private Accounts in Central and Eastern Europe

Country	First Tier	Second Tier	Third Tier
Bulgaria	Reformed PAYGO	Mandatory private individual account	Voluntary supplementary account
Croatia	Reformed PAYGO	Mandatory private individual account	Voluntary supplementary account
Estonia	Reformed PAYGO	Mandatory private individual account	Voluntary supplementary account
Hungary	Reformed PAYGO	Mandatory private individual account	Voluntary supplementary account
Kazakhstan	Mandatory private individual account	Voluntary supplementary account	None
Latvia	Reformed PAYGO	Mandatory private individual account	Voluntary supplementary account
Poland	Reformed PAYGO	Mandatory private individual account	Voluntary supplementary account

Source: Barbara Kritzer, "Social Security Reforms in Central and Eastern Europe: Variations on a Latin American Theme," *Social Security Bulletin*, vol. 64, no. 4, 2002, p. 20.

6

Work, Welfare, and Wanderlust

Immigration and Integration in Europe and North America

Randall Hansen

Europe and North America have long diverged in their immigration policy. Simply put, Europe was from the early 1800s until the 1950s a continent of emigration, whereas the United States and to a lesser degree Canada were quintessential countries of immigration. Canada and the United States encouraged Northern European immigration with the goal of building white, Anglo-Saxon settler societies; Europe encouraged emigration with the goal of exporting surplus population and unemployment (Germany, Italy) and/or empire building (the United Kingdom). In the postwar years, divergence continued. The United States and Canada abandoned the race-based, exclusionary inflection of their immigration policies, and opened their doors to an extraordinary migration from East and South Asia, the West Indies, Latin America, and Africa. European nation-states tried to have their cake and eat it too: They tried to harness the economic benefits of mass unskilled labor while ensuring that the migration was temporary. These efforts largely failed: The liberal constitutional order that is common to Europe and North America meant that the immigrants were not simply workers but rights-bearers, and European courts frustrated national efforts to guarantee the migrants' return.

The result, by the 1990s, was a demographic makeup that looked broadly similar on both sides of the Atlantic. European and North American societies were multi-ethnic; the bulk of migrants and ethnic minorities lived in their cities; and (with Canada partially excepted) the migration patterns were dominated by family reunification. For institutional reasons, their immigration policies (Britain excepted) remained modestly expansive despite public opposition to immigration. Where the two continents continued to diverge was on the national story that accompanied migration. Although it is in fact exceedingly difficult to migrate legally to the United States, and America's immigration policy was shot through with racist intent until the 1960s, immigration is a fundamental part of the country's founding myths. The opening of U.S. immigration policy to non-Europeans in 1965 coincided with the civil rights movement, and there are important links between the two. Multiculturalism everywhere owes its existence to the postwar human rights revolution, of which the civil rights movement was a symbol and to which it contributed. In the United States, therefore, multiculturalism cannot be separated from the particular experience of African Americans.[1] In Canada, multiculturalism, although of even more recent vintage than the United States' color-blind immigration policy, is now a fundamental part of the country's national identity. It is, to be sure, taken more seriously by the Torontonian elite than Western Canadians or Quebeckers, but support for both multiculturalism and immigration is higher in Canada than in almost any other country in the world. By contrast, with the partial exception of France, European nation-states did not base their identity on immigration. The point here is conceptual: It was always very grating to see scholars, often with undisguised glee at their cleverness, point out the supposed contradiction between Germany's official claim that it was "not a country of immigration" and the reality of substantial migration. There was in fact no contradiction: The statement was about whether Germany derived its identity from immigration and whether immigration was wanted. It did not, and it was not. Neither Germany nor the rest of Europe pursued a policy of encouraging immigration; on the contrary, all European countries pursued until recently the chimerical goal of zero immigration.

Since the millennium, there have been two important shifts in European immigration and integration policy, one that brings Europe closer to the United States and another that pulls it further away. First, since 2000, Britain, Germany, and Spain have expanded opportunities for skilled and unskilled migration, the United Kingdom explicitly copied the Canadian points system (which assigns points based on age, education, and experience, and grants entry to those with enough points), and France's President Nicolas Sarkozy proposes to follow suit. Policy makers in these countries view themselves as competitors with the classic settler countries over skilled migrants. Second, this new openness to immigration has been matched by a new emphasis on integration and hostility to multiculturalism, particularly (but not only) in the Netherlands and Denmark.

---

[1] Christian Joppke and Ewa Morawska, "Integrating Immigrants in Liberal States: Policies and Practices," in Christian Joppke, ed., *Toward Assimilation and Citizenship. Immigrants in Liberal Nation-States* (Houndmills: Palgrave, 1999).

This chapter compares immigration and integration policy in Europe and North America. It is divided into three sections. The first provides a brief historical overview of migration to the two continents. The second examines immigration policy itself, paying particular attention in Europe to France, Britain, and Germany. The third compares post-2000, post-9/11 immigration and integration policy. It makes two arguments. First, policy toward labor migrants on both continents has been largely unaffected by events since the millennium; rather, it is driven by the position of both North America and Europe in the global economy, and in Europe by demographic demands. Second, whereas the clearest effect of 9/11 in the United States has been a restriction of civil liberties for permanent residents, immigrants, and citizens, in Europe the clearest effects have been in integration policy: Naturalization requirements have been tightened, loyalty requirements have been introduced, and family reunification has been subjected to more stringent requirements. In Europe, events since the turn of the century have magnified pre-2000 concerns about inadequate language skills, social segregation, and economic failure on the part of Europe's large ethnic minority populations. These poor integration outcomes, the chapter concludes, can be partially explained by a further basic difference between immigration policy in Europe and North America: Whereas North America integrates immigrants into work, Europe integrates them into welfare.

Migration to Europe

Postwar migration to Europe was a market-driven phenomenon: Migrants traveled to and within Europe in response to the needs of the buoyant postwar economy, particularly in the Franco-German core. Migrants arrived in response to this demand through two distinct channels. The first were the guestworker schemes operated by Austria, Belgium, Denmark, France, Germany, Norway, Sweden, and Switzerland. All these countries sought to fill labor shortages with those migrants regarded as the least troublesome and most likely to return: Southern Europeans. Large numbers of Italians, Greeks, Spanish, and Portuguese migrated north for work. Once this initial pool of workers had been exhausted, these labor-importing countries had to look outside Western Europe. Austria, Switzerland, and Germany had no colonies. As a result, they expanded their guestworker programs to include Yugoslavia and Turkey.

It was at this time that the second migration channel emerged. Unable to compete with Swiss and German wages, Britain, France, and the Netherlands found themselves increasingly reliant on colonial migration. The process was a passive one insofar as none of these countries was keen to encourage large-scale, nonwhite colonial migration. Nonetheless, they all maintained citizenship and/or migration schemes that provided privileged access for colonial migrants. The combination of labor market demand and open or relatively open immigration channels could only have one consequence: West Indians and South Asians migrated to Britain, North Africans to France, and Surinamese to the Netherlands. Most of these migrants were young men, and they later brought their wives and had families. The same process occurred in the guestworker countries. Although many guestworkers did return home, enough stayed – 3 million (out of 14 million) in the case of Germany – to ensure that, following family reunification, these countries would have substantial ethnic minority populations. Some halfhearted efforts were made to ensure that guestworkers would return and to limit family reunification once it was clear that they wouldn't, but these were blocked by domestic courts. A defining case was heard in Germany.[2] It involved an Indian national who had entered Germany on a temporary work visa, which he regularly renewed. As the deadline for his departure approached in 1972, he applied for German citizenship. While his application was pending, the authorities withdrew his work permit in 1973 on the (not unreasonable) grounds that he intended to stay in Germany permanently, and ordered his departure. The matter went before the constitutional court, however, which argued in a landmark 1978 decision that the repeated renewal of the work permit had built up a "reliance interest" on his part. His deportation would thus violate the "protection of legitimate interests" principle of article 19 of the German constitution.

In this and other key legal decisions, activist courts, imbued by a post-war, post-Holocaust concern for individual rights against a heavy-handed state, drew on national constitutions and jurisprudence to ensure the guestworkers' stay. For their part, colonial migrants entered mostly as citizens and they could not be compelled to leave. Many countries introduced incentives for voluntary return, but these programs were limited, symbolic in intention (designed to placate the restrictionist right), and rarely used except by those migrants who had intended to return anyway. The result, by the mid-1970s, was a large and stable migrant population – numbering in the millions in the larger Northern European states. When the European economy entered recession in the early 1970s, all the northern receiving

---

[2] Phil Triadafopoulos, "Shifting Boundaries: Immigration, Citizenship, and the Politics of National Membership in Germany and Canada," unpublished Ph.D. thesis, New School for Social Research, 2004.

countries ended primary migration (consisting of migrants with no familial ties to the destination country) and limited new migration to family reunification.

Migration to the United States

Immigration to the United States took place in four waves.[3] The first wave occurred before 1820. Some 60 percent were English immigrants, but there were also German sectarians seeking religious freedom in Pennsylvania and Spaniards seeking converts in Florida and the Southwest.[4] The second wave occurred from 1820 to 1860, when 5 million immigrants – 40 percent of which were Irish – traveled to the United States to settle the frontier. In 1890, the American frontier was closed, and the third wave of migration, beginning in 1880, was diverted to industrial cities in the Northeast and Midwest.

From 1875, Congress passed a series of restrictive measures – designed to keep prostitutes, coolies, and Chinese migrants out – but immigration remained at high levels. As the new century approached, however, the composition of the migrant streams altered. In 1882, 87 percent of migrants came from Northwestern Europe and 13 percent from Southern and eastern Europe. Economic boom reduced emigration pressure from Western Europe, and by 1907 the proportions had reversed: Eighty-one percent of migrants came from eastern and Southern Europe, including large numbers of Jews, and only 19 percent were from Northwestern Europe.[5] This development set the stage for a policy change that was meant to mark the end of America's immigration history.

As immigration soared, pro-immigration business battled restrictionist politicians and interest groups – notably the populist American Protection League and the elitist Immigration Restriction League (which was founded by three Harvard alumni). After a war-induced cessation in immigration, the restrictionists won the argument. The Immigration Act of 1917 all but ended Asian immigration, and the National Origins Acts of 1921 and 1924 introduced a quota system that capped the annual intake of U.S. immigration through a system of country-based quotas.[6] Inspired by eugenic

---

[3] P. Martin, "U.S. Immigration," in M. Gibney and R. Hansen, eds., *Immigration and Asylum from 1900 to the Present* (Santa Barbara: ABC-CLIO, 2005).
[4] Ibid.
[5] Ibid.
[6] Desmond King, *In the Name of Liberalism: Illiberal Social Policy in the USA and Britain* (Oxford: Oxford University Press, 1999).

ideas about racial inferiority,[7] the legislation limited yearly immigration from any country to 2 percent of that country's citizens' total population in the United States under the 1890 census. Given the overwhelmingly white, Northern European character of U.S. immigration in 1890, the legislation effectively prevented nonwhite (and particularly non-Northern European) immigration. With the exception of African Americans, who were spatially and institutionally segregated from mainstream U.S. society, the National Origins Acts froze the white, European makeup of late nineteenth century America.

The legislation stayed on the books until 1965, and as emigration pressure in Europe eased, so did immigration to the United States. The 1952 McCarran-Walter Act reaffirmed the quota system, and extended it to ensure that citizens of Europe's colonies were excluded. Scholars in the 1950s and early 1960s thought immigration to the United States was largely over,[8] and no one would have predicted the massive non-European migration that began in the 1970s and continues to this day. The change that made it possible occurred in 1965. Inspired by President John F. Kennedy's assassination, President Lyndon B. Johnston's landslide victory, and a post–Civil Rights Act sympathy for ethnic minorities, Congress passed the Immigration Act of 1965.[9] The legislation scrapped the national origins quota, replaced it with a per-country limit of 20,000 and subjected the Western Hemisphere to a first-ever limit of 120,000. It also established a seven-category preference system based on family ties, labor skills, and Cold War refugee claims. International disparities of wealth, the spread of cheap international travel, and the pull of the American economy made the United States attractive to non-European immigrants. The 1965 legislation gave them, for the first time in four decades, the chance to immigrate.

Successive acts have tinkered with the system – the Western Hemisphere was placed under the per-country limits in 1976, in 1978 a worldwide quota of 290,000 was established (allowing the admission of Indochinese refugees), and in 1990 Congress raised the quota to 675,000 – but the basic structure of the 1965 act remains intact. Today, there are four major types of immigration to the United States.[10] The largest category consists of relatives

---

[7] Randall Hansen and Desmond King, "Eugenic Ideas, Political Interests, and Policy Variance: Immigration and Sterilization Policy in Britain and the US," *World Politics*, vol. 53, no. 2, 2001, pp. 237–63.

[8] Nathan Glazer, *We Are All Multiculturalists Now* (Cambridge: Harvard University Press, 1997).

[9] P. Schuck, "Lottery Program (U.S)," in Gibney and Hansen, *Immigration and Asylum*.

[10] Martin, "U.S. Immigration."

of U.S. immigrants; of the 850,000 immigrants admitted in 2000, 583,000 (69 percent) were family members sponsored by a relative in the United States. The second category is comprised of migrants (and their families) admitted for economic or employment reasons – 107,000 (13 percent) in 2000. Almost all of these individuals are already in the United States (for example, on a high-skilled temporary-work visa) and readjust their status. The third group is made up of "diversity" immigrants. Most of these enter through the controversial lottery program, which randomly grants full residence rights to fifty thousand people annually. Many of those receiving them are already in the United States illegally. The lottery system has been criticized for being highly politicized – between 1990 and 1994, forty thousand were reserved for Ireland – and for favoring the lucky over those who have patiently waited in line for years.

In addition to these legal flows, there is substantial, probably massive, illegal immigration to the United States each year. Hundreds of thousands of clandestine migrants enter the country every year, the result of the combination of proximity to poor sending countries (above all Mexico), near-insatiable demand in the informal economy (for cheap laborers, nannies, housekeepers, and so on), and a reluctance on the part of officials to enforce employer sanctions against those hiring illegal workers. Government efforts to combat such illegal immigration have focused on border control – expanded patrols, and a controversial fence between the United States and Mexico – but arrivals remain high.

Migration Policy in Europe

From the early 1970s to the late 1990s, all European countries pursued zero-immigration policies and, as noted, unsuccessfully attempted to reduce their foreign populations through (forced and voluntary) return and through limited family reunification. At the same time, all EU member states are signatories to the 1951 United Nations convention relating to the status of refugees, and they all have developed complex and lengthy legal mechanisms for processing asylum claims.[11] Most individuals who apply for asylum under the 1951 convention do not get it ("recognition rates" are 10–30 percent across the EU), but due to legal, financial, and moral constraints on deportation, they are not returned either. In practice, asylum has been, and is recognized

---

[11] Matthew Gibney and Randall Hansen, *Deportation and the Liberal State* (New York: United Nations High Commissioner for Refugees [UNHCR], 2006).

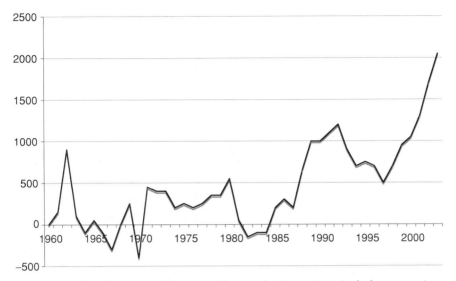

FIGURE 6.1. Net Migration, EU-15, in Thousands. *Note*: Data includes corrections due to population censuses, register counts, and so on, which cannot be classified as births, deaths, or migration. *Source*: *Eurostat Yearbook 2005*, Office for Official Publications of the European Communities.

to be by traffickers and migrants, an effective channel for lengthy if not permanent migration to Europe. The result of these two channels was net migration to Europe that ebbed and flowed not in relation to policy change but rather the strength of Europe's economy (a pull factor) and economic, political, and environmental crises abroad (push factors). Figure 6.1 provides an overview of net migration to Europe since 1970.

The only way in which zero-immigration policies were effective was in blocking the one type of migration in which European states have an interest: labor migration. Until recently, it was exceptionally difficult for labor migrants without family in Europe to migrate there. In the U.K., employers could apply for a temporary work permit and, after four years, the work permit holder could apply for permanent residence. Work permits were, however, only exceptionally granted and were subject to intrusive Home Office scrutiny. In Germany, postguestworker, nonethnic immigration was effectively nonexistent. Across Europe, due to the migration "stop" of the early 1970s, only two migrant channels were open: family reunification and asylum seeking. In Germany during the 1990s, 90 percent of net migration was made up of family migrants (75,000), asylum seekers (100,000), and ethnic Germans (100,000).[12] In France from 1993 to 1999, 78 percent of the migrants arriving annually were family members (37,600) or asylum seekers (23,000).[13] In the United Kingdom in the mid-1990s, 68 percent of arriving migrants were family members (48,400) or asylum seekers (3,700).[14]

Migration Policy in the United States

Every year, some 800,000 to 1,000,000 people migrate to the United States legally, and another 300,000 to 400,000 (although no one knows definitively) slip in illegally, making the country the world's largest single receiver of immigrants. Despite this, the fact that the system is organized around family sponsorship means that it is exceedingly difficult for anyone without those ties to migrate to the United States. There is no equivalent to the Canadian points system, which allows individuals to migrate to Canada solely on the basis of their skills (although one is proposed, as discussed later in this section). The closest thing the United States has to a direct immigration channel is the lottery system, and the average applicant is likelier to gain admission to Harvard than win a lottery visa. As a result, would-be migrants either need family in the United States or must come to the United States through some nonmigrant legal channel and adjust their status later. The most common way for skilled migrants to do this is to obtain an H1-B visa granted to workers with a bachelor's degree or higher level of education. The annual number of H1-Bs is capped at 65,000 (it was temporarily raised to 195,000 during the technology boom), a figure that is remarkably low for the world's premier immigration country. The United Kingdom, a country one-fifth of the size of the United States, grants over 100,000 work permits per year, the majority of which go to high-skilled professionals. After six years, the employer of H1-B visa holders can apply to sponsor them for immigrant visas, but they have to seek certification from the U.S. Department of Labor that no American worker can fill the position. The task is time consuming, often lasting several years, and it tries the patience of the saintliest employers and visa holders.

---

[12] Martin, "U.S. Immigration."

[13] J. F. Hollifield, "France: Republicanism and the Limits of Immigration Control," in W. A. Cornelius, T. Tsuda, P. L. Martin and J. F. Hollifield, eds. *Controlling Immigration: A Global Perspective* (Stanford CA: Stanford University Press, 2005).

[14] Z. Layton-Henry, "Britain: From Immigration Control to Immigration Management," in Cornelius et al., *Controlling Immigration*.

The fact that only some 10 percent of immigrant visas are given to labor migrants has led some commentators to call for a reduction in family immigration. Harvard economist George Borjas in particular caused a stir when he attributed poor economic performance among recent migrants to excessive arrivals from developing countries such as Mexico.[15] He argues that the appeal of a particular country for a would-be migrant is a function of the migrant's skills, the financial incentive structure of the country of origin, and the financial incentive structure of the home country. The highly skilled have an incentive to migrate from countries with high, progressive tax regimes (such as the Scandinavian countries, France, Germany, and Austria) to the United States, where their skills provide much higher returns. By contrast, they will have an incentive to remain in developing countries, where the tax system and inequality make these returns higher than they are in the United States (it is common for a member of Pakistan or India's much smaller middle class to have a larger house, a driver, and servants). The reverse is true for the unskilled: They will have an incentive to remain in Europe, where the rewards to skill are lower, and an incentive to migrate from developing countries to the United States. The United States thus faces two potential migration schemes: the skilled from Europe, and the unskilled from the developing world. Its immigration policies block the former while encouraging the latter. Because of the limited entry opportunities for skilled migrants, few come, whereas the ample opportunities (legal and illegal) for unskilled migration have predictable consequences: They arrive yearly in the hundreds of thousands.

To change this situation, Borjas recommends expanding skilled migration and limiting family migration. His model is Canada, whose point system, he argues, is a national quota system in everything but name. The recommendation has much intellectual and political support, but it is exceedingly difficult to implement. In an important piece, Gary Freeman explained why. Migration policy in the United States, he concluded, is dominated by clientelistic politics in which benefits are concentrated (on the employer and the immigrant) and the costs (for roads, health care, pensions, and so on) diffuse.[16] Added to this is the fragmented nature of the U.S. party system, which renders Congress highly porous to interest group pressure, and where organized migrant, business, and ethnic lobbies are able to exercise

---

[15] George Borjas, *Heaven's Door: Immigration Policy and the American Economy* (Princeton: Princeton University Press, 1999).

[16] Gary Freeman and James Jupp, eds., *Nations of Immigrants* (Oxford: Oxford University Press, 2003).

disproportionate influence. Public opinion remains hostile to immigration, but the anti-immigration interest groups through which this hostility is channeled are poorly resourced relative to business groups, and they face the limiting affects of the antipopulist norm – the postwar, post-Holocaust delegitimization of arguments against multicultural diversity and in favor of an ethnic homogeneity. One can also point to immigration's distributional effects. The federal government is a net winner through taxes, and the states, which have to pay for most infrastructure and social services used by immigrants, are net losers. Immigration policy is made by Congress, not the states.

The result is that immigration policy in the United States has a structural tendency to being modestly expansive. In passing the 1990 immigration reform, Congress began with the intention of reducing family migration while expanding skilled migration, but was only able to increase skilled migration by considerably expanding all categories of migration, particularly family reunification.

Immigration Policy since 2000

Following September 11, 2001, there was much talk about how terrorism would transform immigration policy. Conferences were organized around the issue, and liberal academics fretted about conservatives' supposed draconian intentions. In fact, it is difficult to identify a single immigration measure that can be directly related back to 9/11. On both continents, economic demands drove immigration policy. In the United States, the cap of 65,000 per year on H1-B visas proved, particularly in the heady days of the technology boom, inadequate. Following pressure from the business lobby, Congress raised it to 115,000, and then again to 195,000.[17] In 2004, implementing a decision taken before the terrorist attacks, the figure fell back to 65,000, prompting another round of complaints from the business community. Until recently, the terrorist attacks' most noticeable effect in this area seemed to be keeping something from happening, namely Karl Rove's dream of moving Latino voters into the Republican column by instituting legalization and guestworker schemes for Mexican workers. Policy now appears to be moving in this direction, although it is driven by the White House and Democrats rather than Congressional Republicans. At the time of writing (June 2007), a comprehensive immigration bill is before the U.S. Senate. It has three components: a legalization program for anyone living in the United States before 2007; a temporary guestworker program (for between

[17] Martin, "U.S. Immigration," p. 57.

two hundred thousand and four hundred thousand people a year) for low-skilled workers; and the replacement of extended family migrants' right to enter the United States with a points system. If the bill succeeds, it will represent a massive shift in U.S. immigration policy. It remains an open question, however, whether the bill will survive the aforementioned institutional constraints.

The effects of 9/11 were indirect and secondary. The first was institutional. From 1940, border control and immigration had been managed by the Immigration and Naturalization Service (INS), located within the Department of Justice. The organization had few friends. Conservatives saw it as a profligate and incompetent bureaucracy; liberals viewed it as inhumane and dogmatic. The INS signed its own death warrant in February 2002, when it issued student visa extensions for two of the dead 9/11 hijackers, and in 2003 the Department of Homeland Security took over all border-control and immigration functions.

The second concerned internal controls. Since the attacks, Congress has substantially expanded state power over aliens in and citizens of the United States. Its first post-9/11 act was passing the "Uniting and Strengthening America by Providing Appropriate Tools Required to Intercept and Obstruct Terrorism Act of 2001" – a mouthful of a title elaborated to produce the acronym USA PATRIOT Act.[18] The legislation broadened grounds for deportation, expanded the government's powers to tap phone and Internet communication and to access private data (including health and financial records), allowed the Justice Department to investigate criminal behavior by citizens and residents without probable cause, and tripled the number of U.S. border control personnel, customs personnel, and immigration inspectors along the northern border. The State Department, immediately after the attacks, subjected male visa applicants from twenty-six Middle Eastern nations to particular scrutiny, and referred the applications to Washington for final approval. Finally, in late 2001, the Department of Justice launched a controversial roundup of foreign Muslims in the United States. They were subject to questioning and, at the Justice Department's discretion, indefinite detention. The latter led to a lengthy battle between the courts and the Justice Department, and the effort proved largely ineffective. Because of the broader absence of systematic internal controls in the United States (such as identity cards and mandatory registration of addresses), it was easy for foreign visitors to avoid detection and many simply disappeared. In spring of 2002, the

---

[18] Aristide Zolberg, "Visitors, Immigrants, and U.S. Border Security after September 11, 2001," in Gibney and Hansen, *Immigration and Asylum*.

Justice Department admitted that it could find relatively few of 5,000 young Muslim foreign visitors it intended to question, and that not one of the 762 individuals it detained was deemed a terrorist.[19]

In Europe, the consequences of the attacks for immigration policy have been similarly unremarkable, despite the fact that three of the September 11 bombers were members of a Hamburg terrorist cell. In particular, the attacks had no influence on a trend toward more open immigration policy, particularly for skilled immigrants. From 1997, the United Kingdom increased the number of work permits it issued, doubling from some fifty thousand to over one hundred thousand within a few years, and in 2002 it introduced the High Skilled Migrant Programme (HSMP). Under the program, the British interior ministry (the Home Office) awards applicants points for age, education, skills, and profession, and if they receive a sufficient number of points, they are granted a renewable temporary residence permit. In March 2006, the British Parliament considered an immigration bill that would subsume all migration programs, including the HSMP and the work permit scheme, under a single, four-tiered points system. Both the (traditionally pro-migrant) Liberal Democratic and (traditionally antimigrant) Labour parties express public support for immigration.

In 2002, Germany drafted a comprehensive immigration bill that provided for the first time channels for permanent labor migration to Germany. Under it, highly qualified personnel with a job offer in Germany can apply for a combined work and permanent residence permit. The new law, which took effect January 1, 2005, extends work permits to spouses. The interior minister at the time, Otto Schily, also called for a points system for selecting migrants without jobs in Germany, but one has yet to be created.

Countries elsewhere in Europe have followed this expansionist trend. In early 2005, Spain adopted a legalization program (following early programs in 1986, 1991, 1996, and 2000–1) for hundreds of thousands of clandestine migrants resident in the country. Some seven hundred thousand people applied by the deadline. At the same time, the government created a catalogue of high-demand jobs – truck driving, catering, domestic labor, and restaurant staff – for which employment visas are easily obtainable. The program is notable in that it explicitly and publicly targeted unskilled workers. Previous immigration reforms in Europe (such as Germany's) have targeted skilled workers.

In some cases, the numbers have been unimpressive – both the British High Skilled Migrant Programme and (particularly) Germany's immigration

---

[19] Ibid., p. 675.

law have had low take-up rates, but the direction of policy change is clear and significant. After two decades of expressing opposition to immigration, European governments have embraced it as inevitable and, overall, desirable.

The shift has multiple causes, but the most important concerns the position of the European economy within the global market. Starting in 1995, American economic growth accelerated. It appeared for a time that the United States had managed to double its noninflationary growth rate, from an average of 2–2.5 percent common to most Organization for Economic Cooperation and Development (OECD) countries after the rise of the Organization of Petroleum Exporting Countries (OPEC) to (albeit briefly) one of 4–5 percent. The source of the new growth potential was said to be a productivity increase occasioned by new applications of information technology (IT).

The competition from the United States had two effects on Europe. First, the major European economies faced labor shortages in the IT sector; during the 2000 IT boom, Germany reported seventy-five thousand unfilled vacancies. Second, policy makers saw in the labor shortage one clear source of European sluggishness vis-à-vis the United States: the latter's immigration policy on H1-B visas for highly skilled workers, through which Indians, Koreans, Chinese, and (even) brain-drained Europeans had worked in the United States. The American shadow stood behind Germany's first attempt to attract skilled immigration: its policy of issuing twenty thousand visas for high-skilled, high-wage jobs, earning more than Euro 51,129 (DM 100,000) per year, which was dubbed misleadingly (because of its five-year contractual limit) the "green card" program. Importantly, Germany announced this policy during a time of high unemployment and continued opposition to new immigration.

The policy is also designed to address a demographic time bomb. In virtually all European countries, birthrates are below replacement levels: Italy's and Germany's rates are especially low, at approximately 1.2 and 1.3 births per woman, respectively. Certainly, migration alone will not address Europe's reproductive shortfall. If the number of births remains constant, then Germany would actually require a net total of six hundred thousand to seven hundred thousand migrants per year to make up the difference. By most measures, this figure is beyond Germany's integration capacity. But immigration can have the effect of rendering the depopulation process less difficult, and can affect the age structure in a manner that might cushion – particularly in the context of later retirement ages – government programs under pressure through an aging population.

As in the United States, the most important changes since 2001 have occurred in domestic policy. Here the continent has become something of the mirror image of what it was. Whereas from 1973 until the 1990s Europe treated old migrants with relative generosity while shutting out new migrants, since the 1990s Europe has become relatively open to new migrants while hardening its attitude and policy toward old ones. Following the events in New York and Washington, and particularly following terrorist attacks in Madrid and London, EU member states have expanded powers of detention and deportation. In Germany and the United Kingdom, high-profile radical Islamists have been arrested and deported. In the United Kingdom, the home secretary, shortly after 9/11, passed legislation giving the government the right to detain indefinitely terror suspects whom it could not deport. In 2004, the House of Lords ruled that indefinite detention violated the European Convention on Human Rights. In 2005, the government proposed to replace the provision with legislation allowing terrorists to be detained for ninety days without charge, but the proposal was defeated in the House of Commons.

The significant intellectual and policy shift in Europe has occurred in integration policy. Christian Joppke identifies four pillars of Europe's new integration framework:[20] inclusion (where inclusion is understood as a two-way process through which migrants and the receiving society changes); a respect for the basic liberal political values of the EU (with an attendant lowering of emphasis on cultural recognition and cultural diversity); work (employment is a fundamental part of the integration process); and language acquisition. The first pillar can be viewed as at least partially hyperbolic and rhetorical. As Joppke notes, the claim that integration, to use the words of official EU publications, "is a dynamic two-way process of mutual accommodation" requiring changes on the part of migrants and the host society

...has become a platitude, but one should not forget its extreme improbability. Ever since the transition from nomadic to settled life during the Neolithic Revolution, settled populations expected newcomers to adapt to their ways – when in Rome do as the Romans do. The idea that something as complex and massive as the receiving society should change in response to the arrival of numerically inferior migrants – who, as individuals, are ontologically different from a society – is unheard of. That a settled society *would* change as a result of migration is, of course, inevitable,

---

[20] Christian Joppke, "Immigrants and Civic Integration in Western Europe," in Keith Banting, Thomas J. Courchene, and F. Leslie Seidle, eds., *Art of the State*, vol. 3, *Belonging? Diversity, Recognition and Shared Citizenship in Canada* (Montreal: Institute for Research on Public Policy, 2007).

but elevating this to an ethnical maxim – a *should* – is an unprecedented stance to take.[21]

The last three principles can be thus viewed as the most important. Across Europe, a range of policies have been implemented that aim to increase migrants' and migrant children's ability to enter the labor market and to ensure their loyalty to basic liberal values. In the former, the third and fourth pillars – work and language – are mutually reinforcing. In a skills-based economy, mastery of the national language is basic to securing employment, and in Germany, Austria, and the Netherlands, there is evidence of poor, stagnating, and in some cases declining language competence among even established ethnic minority communities. Declining language competence is believed to result from marriages (often arranged) with individuals from the home country who do not speak the host society's language and reinforce a tendency to speak the sending country's language at home. A recent Dutch report on arranged marriages makes the claim that 70 percent of Turkish youngsters, 60 percent of Moroccan women, and 50 percent of Moroccan men marry someone from their home country.[22]

As a result, following the Netherlands' lead, Austria, Denmark, Finland, France, and Germany have all introduced obligatory or semi-obligatory (as in Germany) language courses that migrants must enter immediately upon entry (or in the case of the Netherlands, before entry), with a financial penalty or denial of permanent residence as a sanction for noncompliance.[23]

The "respect" or "loyalty" requirement has two variants. The first concerns potential citizens, who must attend integration courses and/or take tests before naturalizing. In the United Kingdom, candidates for naturalization must prove their language ability, write a test on British history, institutions, and society, and take an oath of allegiance. The language test was introduced in part because local officials noted that some of those naturalizing could not repeat the sentence-by-sentence oath and evidently did not understand what they were saying. In Germany, two states – Baden-Württemberg and Hesse – introduced citizenship tests (Germany's naturalization law is administered by the Länder), and Bavaria plans to follow suit. Most of the questions concern German institutions, history, society, and culture, but some apparently have Muslim migrants in mind. Baden-Württemberg's test asks about the applicant's views on forced marriage, homosexuality, and women's rights, and Hesse's test asks whether they believe in Israel's right to exist and a

[21] Ibid., p. 326.
[22] Ibid.
[23] Ibid.

woman's right to be allowed out of the home without the company of a male relative. The tests have been suspended pending court decisions on their constitutional validity.

The second concerns potential migrants, and requires them to take courses and/or write tests as a condition of their migration. In France, since 2003, 90 percent of new migrants sign a "contrat d'accueil et de l'intégration," requiring one day of civics instruction and, when deemed necessary, five hundred hours of language instruction. As most family migrants to France come from ex-colonies or Algeria, only one-third of migrants are enrolled in the language classes. In Germany, since 2004, new migrants (and, interestingly, ethnic Germans) take thirty hours of civics instruction and six hundred hours of language classes. In a typically German compromise between the hard-nosed right and the guilt-ridden left, the civics classes emphasize the multicultural and non-German nature of German culture (French baguettes, American music, Turkish pitas), and, although the courses are obligatory, there is no sanction for nonattendance. In the Netherlands, which embraced multiculturalism with an enthusiasm unparalleled in Europe and which is now rejecting it with equal enthusiasm, integration tests are compulsory for both new *and* settled immigrants. They cost 350 Euros, last one hour, and cover language, geography, and history. New migrants are subject to additional hurdles: Before even taking the full test, they have to pass a series of over-the-phone examinations with Dutch officials, which, if passed, permit them to take the full, written test at Dutch embassies. The preparation tests cost 63 Euros, and include a video showing two men kissing and a topless woman (scenes that were edited out of films for some, mostly Islamic, countries). Newcomers who fail to take the full test within five years are fined. Finally, family reunification now has a specific class basis: Those wishing to bring a spouse must be twenty-one and earn at least 120 percent of the minimum wage.

Integrating into What?

The previously identified patterns suggest two conclusions. First, there has been a convergence – in policy, if not in numbers – between Europe and the United States on maintaining or expanding immigration channels for skilled (and sometimes unskilled) migrants. Indeed, in purely formal, legal terms the United Kingdom and Germany are now countries of immigration to a greater degree than the United States; both provide direct channels for migrants with no family connections. These developments are driven by one factor common to both Europe and North America – the perceived need to attract skilled migrants to compete in the global economy – and one factor unique to Europe – the need to increase numbers to stave off a demographic crisis. In this policy area, Europe and the United States appear to be growing together rather than growing apart. Second, the effects of 9/11 and the events since have been concentrated on both continents in the domestic sphere, but in different areas. In the United States, legislators have sought to expand powers to detain, question, and deport suspected terrorists; to expand powers of surveillance; and to increase (or create the impression of increasing) their control over the country's borders. In Europe, policy makers have focused their efforts on individuals who are in many cases no longer immigrants: long-term residents. A series of measures, which commentators view as punitive (although they rarely offer alternatives), have been implemented with the goal of increasing residents' language skills and ensuring their loyalty to the host society and its values.

This combination of playing good cop – expanding immigration – and bad cop – demanding evidence of loyalty and integration – might appear contradictory, but it is not. It rather reflects a further basic difference between Europe and the United States' experience of immigration: Whereas the United States integrates migrants into work, Europe integrates them into welfare.[24] Table 6.1 provides data on ethnic minority/migrant unemployment rates in the two countries.

The results are striking.[25] In continental Europe, unemployment rates among immigrants are at best double that of the national average, and at worst over three times the national average. In North America, the gap is at most 1.3 percent. What's more, the lines move in opposite directions over time: The longer migrants are in Canada or the United States, the less likely they are to claim welfare benefits, whereas in Europe the reverse is true. Thus, the relative unemployment rate for foreigners in Europe – which includes

---

[24] I owe this phrase to Phil Martin.

[25] Most unemployment figures are from 1998. The OECD has not produced new data, and the difficulty of comparing national statistics prevents the culling of these data from national sources. Recent data on ethnic minority unemployment rates (which, of course, include migrants, permanent residents, and citizens) suggest that the gap has remained. Indeed, the relative unemployment rate between ethnic minorities and whites has been constant in periods of recession and periods of growth. See Randall Hansen, "Diversity, Integration and the Turn from Multiculturalism in the United Kingdom," in Keith Banting, Thomas J. Courchene, and F. Leslie Seidle, eds., *Art of the State: Belonging, Diversity, Recognition and Shared Citizenship in Canada* (Montreal: Institute for Research on Public Policy, 2007); Ruud Koopmans, "Tradeoffs between Equality and Difference: The Failure of Dutch Multiculturalism in Cross-National Perspective," paper presented at the conference on Immigrant Political Participation, Harvard University, April 22–23, 2005.

TABLE 6.1. *Relative Unemployment in Percentage of the Labor Force by Origin, 1995*

Country	Unemployment in % of Labor Force			Relative Unemployment Born Overseas/ Born in the Country
	Born in the Country	Born Overseas	Total	
Belgium	8.3	19.5	9.3	2.3
Canada[a]	10.1	10.2	10.2	1.0
Denmark	6.7	14.6	7.0	2.2
France	11.1	17.5	11.9	1.6
Germany[b]	7.5	15.0	8.2	2.0
Netherlands	6.0	19.6	7.2	3.3
Sweden	7.1	21.7	8.1	3.0
United Kingdom	8.4	12.6	8.7	1.5
United States[c]	6.2	7.8	6.3	1.3

[a] Data for Canada are from 1991.

[b] For Germany, data are not divided by place of birth but rather by "citizen" versus "non-citizen."

[c] Data for the United States are from 1990.

Source: International Migration Data, OECD.

both recent immigrants and long-term residents (and sometimes their children) – ranges from 2.2 percent in Germany and the United Kingdom to 5.4 percent in the Netherlands and Sweden.

What explains this difference? Europeans suggest that the migrants to North American have higher skills and more education. The data do not support this interpretation. Although there is a marked difference between the educational achievements of migrants to Canada and migrants to Europe (which is unsurprising given Canada's points system), the difference between migrants to the United States and those to Europe is small (see Table 6.2).

Thus, more immigrants to the United States have completed postsecondary education than immigrants to *some* European countries (France, Belgium, or Germany), but there are also more immigrants (twice as many as those in Sweden) who have not finished high school. Migrant educational levels are roughly similar between the United States and Europe.

The political left would argue that higher levels of social exclusion, racism, and Islamophobia in Europe prevent migrants from entering the labor market. Taking the lattermost first, racism no doubt plays a role, but it cannot explain why certain ethnic minorities – such as the Indians and the Chinese

TABLE 6.2. *Relative Level of Education of the Labor Force, 1995*

Country		Less than First Level of Secondary Education (%)	Completed Secondary Education (%)	Completed Tertiary Education (%)	Other (%)
		Relative Level of Education			
Belgium	Born in country	33.2	36.5	30.3	—
	Born overseas	41.2	32.1	26.7	—
Canada[a]	Born in country	3.3	34.6	62.1	—
	Born overseas	7.1	27.3	65.6	—
Denmark	Born in country	14.7	54.5	30.8	—
	Born overseas	22.2	39.1	38.7	—
France	Born in country	30.5	47.8	21.7	—
	Born overseas	47.4	30.9	21.7	—
Germany[b]	Born in country	9.9	60.4	26.1	3.6
	Born overseas	39.5	39.8	15.0	5.8
Netherlands	Born in country	13.6	60.0	26.0	0.4
	Born overseas	27.6	50.2	21.1	1.0
Sweden	Born in country	20.3	49.3	30.3	—
	Born overseas	22.9	42.5	33.8	—
United Kingdom	Born in country	40.5	34.2	25.1	0.2
	Born overseas	51.8	19.9	28.1	—
United States[c]	Born in country	23.0	31.1	45.9	—
	Born overseas	41.2	19.6	39.2	—

[a] Data for Canada are from 1991.
[b] For Germany, data are not divided by place of birth but rather by "citizen" versus "noncitizen."
[c] Data for the United States are from 1990 and calculations are based on figures for the population rather than labor force.
Source: International Migration Data, OECD.

in the United Kingdom – do as well if not better than the overall population. Racists are unlikely to distinguish between different groups of Asians. The same point applies to the currently fashionable concept of Islamophobia: It is doubtful that racists could differentiate Indian/Pakistani Hindus and Muslims in theory, or that they would want to in practice.

A more plausible explanation concerns the incentive structure faced by migrants and their children. Although the pro-migrant lobby – Proasyl in Germany, No One Is Illegal in the United Kingdom – often speak as if migrants are invariably hapless victims, they are in most cases willful and determined actors. Migrating is not easy; it requires considerable resources – financial and personal – and more often than not guile. Individuals have to leave friends and family; to educate themselves on the legal (or illegal) entry points to developed countries; and to raise funds for travel or, in the case of most illegal migrants, traffickers. They are, in short, rational actors who will respond to the incentives they face on arrival. In the United States, arriving migrants receive little or no social support, and have to rely on their own initiative and the support of their communities. In Europe, legal migrants are granted the full range of benefits – housing, health care, subsistence level social support – available to permanent residents and citizens. Much the same is true of illegal migrants. If they claim asylum, as any rational migrant will do, they are entitled to extensive, if not overly generous, social support, health care, and housing.

The result is that a legal migrant arriving in Europe will face the choice between, on the one hand, seeking a job in an often less-than-buoyant market and (because her qualifications will likely not be recognized) accepting a poorly paid and unrewarding position and, on the other, accepting comfortable, clean social housing and sufficient monthly support to eke out a living. The choice should be clear. In the United States, a legal migrant will face the choice between work and starvation. The choice should be equally clear, and it is borne out by the data in Table 6.2. Despite broadly similar educational levels, migrants to the United States work, and migrants to Europe do not. During the 2005 riots in Paris's suburbs and elsewhere, much was made of the social deprivation affecting these areas. What was not mentioned was that the standard of housing, welfare benefits, and public safety were all at a level far above that of American urban ghettos; what was as bad, if not worse, was unemployment, often reaching 40 percent.

The obvious solution for Europe would be a bit of tough love: Reduce or remove welfare benefits for migrants, and make it clear to them that that they are welcome, but that their welcome is contingent on their willingness to enter the labor market. In practice, the matter is much more complicated, for two reasons. First, many Europeans would view with repugnance the idea that migrants are told to work or starve. Second, and more importantly, courts' jurisprudence in Europe allows less for distinguishing between citizens and residents, and any effort to strip legal residents of social rights enjoyed by citizens might not survive a court challenge.[26] What this likely means is that a European government intent on rolling back migrant rights to social entitlements would have to embed this in a general rollback of welfare

[26] Yasmin Soysal, *The Limits of Citizenship* (Chicago: University of Chicago Press, 1994).

state provision. Such a reform effort would naturally face substantial social opposition.

Where does this leave Europe? In a bind. Due to the previously cited demographic developments, Europe will need substantially larger numbers of immigrants. Given intense international competition for skilled migrants and the greater attractions of the United States (the English language, lower taxes, and less regulation) for many skilled migrants, a substantial portion of these migrants will have to be unskilled. Yet in the absence of a substantial reform of social provision, European migration history risks repeating itself: low levels of employment, high levels of welfare dependency, and alienation among ethnic minority communities. Perhaps Europe's main hope lies in the fact that other pressures are pushing in this direction anyway. In France, Germany, and the United Kingdom, which collectively constitute almost two-thirds of Europe's total GDP, the pressures of international competition have led (in the case of the United Kingdom) or are leading (in the cases of France and Germany) to a loosening of the labor market and a reduction of social provision. The United Kingdom went down this road long ago, but France and Germany have more recently followed. In Germany, welfare benefits for the long-term unemployed have been reduced, and welfare has in some cases been made conditional on work. In France, during the spring of 2006, the conservative government sought to ease restrictions on the firing of workers. It is unclear whether or not these efforts will ultimately succeed. If they do, these countries may be better prepared to cope with the sort of immigration levels viewed as normal in the United States. The corollary of this is, of course, that Europe may eventually look, in matters of social solidarity and economic inequality, more like the United States. Europe's current divergence in matters of work, welfare, and immigration may hold the causes of their ultimate convergence.

7

Lost in Translation

The Transatlantic Divide over Diplomacy

Daniel W. Drezner

Introduction

Asserting that Americans and Europeans have had different diplomatic styles since the turn of the century would be one of the easier calls in current affairs.[1] As Robert Kagan famously put it, "on major strategic and international questions today, Americans are from Mars and Europeans are from Venus."[2] Since George W. Bush came into office, the United States has rejected or stalled a plethora of international treaties, organizations, and understandings. In 2002, a Pew Global Attitudes survey found that pluralities in most of the nations surveyed complained about American unilateralism – and those attitudes have only hardened over time.[3] Richard Haass, Bush's first director of policy planning at the State Department, made it clear that unilateralism has been a significant component of Bush's foreign policy.[4] At the same time, the European Union has grown more assertive in calling for

---

[1] Some of the ideas expressed in this chapter previously appeared in *The New Republic* Online in February 2003, and were presented at Williams College in April 2003. I am grateful to Ralph Bradburd, Henry Farrell, Jeffrey Kopstein, Jacob Levy, James McAllister, Gideon Rose, Noam Scheiber, Sven Steinmo, Steven Teles, and especially Mark Blyth for their feedback. I am grateful to Craig Kennedy and the German Marshall Fund of the United States for their financial support during the drafting of this chapter.
[2] Robert Kagan, "Power and Weakness," *Policy Review*, no. 113, June 2002.
[3] For 2002 attitudes, see Pew Research Center, "What the World Thinks in 2002," December 2002, available online at http://people-press.org/reports/display.php3?ReportID=165. For the hardening of public opinion, see Pew Research Center, "Islamic Extremism: Common Concern for Muslim and Western Publics," July 2005, available online at http://pewglobal.org/reports/display.php?ReportID=248; Andrew Kohut and Bruce Stokes, *America against the World: How We Are Different and Why We Are Disliked* (New York: Times Books, 2006).
[4] Richard Haass, "The Case for 'Integration,'" *National Interest*, no. 81. Fall 2005, pp. 22–9.

law-based forms of global governance, all the while expanding its own membership beyond the northwest portion of the continent. On issues ranging from nonproliferation to war crimes to genetically modified foods to competition policy, the EU and its member states have relentlessly pushed for the principle of multilateralism to regulate world affairs.

Wrapped up in this transatlantic divide is the general perception that the Bush administration has diverged from prior administrations in both foreign policy substance and style. On the substantive side, the United States appears to be walking away from international institutions of its own creation in order to pursue the foreign policy aims set forth in Bush's September 2002 National Security Strategy (NSS), the March 2006 follow-up NSS, and his second inaugural address.[5] With regard to style, the Bush administration's first term appeared at times to be an exercise in rudeness. Beyond Bush's coining of the "Axis of Evil," close allies such as Canada, Germany, Mexico, South Korea, and Turkey were on the receiving end of some sharp rhetoric from Bush administration officials. Fareed Zakaria concluded in 2003 that U.S. officials had "developed a language and diplomatic style that seemed calculated to offend the world."[6]

A closer look, however, reveals some discordant information beneath the surface. In reaction to the September 11 terrorist attacks, the Bush administration enlisted a healthy number of multilateral institutions, for example. In some international organizations, such as the World Trade Organization (WTO), it is the United States that has played good cop to the EU's bad cop. The United States has expended some political capital to bring China and India into the concert of great powers within the international financial institutions. As for diplomatic style, both George W. Bush *and* French President Jacques Chirac seemed plucked from central casting to substantiate the worst stereotypes about their respective countries. In the run-up to the second Gulf War, neither Chirac nor German Prime Minister Gerhard Schröder lacked for rudeness. Has there really been a transatlantic divide over diplomacy? If so, what is the cause?

This chapter argues that there is a transatlantic divide over the utility of international organizations – and diplomacy more generally. Contrary to public perceptions, however, this divide is not because the United States is reflexively unilateralist and EU members are always multilateralist. Rather,

---

[5] "National Security Strategy of the United States," September 2002, available online at http://www.whitehouse.gov/nsc/nssall.html. Second inaugural address is available online at http://www.whitehouse.gov/news/releases/2005/01/print/20050120-1.html.

[6] Fareed Zakaria, "The Arrogant Empire," *Newsweek*, March 24, 2003.

the fundamental transatlantic clash is about process more than outcome. For Americans, multilateralism is strictly a means to an end; for Europeans, multilateralism remains a desired end in itself. The Bush administration has taken the American view to its logical extreme – the difference in diplomatic style between this administration and the ones that preceded it is one of degree rather than kind. If world politics is a Prisoner's Dilemma, the Bush administration has chosen to pursue a "grim trigger" strategy to deal with it. This renders traditional diplomacy of little use – a fact that has caused its own backlash on the European continent.

Will this divergence over multilateralism persist? Many international relations commentators have argued that because of the growing divide in capabilities between the United States and EU, the answer is yes. However, there are reasons to believe that the long-term distribution of power, the medium-term distribution of threats, and the shared sense of social purpose on many issues will prevent a long-term rupture. The United States and Europe will always have issues to contest, but compared to the rest of the world, American and European interests coincide much more than they conflict.

The Costs and Benefits of Multilateralism

There are as many definitions of multilateralism as there are multilateral institutions.[7] For the purposes of this chapter, multilateralism is the diplomatic tactic of acting in concert with several countries under the aegis of an international regime, using previously agreed-upon rules and procedures for achieving policy coordination. International relations scholars and foreign policy analysts have debated the merits of multilateral institutions as long as the study of international relations has existed. This debate, however, has taken on a renewed sense of urgency with the Bush administration's ascent to power and the September 11 attacks.

From a great power's perspective, the relative pros and cons of multilateralism are straightforward.[8] On the plus side, multilateralism enhances both the material and nonmaterial incentives for promoting global governance. Materially, international organizations make it easier to monitor multilateral agreements. Beyond achieving a common policy position, multilateralism makes it easier for governments to reassure each other if or when

---

[7] See, for example, John Gerard Ruggie, ed., *Multilateralism Matters* (New York: Columbia University Press, 1993).

[8] For a nice contrast in takes, compare John Ikenberry, *After Victory* (Princeton: Princeton University Press, 200) with John J. Mearsheimer, *The Tragedy of Great Power Politics* (New York: W. W. Norton, 2001).

circumstances change. Multilateralism also facilitates the enforcement of global rules and regulations; sanctions imposed with the imprimatur of a multilateral institution are far more likely to succeed in obtaining compliance from the targeted country.[9] Beyond multilateralism's material effects, the logic of appropriateness also applies to international organizations by enhancing the legitimacy of foreign policy.[10] International organizations can foster a sense of legal obligation for states to comply with the promulgated set of rules.[11] The more countries that participate in a multilateral enterprise, the greater the normative desire of all countries to avoid belonging in the "out group."[12] Ideally, multilateralism can "lock in" what great powers want to do in the first place.[13]

The drawbacks of multilateralism for the great powers are equally clear.[14] First and foremost, there is the possibility that multilateral agreements will create a false sense of security. The history of international law suggests that states will choose to defect from international agreements when such action is conducive to their interests.[15] If a state believes that multilateralism will compel cooperation when it doesn't, then that state could be in for a rude surprise in the future.[16] For example, both the United States and the International Atomic Energy Agency (IAEA) were surprised, following the end of the first Gulf War, just how far Iraq had proceeded with its nuclear weapons program despite being an IAEA member and a signatory to the Nuclear Nonproliferation Treaty. Iran's twenty-year clandestine nuclear program under the same strictures is a cause for even greater concern.

---

[9] Daniel W. Drezner, "Bargaining, Enforcement, and Multilateral Economic Sanctions: When Is Cooperation Counterproductive?" *International Organization*, no. 54, Winter 2000, pp. 73–102.

[10] James March and Johan Olsen, "The Institutional Dynamics of International Political Orders," *International Organization*, no. 52, Autumn 1998, pp. 943–69.

[11] Kenneth Abbott and Duncan Snidal, "Why States Act through Formal International Organizations," *Journal of Conflict Resolution*, no. 42, February 1998, pp. 3–32; Kenneth Abbott et al., "The Concept of Legalization," *International Organization*, no. 54, Summer 2000, pp. 401–20; Kenneth Abbott and Duncan Snidal, "Hard and Soft Law in International Governance," *International Organization*, no. 54, Summer 2000, pp. 421–56.

[12] A. Iain Johnston, "The Social Effects of International Institutions on Domestic (Foreign Policy) Actors," in Daniel W. Drezner, ed., *Locating the Proper Authorities* (Ann Arbor: University of Michigan Press, 2003).

[13] Ikenberry, *After Victory*.

[14] Stephen Brooks and William Wohlforth, "International Relations Theory and the Case against Multilateralism," *Perspectives on Politics*, no. 3, September 2005, pp. 509–24.

[15] Jack Goldsmith and Eric Posner, *The Limits of International Law* (New York: Oxford University Press, 2005).

[16] John J. Mearsheimer, "The False Promise of International Institutions," *International Security*, no. 19, Winter 1994/95, pp. 5–49.

Even if multilateral agreements do lead to effective outcomes, they can also be cumbersome and time-consuming to negotiate. Obviously, the greater the number of voices that need to be heard, the tougher it becomes to foster a common position on anything. Prior research shows that superpowers expend considerable resources to attain multilateral cooperation. Great powers must bear considerable costs to convince other participants in multilateral bodies of their seriousness of intent.[17] Even if that is achieved, superpowers will often lose out on burden sharing because other states will free-ride off of them, enjoying the provision of public benefits without paying much for them.[18] Most significantly, great powers must be concerned that strict adherence to the principle of multilateralism will constrain their foreign policy actions. For the great powers, multilateralism can be like golf – a game in which strange rules and ill-fitting tools make it very difficult to achieve what would otherwise be a relatively simple task.

Reviewing the Record

Given the relative costs and benefits of multilateralism, did the Bush administration simply decide that the costs always outweighed the benefits? It is easy to make the argument that the United States veered toward unilateralism after 2001. Within its first six months, the Bush administration abruptly pulled out of the Kyoto Protocol and the International Criminal Court (ICC), and announced its intention to pull out of the Anti-Ballistic Missile (ABM) Treaty. On a host of other issues, ranging from the United Nations Conference on Racism to the OECD effort to combat harmful tax practices, the administration altered its position at the cost of international comity. The United States invaded Iraq without explicit authorization from the United Nations Security Council, imposed steel tariffs that violated WTO trade rules, and signed a civilian nuclear deal with India that violated the nonproliferation norm. What more evidence is needed to demonstrate the Bush administration's disregard for multilateral initiatives?

The problem is that when you parse actions from rhetoric, this administration has pursued a reasonably multilateralist foreign policy since the September 11 attacks. To some extent, American foreign policy in recent years needs to be watched like a television set put on mute – subtract the

---

[17] Lisa Martin, *Coercive Cooperation* (Princeton: Princeton University Press, 1992).

[18] Mancur Olson and Richard Zeckhauser, "An Economic Theory of Alliances," *Review of Economics and Statistics*, no. 33, August 1966, pp. 266–79; Todd Sandler and Keith Hartley, "Economics of Alliances: The Lessons for Collective Action," *Journal of Economic Literature*, no. 39, September 2001, pp. 869–96.

rhetoric, and the administration's foreign policy looks much less belligerent than it sounds.

The immediate reaction to the terrorist attacks was besotted with multilateral institutions. U.S. military operations in Afghanistan took place with the full blessing of both NATO and the United Nations Security Council. As of this writing, there are more non-American than American troops engaged in Afghan peacekeeping, under the explicit aegis of NATO and the Security Council. The administration's immediate reaction to combating terrorist financing was to strengthen the role of the relevant international bodies – the Financial Action Task Force, the Egmont Group, and the International Monetary Fund.[19]

In its foreign economic policy, the administration has played the part of responsible hegemon whereas the European Union has been the petulant protectionist. Yes, the steel tariffs imposed by the Bush administration in 2002 were problematic, as was the increase in farm subsidies. One can argue, however, that these steps were temporary and necessary evils to secure Congressional backing for trade promotion authority (and pale in comparison to the extent of EU protectionism on agricultural subsidies).[20] The United States took the lead in jump-starting the latest round of WTO talks at Doha, and made early concessions on intellectual property rights in order to secure buy-in from the developing world. On both agricultural and manufacturing barriers, the U.S. trade negotiators demonstrated a willingness to liberalize that made their European counterparts blanch. The Bush administration also complied quickly with the WTO ruling against the steel tariffs. The Doha round might be stalemated – but this is largely due to disagreements between the European Union and the advanced developing countries.[21] The United States has also pushed for more regional free-trade agreements. The Central American Free Trade Agreement has been ratified, the Middle Eastern Free Trade Area has been proposed, and negotiations are ongoing or pending with Southern Africa and Latin America.

Critics would point to the 2002 NSS, with its discussion of preemption and a desire to prevent a peer competitor from challenging U.S. hegemony. Even

[19] Council on Foreign Relations, *Terrorist Financing* (New York: CFR, 2002).

[20] C. Fred Bergsten, "A Renaissance for U.S. Trade Policy?" *Foreign Affairs*, no. 81, November/December 2002; Arvind Panagariya, "Liberalizing Agriculture," *Foreign Affairs*, Special Edition, December 2005, pp. 56–66; Dan Morgan, Sarah Cohen, and Gilbert M. Gaul, "Powerful Interests Ally to Restructure Agriculture Subsidies," *Washington Post*, December 22, 2006.

[21] Daniel W. Drezner, *U.S. Trade Strategy: Free versus Fair* (New York: Council on Foreign Relations Press, 2006).

in that discussion, however, there is a pledge to "coordinate closely with our allies to form a common assessment of the most dangerous threats." Then, in the introduction, there is this: "The United States is committed to lasting institutions like the United Nations, the World Trade Organization, the Organization of American States, and NATO as well as other long-standing alliances." John Lewis Gaddis concluded, "the Bush NSS comes across as more forceful, more carefully crafted, and – unexpectedly – more multilateral than its immediate predecessor."[22]

The administration's post-NSS strategy on nuclear nonproliferation has also been more multilateral. The follow-up document to the 2002 NSS – the December 2002 National Strategy to Combat Weapons of Mass Destruction – had more multilateral language than the NSS itself.[23] The administration's rationale for preemption was the nexus between weapons of mass destruction (WMD) proliferation and terrorism, so one would have expected an extended discussion of this doctrine. But the section in the December document on strengthening nonproliferation emphasized the key roles of bilateral diplomacy, strengthening existing multilateral regimes, and even negotiating new ones. There is no substantive focus on preemption. Since the articulation of that document, the administration has invested considerable effort in jump-starting the Proliferation Security Initiative, a club of states committed to interdicting WMD materials.

As for the world's other trouble spots, the post-9/11 approach has also been multilateral. In the Balkans, the United States consistently deferred to the European Union on policy matters. Washington agreed to threaten aid sanctions against Yugoslavia unless Slobodan Milosevic was extradited to the Hague, and was also willing to let the Europeans take the lead on peacekeeping operations in Macedonia. In the Middle East, the United States willingly participated in policy coordination with the quartet – the United States, EU, Russia, and the United Nations.

For the best test of whether the Bush administration has acted unilaterally, perhaps we should examine its policy toward the three countries identified as the "Axis of Evil" in Bush's 2002 State of the Union speech. In all three cases, the administration acted more multilaterally than perceptions suggest. In the case of Iran, for example, the administration agreed in the fall of 2004 to let the "EU-3" – Great Britain, France, and Germany – take the lead in negotiating with Tehran on that country's alleged WMD program. At every

---

[22] John Lewis Gaddis, "A Grand Strategy of Transformation," *Foreign Policy*, no. 133, November/December 2002.

[23] White House, "National Strategy to Combat Weapons of Mass Destruction," December 2002, available online at http://www.whitehouse.gov/news/releases/2002/12/WMDStrategy. pdf.

stage of the process to date, the administration has worked within the IAEA and United Nations Security Council to maximize support for convincing Iran to comply. The diplomatic result as of this writing was two unanimous Security Council resolutions that imposed multilateral sanctions against Iran.

With North Korea, the Bush administration found itself in the odd position of cajoling both allies (Japan and South Korea) as well as rivals (China and Russia) to approach the problem in a multilateral fashion. Most of these countries would prefer to have the United States alone deal with North Korea, but the United States prefers ensuring that all of North Korea's principal trade and foreign policy partners remain on the same negotiating page. In February 2003, Defense Secretary Donald Rumsfeld had to buttonhole his Russian counterpart on the importance of using the IAEA to help defuse the North Korean crisis.[24] By 2006, North Korea's intransigency led to a unanimous UN Security Council resolution imposing sanctions against Pyongyang – paving the way for a tentative February 2007 agreement at the Six-Party Talks for North Korea to relinquish its nuclear program.

Then there's Iraq. For all of the bluster about Bush's unilateralism, the administration went through the UN Security Council at every step in the bargaining process, even though the Council hardly acted like a rubber stamp on the issue.[25] At the core of Bush's September 2002 UN address was that action against Iraq was necessary to restore the credibility of the United Nations; this was also the essence of Rumsfeld's controversial speech in Munich in February 2003. Jonathan Rauch, summarizing the postinvasion state of affairs in November 2003, reached a similar conclusion:

Obviously much of the world opposed the U.S. invasion of Iraq, but to speak of America as isolated or Bush as unilateralist seems an exaggeration, to be charitable. The administration tried hard to get the Security Council to put teeth in its own resolutions against Saddam Hussein. It went to the council not once but twice, when unilateralists said the right number of times was zero. It received support from dozens of countries, including some European biggies (Britain, Spain, Italy, Poland). It sought and obtained the Security Council's blessing for the occupation. It received $13 billion in reconstruction pledges from many countries. It is getting help from 24,000 foreign troops in Iraq, most of them British and Polish, but with support from more than 30 countries.[26]

Reviewing the record, the one issue area where the Bush administration consistently acted in an unconditionally unilateral manner relates to

---

[24] United States Embassy to Italy, "Background Briefing on Rumsfeld Meetings in Munich," February 2003, available online at http://www.usembassy.it/file2003_02/alia/a3021003.htm.

[25] It is true that the administration did not want to go back to the Security Council in early 2003, but it agreed to do so to help out the leader of a vital ally, Great Britain's Tony Blair.

[26] Jonathan Rauch, "Bush Is No Cowboy," *Reason*, November 2004.

warfighting. The administration adamantly opposed the ICC, largely to protect U.S. soldiers against politically inspired prosecutions.[27] Allied countries participated in the invasions of Iraq and Afghanistan, but the United States was at best indifferent to their support. In large part, this was the hangover from the 1999 NATO bombing campaign in Kosovo. Military experts across the board observed a discernible gap between American and European forces over issues ranging from technological sophistication to combat readiness. On this issue, the Bush administration clearly believed that the freedom of action from acting unilaterally outweighed any benefit of military multilateralism.

Overall, the United States can be accused of threatening to act in a unilateral manner if it doesn't get most of what it wants through multilateral institutions. And as any international relations scholar will attest, this is pretty much how all great powers have acted since the invention of multilateral institutions.

Crossing the Atlantic, there is no question that European leaders have repeatedly preached the virtues of multilateralism in the face of American *"hyperpuissance."* However, other actions and declarations by European officials do call the sincerity of these claims into question. Schröder rescued his electoral prospects in August 2002 by explicitly declaring that Germany would not support an invasion of Iraq *regardless of how the UN Security Council acted*. Chirac blasted the eastern European governments that were signatories to statements supporting the U.S. position on Iraq. In his immortal words, "they missed a great opportunity to shut up."[28] France's defense minister at the time went further, stating explicitly, "We could have expected that the countries that want to join [the EU] strike up a cautious position."[29] France and Germany, along with Belgium, also tried to block NATO from moving military material to Turkey to defend that country's borders in case it was attacked by Iraq – angering the other members of NATO.[30] On the trade front, the EU's agricultural commissioner blasted developing country demands prior to the 2003 Cancun Ministerial, declaring, "If they want to do business, they should come back to mother earth."[31] In 2005, Chirac helped

---

[27] Even here, however, the United States modified its intransigent opposition to give the ICC jurisdiction over possible war crimes in Darfur.

[28] Quoted in "Chirac Blasts EU Candidates," BBC News, February 18, 2003.

[29] Quoted in Ambrose Evans-Pritchard, Kate Connolly, and Matthew Day, "Eastern Europe Rounds on Paris," *Daily Telegraph*, February 19, 2003.

[30] "NATO Crisis over Veto on Plans to Defend Turkey," *Guardian*, February 11, 2003.

[31] Andrew Osborn, "EU Farm Chief Slams Poor Nations' Demands," *Guardian*, September 5, 2003.

sabotage his country's bid for the 2012 Summer Olympics after his anti-British and anti-Finnish comments were published the day before International Olympic Committee voting.[32] Europe has certainly not acted in a consistently unilateral manner – but European leaders have had their moments of pique.

The Diplomacy of the "Grim Trigger"

Why does the Bush administration receive no credit for its multilateralism? To explain this, we need to take a little detour into game theory and familiarize ourselves with the mysteries of the Prisoner's Dilemma and the grim trigger.

Scholars of international relations think of world politics as a variation of the Prisoner's Dilemma (PD).[33] PD participants face a simple choice: Cooperate or Defect with each other. The fundamental attribute of the Prisoner's Dilemma game is that all players are better off with an outcome of mutual cooperation than mutual defection, but each player is best off defecting when everyone else is cooperating. If the PD game is played only once, the dominant strategy is always to defect. When played repeatedly, there are a plethora of equilibrium strategies, which can lead to outcomes of repeated cooperation, repeated defection, or a combination of both.[34] The ones that yield the results with the greatest combined payoffs start with cooperation while demonstrating a willingness to defect if other players cheat.

The key variable in these strategies is how much to punish other players who decide to defect. A tit-for-tat strategy, for example, punishes one-time defections with corresponding one-time defections. Tit-for-two-tats strategy is more forgiving; punishment takes place only when another player defects twice in a row. The grim trigger is the *ne plus ultra* of punishment strategies. A player who uses the grim trigger starts out cooperating. If another player cheats at any point, however, then the punishment is infinite – that is, the player will refuse to cooperate for the rest of the game. There is no give to the grim trigger – once the punishment starts, it never stops. Compared to other strategies, the grim trigger employs the biggest stick in its punishment stage.

---

[32] Andrew Fraser, "Chirac Gives Voters Food for Thought," BBC Sports, July 5, 2005; Steven Downes, "Athletics Chief 'Switched from Paris to London,'" *London Times*, July 6, 2005.

[33] For a fuller explanation, see Robert Axelrod, *The Evolution of Cooperation* (New York: Basic Books, 1984).

[34] Drew Fudenberg and Eric Maskin, "The Folk Theorem in Repeated Games with Discounting or with Incomplete Information," *Econometrica*, no. 54, May 1986, pp. 533–54.

Thinking in terms of foreign policy, the principal advantage to the grim trigger is that it can compel a larger class of governments into cooperating than other strategies.[35] Because the punishment associated with the grim trigger is so great, rational governments that would not be deterred by a simple tit-for-tat punishment would find an incentive to cooperate when interacting with a grim trigger government. The key, of course, is that these governments decide to cooperate *before* the grim trigger is actually pulled; it's the *threat* of punishment that compels cooperation.

A reputation for resolve is a necessary condition for the grim trigger to work properly. Because the strategy imposes costs on the government that plays it as well as everyone else, governments with an incentive to defect must believe that the country in question will actually execute the strategy properly. If there is doubt in other players' minds, then the utility of this strategy declines dramatically.

Game theory is, of course, theoretical; what would the diplomacy of the grim trigger look like in practice? It would require a government to announce publicly in advance what it viewed as examples of noncooperative behavior, and to state repeatedly that such actions would meet with the gravest of retaliations. Such a government will commit to multilateral initiatives only if these institutions follow through on their commitments – and punish those states that choose to renege. Because of the importance of reputation, a grim trigger approach has little room for hypocrisy; a government would need to do what it said to ensure that its reputation for resolve remains intact.

Most important, the actual practice of diplomacy would be of little use to a grim trigger government beyond the issuance of ultimatums. If diplomacy consists of the private conveyance of information, consultation in the interest of coordinating policy, or an indication of a willingness to alter negotiation terms, it serves little purpose in advancing the grim trigger. Indeed, normal diplomacy and bargaining would actually be counterproductive, because that would signal a flexibility that no grim trigger state would want to broadcast.

The last few paragraphs bear more than a passing resemblance to the Bush administration's foreign policy in the early part of this decade. Seen through the lens of the Prisoner's Dilemma, the style and substance of the Bush administration's approach to multilateralism bears a remarkable similarity to the grim trigger. Because of the importance of reputation, the American view

---

[35] Formally, a class of actors with a shorter shadow of the future will cooperate against the grim trigger but would choose to defect against tit-for-tat strategies.

of multilateralism differs from most other countries. For the United States, multilateralism serves only as a means to an end. The 2002 National Security Strategy explicitly stated: "In all cases, international obligations are to be taken seriously. They are not to be undertaken symbolically to rally support for an ideal without furthering its attainment." The March 2006 NSS reinforced this point: "The potential for great power consensus presents the United States with an extraordinary opportunity.... Where existing institutions can be reformed to meet new challenges, we, along with our partners, must reform them. Where appropriate institutions do not exist, we, along with our partners, must create them."[36] This administration is consistent on this point – when multilateral rules are broken, be they IMF lending agreements or UN Security Council resolutions, the United States will use the necessary means to enforce the norms underlying those multilateral institutions. Multilateral institutions that fail to enforce their own norms – such as the UN – end up becoming the object of scorn. The Bush administration gives greater deference to those institutions that are seen as effective, such as the WTO. This does not mean that the Bush administration rejects multilateralism out of hand – but it does mean that it will engage in forum shopping when an international organization fails to follow through or appears to be dysfunctional. Most commonly, the administration has switched tracks from a formal international governmental organization with near-universal membership to a more informal club of like-minded states.[37] On nonproliferation, for example, the Bush administration has shown little interest in the recent review of the Nuclear Nonproliferation Treaty (NPT), because in the administration's eyes, the NPT is a failed regime. Instead, officials have voiced a willingness to shift nonproliferation responsibilities away from the near-universal membership of the NPT/IAEA and toward the G-8, the Nuclear Suppliers Group, the aforementioned Proliferation Security Initiative (PSI), or bilateral agreements with countries such as India.[38] The PSI in

---

[36] Executive Office of the President, *The National Security Strategy of the United States of America*, September 2002, p. vi, available online at http://www.whitehouse.gov/nsc/nss.pdf; Executive Office of the President, *The National Security Strategy of the United States of America*, March 2006, p. 36, available online at http://www.whitehouse.gov/nsc/nss/2006/nss2006.pdf.

[37] For more on this phenomenon, see Daniel W. Drezner, *All Politics Is Global: Explaining International Regulatory Regimes* (Princeton: Princeton University Press, 2007); idem, "The New New World Order," *Foreign Affairs*, no. 86, March/April 2007, pp. 34–46.

[38] David Sanger, "Months of Talks Fails to Bolster Nuclear Treaty," *New York Times*, May 28, 2005, p. A1; James Cotton, "The Proliferation Security Initiative and North Korea: Legality and Limitations of a Coalition Strategy," *Security Dialogue*, no. 36, June 2005, pp. 193–211.

particular played a crucial supporting role in convincing Libya to renounce its nuclear aspirations.[39] On global warming, the United States withdrew from the Kyoto Protocol, objecting to the unfair distribution of costs and the lack of enforcement measures.[40] In July 2005, the United States launched the Asian Pacific Partnership for Clean Development and Climate with Australia, China, India, Japan, and South Korea. Press reports intimated that its creators believed the arrangement to be an improvement over the Kyoto Protocol.[41]

This approach also helps to explain some of the administration's bilateral approaches as well. For example, the administration evinced a willingness to cooperate with the Palestinian Authority (PA) under Yassir Arafat – until a cargo ship laden with PA-purchased weapons from Iran was uncovered in January 2002.[42] From that point on, the United States refused to cooperate with Arafat and refused to condemn Israel for any actions it took in the occupied territories. It took Arafat's death for the Bush administration to reengage the Palestinians. Clearly, the grim trigger had been pulled. The United States acted in a similar fashion in response to Hezbollah's rocket attacks on Israel in the spring of 2006. Rather than treat Hezbollah as an entrenched actor that required some kind of engagement, the Bush administration chose to ignore it and stand resolutely by Israel.

One can argue that this strategy has yielded cooperative outcomes that would not have happened using another strategy. Game theory would predict that the grim trigger yields results with states reluctant to cooperate when faced with less threatening diplomatic practices. Pakistan has provided significant levels of cooperation since the September 11 terrorist attacks, despite the domestic unpopularity this brought President Pervez Musharraf. In part, Pakistani cooperation has been due to the clear U.S. message of the costs of noncooperation. In his memoirs, Musharraf said the Bush administration made it clear to him that punishment for noncooperation would be severe.[43]

---

[39] Robin Wright, "Ship Incident May Have Swayed Libya," *Washington Post*, January 1, 2004, p. A18.

[40] Scott Barrett, "The Political Economy of the Kyoto Protocol," *Oxford Review of Economic Policy*, vol. 14, no. 4, 1998, pp. 20–39; John Heilprin, "Bush Advisers Say Withdrawal from Climate Treaty Aids Economy," *Boston Globe*, July 12, 2002.

[41] Quoted in Richard Lloyd Parry, "We Will Find a Cleaner Way, Say World's Big Polluters," *London Times*, July 29, 2005.

[42] Todd Purdum, "President Assails Palestinian Chief on Arms Shipment," *New York Times*, January 26, 2002.

[43] Pervez Musharraf, *In the Line of Fire: A Memoir* (New York: Free Press, 2006).

Similarly, Libya has renounced its WMD aspirations and agreed to cooperate with the United States. Libya's leader, Muammar Ghadhafi, articulated a link between his decision and Bush's decision to invade Iraq.[44] Despite arguments about the administration's foreign policy causing blowback among Muslims, public opinion surveys also demonstrate a decline in public support in the Middle East for suicide bombings.[45] There is evidence that in the spring of 2003, when Operation Iraqi Freedom appeared to be a success, Iran sent out diplomatic feelers to negotiate a "grand bargain" with the United States about a variety of issues.[46]

There are, however, significant downsides to the grim trigger strategy – many of which also crop up in any dissection of recent American foreign policy. For one thing, a grim trigger approach renders traditional diplomacy superfluous. The trademarks of traditional diplomacy are discretion, consultation, tact, and sensitivity to the position of others. The grim trigger strategy is its complete obverse. For the strategy to work, its practitioner must be blunt, unyielding, public, and, in essence, trigger-happy. Although such an approach might yield results from adversaries or potential adversaries, it can backfire when dealing with even mildly recalcitrant allies.

This helps to explain the Bush administration's abject failure at "gardening" – a term former secretary of state George Schultz used to describe the careful cultivation of allies through repeated, routinized consultations.[47] Gardening was a key part of Bush's foreign policy mantra as a candidate, but he did not implement it across the administration. During Bush's first term in office, allies (except for Tony Blair) routinely carped about being out of the loop when the United States makes foreign policy decisions. Face-to-face consultations between high-ranking U.S. officials and allies practically disappeared. Colin Powell was the least-traveled secretary of state in thirty years; Bush was the least-traveled president in forty years. In his first three years of office, Vice President Richard Cheney traveled abroad only once.[48] This led to some process-oriented mistakes, such as peremptorily withdrawing from the Kyoto Protocol without ever consulting with any European

---

[44] Patrick Tyler and James Risen, "Secret Diplomacy Won Libyan Pledge on Arms," *New York Times*, December 21, 2003. For a more nuanced take, see Bruce Jentleson and Christopher Whytock, "Who 'Won' Libya?" *International Security*, no. 30, Winter 2005/6, pp. 47–86.

[45] Pew Research Center, "Islamic Extremism."

[46] Floyd Leverett, "Iran: The Gulf between Us," *New York Times*, January 24, 2006.

[47] George Schultz, *Turmoil and Triumph* (New York: Simon and Schuster, 1993), p. 128.

[48] Zakaria, "The Arrogant Empire"; Glenn Kessler, "Powell Flies in the Face of Tradition," *Washington Post*, July 14, 2004.

allies. Even Bush administration officials acknowledged that they should have handled that episode with more grace.[49] Without gardening, a poorly worded utterance – a German justice minister comparing Bush to Hitler, or a U.S. defense secretary comparing Germany to Cuba – poured salt into deepening transatlantic wounds.

There are other drawbacks to this type of grand strategy. This strategic approach potentially overemphasizes the importance of reputation in international affairs. It remains an open theoretical question whether governments think about another country as having a single reputation for bargaining.[50] Even if this were the case, however, recent research suggests that a reputation for resolve may matter less in crisis diplomacy than a reputation for honesty.[51] Furthermore, the grim trigger cannot cope with the possibility of cross-issue linkages, because a concession in one arena of bargaining would be seen as a willingness to horse-trade. The inability to trade across issues also undermines a clear benefit of multilateralism, which is to allow for the kind of pork-barrel political exchanges that routinely take place in domestic legislatures.[52]

The final and most obvious problem with the grim trigger is the brittle nature of the strategy. The grim trigger never forgives and never forgets – any defection from another government triggers the eternal punishment phase. However, there can be many reasons for defection, and not all of them are intentionally designed to sour relations.[53] When Schröder declared that Germany would ignore even a Security Council mandate, his targeted audience for that message was domestic. Running for reelection, Schröder was willing to make statements and take positions that he knew he would have to walk back later. Sure enough, after he won, he backed away from his anti-American statements. However, for the United States, the grim trigger was essentially pulled, souring German–American relations for the rest of Schröder's term. The grim trigger can therefore lead to unnecessary

---

[49] Eric Pianin, "EPA Chief Lobbied on Warming before Bush's Emissions Switch," *Washington Post*, March 27, 2001.

[50] Brooks and Wohlforth, "International Relations Theory and the Case against Unilateralism"; George Downs and Michael Jones, "Reputation, Compliance and International Law," *Journal of Legal Studies*, no. 31, January 2002, pp. S95–S114.

[51] Anne Sartori, *Deterrence and Diplomacy* (Princeton: Princeton University Press, 2005).

[52] On this point, see Daniel W. Drezner, "The Trouble with Carrots: Transaction Costs, Conflict Expectations, and Economic Inducements." *Security Studies*, no. 9, Autumn 1999/Winter 2000, pp. 188–218.

[53] See Jonathan Mercer, "Reputation and International Relations," and Daniel W. Drezner, "The Cohesion of International Regimes," both presented at the 94th annual meeting of the American Political Science Association, Boston, September 1998.

diplomatic ruptures, whereas more permissive approaches are robust enough to cope with the occasional disagreement.

The Diplomacy of Communicative Action

Another obvious problem is the extent to which a grim trigger strategy clashes with the style of European diplomacy. The stereotype of European diplomacy is that multilateralism remains an end in itself.[54] Substantial disagreements are papered over with either vague communiques or a pledge to continue negotiations in the future. Put crudely, outright violation from international agreements is handled with a chorus of "Stop, or I'll say 'stop' again!"

This stereotype overlooks the mix of sincere and strategic components to European diplomacy. Among European international relations scholars, there is a strong belief that Habermasian discourse has the capacity to lead eventually to multilateral cooperation. Even when no agreement is achieved, communicative action can achieve a purpose. Thomas Risse explains:

Argumentative and deliberative behavior is as goal oriented as strategic interaction, but the goal is not to attain one's fixed preferences, but to seek a reasoned consensus. Actors' interests, preferences, and the perceptions of the situation are no longer fixed, but subject to discursive challenges.[55]

The hope is that a sufficient amount of Habermasian communication will eventually generate an unforced consensus. This is particularly true if the issue area involves technical, scientific, or otherwise abstruse information.[56]

Some scholars and diplomats go even further in praising the powers of talk. For them, communication and debate are not merely useful for facilitating agreement, they are essential features to giving legitimacy to any international agreement. Jennifer Mitzen asserts, "we take for granted that public, interstate talk matters for legitimacy; it is part of our common sense about contemporary world politics."[57]

In point of fact, there is also a strategic logic to the European policy of communicative action. It is true that in the short term, multilateral diplomacy can look both ineffective and hypocritical. If participants cannot achieve a common position, then nothing appears to have been accomplished.

---

[54] Kagan, "Power and Weakness."

[55] Thomas Risse, "Let's Argue! Communicative Action in World Politics," *International Organization*, no. 54, Winter 2000, p. 7.

[56] Anne-Marie Slaughter, *A New World Order* (Princeton: Princeton University Press, 2004).

[57] Jennnifer Mitzen, "Reading Habermas in Anarchy: Multilateral Diplomacy and Global Public Spheres," *American Political Science Review*, no. 99, August 2005, p. 410.

If an agreement is reached, it is often honored only in the breach. The gap between what governments say and what they do can seem quite large at times. However, the communicative approach has the advantage of preventing the lock-in of undesirable policies. As Kagan has pointed out, the strategy of multilateral diplomacy looks desirable when a government lacks the power resources to bargain in alternative fora.[58]

In the long term, agreements that are not initially honored can acquire greater normative cachet. For example, at the time they were signed, the human rights components of the Helsinki Accords were thought to be completely irrelevant. These "Basket Three" arrangements, however, played an important role in toppling communist governments in eastern Europe.[59] Similar arguments have been made for a broad swath of issue areas, including the abolition of slavery, humanitarian interventions, and the environment.[60]

This approach to diplomacy has yielded some significant successes for European statesmen. The most significant example is the European Union itself. It is the most integrated, rule-bound supranational organization in existence. Each step toward integration required painstaking, laborious negotiations. However, reverses never led to defeat. Those who doubt the ability of the European project to overcome the French and Dutch rejections of a proposed EU constitution would do well to remember that in the 1970s, monetary integration looked like it would remain a nonstarter.[61]

This approach to multilateralism is antithetical to the grim trigger strategy. The latter calls for action when words fail, whereas the former consists only of words. For Europeans, the call to action is *in and of itself* a signal that diplomacy has failed. If Habermasians believe that public talk has legitimating purpose in world politics, then the resort to action must be seen as delegitimating such an approach. Not surprisingly, the instances in which Europeans have acted rudely have been those in which the United States or other countries have rejected the diplomatic route in favor of coercive threats.

Predicting the Future

There has been much gnashing of teeth over the prospect that the United States has said goodbye to multilateralism for good.[62] In 2002, Kagan

---

[58] Kagan, "Power and Weakness."

[59] Xinyuan Dai, "Information Systems of Treaty Regimes," *World Politics*, no. 54, July 2002, pp. 405–36.

[60] Neta Crawford, *Argument and Change in World Politics* (Cambridge: Cambridge University Press, 2002).

[61] Andrew Moravcsik, *The Choice for Europe* (Ithaca: Cornell University Press, 1998).

[62] John Ikenberry, "Is American Multilateralism in Decline?" *Perspectives on Politics*, no. 1, September 2003, pp. 533–50.

asserted that the growing power gap between the United States and European countries was responsible for the divergence in transatlantic diplomacy.[63] Economic and demographic trends will only reinforce this power gap. Does this mean that the United States and the European Union will remain divided over the common language of diplomacy?

There are excellent reasons to believe that much of this divide is temporary. American power is impressive but hardly unlimited. As Iraq bogged down American men and material, and as oil prices continued to rise, the Bush administration simply lacked the capacity to use the grim trigger repeatedly. With this relative weakness came a shift away from the grim trigger and toward more permissive strategies in the second term.[64] Personnel turnovers replaced many of the most ardent grim trigger neoconservatives with more diplomatic officials. Face-to-face consultations also increased dramatically since Condoleezza Rice replaced Colin Powell.[65] The greater degree of consultation with allies, combined with a willingness to let them take the negotiating lead with Iran, suggests that the grim trigger might be used more sparingly. Bush's departure from the White House will only accelerate this trend.

The distribution of threats and power will also lead the United States and the European Union into a more cooperative posture. In terms of threats, the global war on terrorism will not disappear anytime soon. Despite all the bluster, both Americans and European recognize a common foe in that arena – and cooperation in technical areas such as terrorist financing has persisted despite high-profile transatlantic blowups. In terms of power, both the United States and the European Union must be concerned about relative losses. Economic and demographic trends suggest that the growth of India and China will shift what is currently a bipolar economic distribution of power into a more multipolar world.[66] The rise of new centers of power with preferences that sharply diverge from those of the West may also force the American and Europeans to cooperate more closely.[67]

---

[63] Kagan, "Power and Weakness."

[64] Philip H. Gordon, "The End of the Bush Revolution," *Foreign Affairs*, no. 85, July/August 2006, pp. 75–86; Drezner, "The New New World Order."

[65] Elaine Shannon, "What Makes Condi Run?" *Time*, March 21, 2005; Romesh Ratnesar, "The Condi Doctrine," *Time*, August 15, 2005.

[66] On the economics, see Dominic Wilson and Roopa Purushothaman, "Dreaming with BRICs: The Path to 2050," Goldman Sachs Global Economics Paper No. 99, New York, October 2003. On the demographics, see Nicholas Eberstadt, "Power and Population in Asia," *Policy Review*, no. 123, February 2004, pp. 1–22.

[67] See, on this point, Timothy Garton Ash, *Free World: America, Europe, and the Surprising Future of the West* (New York: Random House, 2004); Drezner, "The New New World Order."

In the end, however, the fact remains that the current contretemps has more to do with process than substance. Americans and Europeans share a broad degree of consensus about the desired ends in world politics. Polling data show that despite George W. Bush's personal unpopularity in Europe, more Europeans than Americans agree with President Bush's desire for democracy promotion.[68] Disputes over process have been bad before – for example, during the early 1980s, when the United States actually sanctioned Western European firms and hundreds of thousands of Europeans protested the deployment of Pershing II missiles. These storms have been weathered because the desired goals of American and European governments remain unchanged. The transatlantic tiffs over diplomatic style make great head-lines – but they do not fundamentally alter the transatlantic relationship.

[68] *Transatlantic Trends 2005*, available online at http://www.transatlantictrends.org/index.cfm?
id=2.

8

The Atlantic Divide in Historical Perspective

A View from Europe

Laurent Cohen-Tanugi

Introduction

The intensity of the transatlantic crisis over the U.S.-led intervention in Iraq in early 2003 has put into question on both sides of the Atlantic the relevance and the future prospects of the Euro–American alliance in the post–Cold War, post–September 11 world.

The section "Europe and the Politics of Atlanticism" analyzes the different views held in Europe, particularly in France, about the transatlantic relationship, both before and since the Iraqi crisis. The next two sections, "Continental Drift" and "A Resilient Bond," present my own analysis of that crisis, its underlying reasons, and its ultimate impact. Finally, the section "Friends Again: Quick Fix or Strategic Shift?" discusses the present state and future prospects of the Atlantic partnership four years after the invasion of Iraq, in light of the change that occurred in the global geopolitical paradigm since then.

Europe and the Politics of Atlanticism

The range of current European positions about the Atlantic partnership cannot be properly understood without the historical background of the Cold War period, when such positions were first articulated. During the nearly four decades of the East–West confrontation, the relevance of the Atlantic Alliance and the legitimacy of Europe's commitment thereto were, for obvious reasons, not matters for debate. Nevertheless, there were at least three distinct viewpoints within Europe on the subject.

At one end of the spectrum, the British position was inherently Atlanticist, in the sense that Britain placed the Alliance and the "special relationship" with the United States at the core of its foreign and defense policies, over and above its membership in the European Community. At the other end, Gaullist France, although also committed to the Atlantic partnership, made national independence in the diplomatic and security areas – materialized by its autonomous nuclear capability and its permanent seat at the United Nations Security Council – the cornerstone of its foreign policy and its very identity. Of course, the claim for independence only made sense by reference to the United States and NATO, and the French consistently disputed the U.S. military and political leadership over NATO (leading to the withdrawal of France from NATO's integrated military command in 1966). Along the same lines, Europe was seen by France as a natural challenger of the United States, including in the diplomatic and military fields, where France consistently advocated the formation of a "European pillar" of NATO, independent from the United States, a recurring subject of dispute with both Washington and London. Being a "true European," with ambitions for a political Europe, was deemed incompatible with the support of a U.S.-led Atlantic partnership. On the broader international scene, France advocated a "third way" between the ideological systems and hegemonic pretenses of the two superpowers, which Europe would embody for the benefit of developing nations.

Between the French and British positions, the majority of the founding members of the European Community could be characterized as "passively Atlanticist," in the sense that they had no global diplomatic ambitions (for themselves or Europe) and simply entrusted their national security to NATO and, ultimately, Washington. Internally as well, European states (and political leaders) divided themselves along those lines between "Atlanticists" (the majority) and "Europeanists" (mostly French) favoring an independent European defense capability and foreign policy (implicitly modeled after the French ones).

Yet, despite the rhetoric, the constant French–American bickering over NATO's leadership, and France's positioning between East and West, North and South – that is, at the center of the world stage – Paris never defected on important security matters, including in 1983 under socialist rule, when President François Mitterrand supported the installation of the Pershing II missiles at the heart of Europe, vehemently opposed by German pacifists, and again in 1991 when France supported the first Gulf War.

When the Cold War finally came to an end with the victory of the West, the future of the Alliance started to become a subject of intense debate on both sides of the Atlantic. NATO had been created to counter the Soviet threat; with that goal achieved, it seemed no longer to serve any purpose.

In the new geopolitical environment, the Cold War positions about the Alliance took a different shape. As the sole global superpower, the United States struggled to preserve NATO as the cornerstone of Western defense and security policy and to adapt its membership, missions, and organization to the post–Cold War world. France and other Europeanist states stressed the irrelevance of NATO and quietly welcomed its slow death, which meant the removal of longstanding obstacles toward the construction of a "European defense identity" officially programmed in the Maastricht Treaty of 1992. As it was, even to the traditionally Atlanticist European states such as the Netherlands, Denmark, or Portugal, the Atlantic Alliance had lost some of its relevance with the elimination of the Soviet threat to Western Europe and the proclamation of the "end of history." These same reasons, however, kept those states from supporting the building of a strong European defense capability to replace NATO. Throughout the 1990s, except for the United Kingdom, all national defense budgets within Europe decreased significantly.

The turmoil in the Balkans, and the Kosovo war in particular, marked a first turning point in the post–Cold War European attitudes toward the Atlantic partnership. The instability created by the elimination of the Soviet rule from eastern Europe created a new mission for NATO, which the Europeans' military inability to deal with the situation reinforced in their own eyes. NATO's military intervention in Kosovo was at the same time a success in transatlantic cooperation, a demonstration of NATO's continuing relevance and a wake-up call for the Europeans as to their inability to resolve a crisis in their own backyard that was highly meaningful politically but relatively minor militarily. It also revealed the growing gap in military capabilities, particularly in the key area of technological warfare, between the two sides of the Atlantic, threatening the continuing participation of European forces to future NATO missions. It was in fact the concern created by that post-Kosovo realization (rather than a sudden surge of Gaullism at 10 Downing Street) that prompted the British to engage the French to relaunch their bilateral defense cooperation at St. Malo in 1998.

At the end of the 1990s, NATO had managed to survive the disappearance of its original purpose and to reinvent itself, with the inclusion of some of its former eastern European adversaries and the expansion of its missions and geographic coverage. But that did not seem to trouble the Europeanist camp, which had made progress toward a European foreign and security policy and defense capability as well. Euro–American relations were kept in harmony by the promises of the technology-led "new economy," the apparent lack of strategic tensions in the world, and the European honeymoon with the Clinton presidency.

The parenthesis of the 1990s ended with the global shock of September 11, 2001, and one of its principal consequences, the American-led invasion of Iraq. We will return later in this chapter to the actual impact of these major geopolitical events on transatlantic relations, and simply focus here on how they altered the European debate over the future of the Alliance. In spite of the apparent detente in Euro–American relations associated with the early post–Cold War period, differences and tensions had in fact been accumulating between the two sides of the Atlantic over a vast range of "non-strategic" matters such as trade and economic regulation, global warming, development assistance, international law, and societal issues such as human rights and the death penalty. The controversial election of George W. Bush and the undiplomatic attitudes toward European positions of the first few months of his administration crystallized and increased those tensions and anti-American sentiment in Europe.

Against that background, the shock and initial sympathy created by the attacks of September 11 soon gave way to a new surge of anti-Americanism within the European left, fueled by the sudden vulnerability of the "Empire" and the unilateralist reactions provoked by the attacks in the United States. Certain European political and intellectual circles echoed by the media argued more or less explicitly that September 11 was after all the inescapable (if not legitimate) consequence of America's foreign policy, particularly in the Middle East, and of its universal arrogance. In any event, justifiable or not, September 11 was essentially an American affair; Europe had nothing to do with it, other than potentially becoming its indirect victim as a result of its alliance with Washington. Such an attitude, although prevalent in the French left, remained soft-spoken and controversial until the fall of 2002, when the Europeans and the Americans started to quarrel at the United Nations over Washington's plan to intervene in Iraq. The severe transatlantic tensions that followed at the diplomatic level starting in January 2003 and the circumstances of the war themselves produced the most serious crisis in Euro–American relations since 1945 and a rise of European (and global) anti-Americanism unprecedented in intensity and scope.

At the governmental level, Europe divided itself between the old Euro-peanist camp – Jacques Chirac's France, opportunistically joined by Gerhard Schröder's Germany and Vladimir Putin's Russia – and the traditionally Atlanticist states. But the divide was no longer theoretical or doctrinal, as it had been during the Cold War. France and its continental European allies (including Belgium) saw in the Iraqi crisis a unique opportunity to assert Europe's view of the world, its autonomy from the United States, and its role as a counterweight to Americas' global but contested supremacy.

The majority of European governments, enhanced by the fresh Atlanticism of the new central and eastern European member states, maintained their solidarity with Washington against their own public opinion, overwhelmingly opposed to the war in Iraq and hostile to Bush's America.

In contrast with the EU's internal divisions at the governmental level, European public opinion was remarkably united against Washington's foreign policy and the neoconservative vision of the international system. This new form of European anti-Americanism (often mislabeled as anti-Bushism by the Europeans) amalgamated the sense of growing apart on many economic, societal, and cultural issues. This sense developed during the 1990s with the notion that America's superpower had now become a danger to world stability, as illustrated by September 11, and, most convincingly, by the "illegitimate" invasion of Iraq and its disastrous consequences for the region and the West itself. America's conversion from victim of Islamist mass terrorism to global troublemaker status along well-known ideological patterns was skillfully orchestrated in Europe and worldwide by the traditional adversaries of liberal democracy, capitalism, and the United States' traditional support of Israel: the radical left (neo-Marxists, antiglobalists, and the like), now emancipated from their embarrassing association with Soviet communism, and to a lesser extent the old anti-American sovereignist right.

The Bush administration's adventurism in Iraq turned this initially radical view into mainstream European ideology. In transatlantic terms, this translated into what one might call the "separatist theory," under which Europe and America were heading toward a strategic and ideological divorce of historic significance. The separatist theory underlined the contingency of the Alliance on the now defunct Cold War geopolitics and the growing estrangement of American and European cultures, values, and even interests. In the new geopolitical environment, according to that view, the two sides of the Atlantic were bound to diverge, leading to the "end of the West" as a geopolitical concept, and perhaps even as a civilizational one. I call this view "separatist" as opposed to "pessimistic" because its proponents, whether European leftists or sovereignists or American neoconservatives, were generally welcoming the divorce that they were pretending merely to analyze. A variation of separatism advanced the imminent decline of the American empire (a French all-time favorite[1]) as an additional justification for the "rising Europe" (a theme espoused by some American Euro-optimists such as

---

[1] See, for example, E. Todd, *La Fin de l'Empire: Essai sur la décomposition du système américain* (Paris: Gallimard, 2002).

Jeremy Rifkin, Charles A. Kupchan, or T. R. Reid[2]) to turn away from the Alliance.

At the other end of the spectrum of views regarding the nature and seriousness of the Iraqi crisis and the prospects of the Atlantic partnership, the optimistic theory defended by diplomats and traditional Atlanticists stressed the inherently difficult nature of the transatlantic relationship, the occurrence of similar tensions during the Cold War, the "Bush/Chirac" factor in the French–American showdown, and, most important, the strength of the community of interests and values between the United States and Europe, which transcends occasional crises.

Neither of these views is, I believe, accurate. The optimistic (or naive) theory ignores the structural change that has occurred in global geopolitics since the fall of the Berlin Wall, and its impact on the transatlantic partnership. The separatist one exacerbates the Atlantic divide into an ideological "clash of civilizations" within the West in an artificial and often biased and self-interested way. The reality lies somewhere in between: The Atlantic partnership has undergone a structural shift that radically differentiates the recent tensions from what Henry Kissinger used to call the "misunderstandings" of the Cold War era.[3] But the Alliance and the West are here to stay, albeit under a different modus vivendi.

Continental Drift

The transatlantic crisis of 2002 and 2003 over Iraq was not merely a French–American affair, and did not only stem from a clash of personalities; it was much broader and deeper than that, involving, in the absence of a united Europe on the subject, a united European public opinion and a serious transatlantic disconnect. More importantly, the Iraqi crisis did not create the Atlantic divide; it merely revealed it to public opinion (and sometimes governments), and, of course, seriously aggravated it.

The change in the transatlantic relationship began well before the installation of the first Bush administration. It is attributable to the combination of three major events in the recent history of international relations: the end

---

[2] See Charles A. Kupchan, "The End of the West," *Atlantic Monthly*, November 2002; T. R. Reid, *The United States of Europe, The New Superpower and the End of American Supremacy* (New York, Penguin, 2004).

[3] This thesis is fully developed in my book, *An Alliance at Risk: The United States and Europe after September 11* (Baltimore: Johns Hopkins University Press, 2003).

of the Cold War, the emergence of the European Union (EU) as a potential political power, and 9/11 and its aftermath.

After the post–World War II golden age of the Euro–American relationship, which saw the United States help finance the economic reconstruction of Europe and support the first steps of its political unification, the Cold War era started to witness French–American disputes over NATO and an independent European defense, but these clashes remained largely symbolic. The real change occurred with the defeat of communism, the liberation of central and eastern Europe, and the fall of the Soviet Union.

The end of the Cold War eliminated the common threat that had federated Europe and the United States for decades. For Washington, it meant that the now pacified, prosperous, and reunited Europe was no longer a strategic priority; for the Europeans, it meant that they no longer needed U.S. military protection and the Atlantic Alliance, at least to the same degree. Those were the happy years of the "end of history" and the "new economy," celebrated on both sides of the Atlantic, while the key institutions of the postwar international order – NATO, the United Nations, but also the European Community – were suffering a major relevance and identity crisis.

The victory of the "West" over communism coincided with the birth of the EU, created by the Maastricht Treaty of 1992. The EU was meant to embody the "political Europe" that the founding members of the European Economic Community had contemplated from the start. It had a single currency, a common foreign and security policy, as well as ambitious aspirations in the areas of defense and home affairs.

The transformation of Europe from an essentially economic organization to a multinational political entity of unprecedented characteristics made the building of a European identity necessary, both to give European citizens the sense of a common destiny and to position the EU on the world stage. This quest for a common identity was made even more compelling by the prospect of the EU's expansion to the East – another side-effect of the end of the Cold War – with its unavoidably adverse impact on the cohesion and homogeneity of the former European Community.

Defining oneself in opposition to others is a natural way to assert one's existence, and in this instance the natural alter ego of the EU was, of course, the United States, for a variety of reasons. As multilateral trade negotiations began to expand from goods to services to international economic regulation, Brussels and Washington started to conflict over broad policy issues such as the environment, development, social models, and cultural goods and services. As the memory of World War II and of the East–West confrontation faded among the younger generations, asserting European "values" and collective preferences, generally in opposition to the "American model," became one of the key justifications of European unification in the political discourse.

The argument about a growing ideological and cultural distance between the two sides of the Atlantic found support in America's own transformations. Ideologically, the conservative revolution started during the Reagan years produced a new, tougher financial capitalism, the rise of the religious right and related "culture wars," and a new American assertiveness on the world stage that moved the United States away from the old continent. At the same time, the shift of America's centers of economic and political power from the East Coast elites of European descent and Atlanticist culture toward the South and the West of the country further distanced the two longstanding allies from one another. On top of that, throughout the 1990s, the ideological, cultural, and sociological estrangement was compounded by an ever-increasing and troublesome gap between Europe and the United States in economic performance, technological innovation, long-term demographic prospects, and military capability. Divergence, for better or worse, seemed to be the inescapable fate of the transatlantic relationship.

Then came September 11, 2001, and with it the materialization of a lasting and limitless Islamist threat against the United States and the West, as well as that threat's paradoxical impact on the transatlantic relationship. Beyond the solidarity with a longstanding protector and ally, the reappearance of a common threat should have reinforced the Atlantic bond. Yet, it did the opposite, for at least two reasons. First, until the Madrid bombings of March 2004, the Europeans underestimated the impact of September 11 on the American psyche and misunderstood its strategic significance for U.S. foreign policy and global geopolitics generally. For a long while, Americans and Europeans lived on different planets. The sole world superpower had been attacked and felt engaged in a global war against terrorism, whereas the peaceful and defenseless Europe viewed September 11 as largely the product of America's foreign policy, particularly its involvement in the Middle East and longstanding support of Israel. Unlike Soviet expansionism, the terrorist threat and the appropriate method to counter it were assessed differently on both sides of the Atlantic in the light of differences in past experiences, interests, and present situations. September 11 also accelerated the move of Washington's strategic priorities away from Europe and toward Central Asia and the Middle East, where the action was and where Europeans had little to contribute.

These differences reached paroxysm with the U.S. decision to wage war on Saddam Hussein's Iraq, without UN support or convincing evidence of Saddam's possession of weapons of mass destruction or ties to al-Qaeda. European governments divided themselves in terms of the solidarity and support to be provided to Washington in such circumstances, but the breadth and bitterness of the transatlantic public opinion divide was unprecedented. The Americans, misled about the threat presented by Iraq, felt betrayed by ungrateful allies, the French in particular, whereas the Europeans felt ignored and potentially threatened by the unilateral actions of a disdainful and dangerous superpower. The Atlantic Alliance now harbored the clash of two visions of international relations: the American one, focused on regime change through military power, including the unilateral and preemptive use of force when necessary; and the European commitment to multilateralism and diplomacy, even if it meant the preservation of a hateful but stabilizing dictatorship.

A Resilient Bond

The end of the East–West confrontation, the separate and often divergent paths of America and Europe, and the emergence of Islamist radicalism as a long-term factor in global geopolitics have thus altered and seriously challenged the transatlantic relationship. Yet, for all the rhetoric about the "Atlantic divide," this challenge has had little impact on the fundamental justifications of the Alliance and even produced new ones.

Even though the conventionally optimistic view of transatlantic relations misses much of the new dynamics at work since the end of the Cold War, its main articles of faith have not lost their truth and relevance. Transatlantic economic and trade interdependence remains as strong as ever. The United States and the European Union are both each other's most important trading partner and the first foreign investor in the other's territory. This integrated transatlantic economy represents some 60 percent of world GDP and commerce, whereas heavily publicized disputes over aircraft, agricultural, or other subsidies represent less than 5 percent of transatlantic trade. Even at the worst of the Iraqi crisis, this reality remained unaffected.[4]

Similarly, the ritual invocation of shared fundamental values – freedom, democracy, the rule of law, and a free-market economy – does not take away this powerful reality, now reinforced by the common threat of Islamic

[4] See J. P. Quintan, "Drifting Apart or Growing Together? The Primacy of the Transatlantic Economy," Center for Transatlantic Relations (Johns Hopkins University) monograph, 2003.

fundamentalism and related terrorism. In fact, contrary to the commonly held view about an alleged transatlantic divorce with respect to culture and values, a strong case can be made that the two sides of the Atlantic have converged rather than diverged over the past fifty years as a result of economic integration and globalization. Just as trade disputes are only a few drops of water in the ocean of transatlantic economic interdependence, so cultural and philosophical differences over a few powerfully symbolic and heavily publicized subjects such as the death penalty, the International Criminal Court, or climate change seem to be not only exaggerated and partly misunderstood, but in fact marginal in the context of the convergence process that has characterized the development of economies, societies, and ways of living in the New World and the Old since 1945.

Within the Western world, the major historical development of the last half-century has indeed been the convergence of the European and American models around the now-shared norms of the market economy, free-trade, political freedoms, and regulation through law, under the influence of the opening of borders, of European unification, and of the ideological triumph of liberalism over Marxism and communism.[5] As a practical matter, this means that the economies and the democracies of Europe and the United States now function along comparable lines. On either side of the Atlantic, businesspeople, politicians, lawyers, and journalists now speak the same language, and societies are much more transparent to one another even in their peculiarities.

One might object that this convergence is essentially the product of the Americanization of the world, of the conversion of Europe, like other regions of the planet, to the essential values of the American system, in the economic as well as the political and cultural realms. Further, one might argue that this conversion has been accomplished under the influence of ideological, institutional, and economic mediations that are now vigorously challenged, such as neoliberalism, globalization, or even European integration as illustrated by the rejection of the EU constitutional treaty by France and the Netherlands, two of its founding members. However pertinent it might be, the objection nevertheless omits the freely accepted and very broadly positive character throughout Europe of the transformation of closed and administered economies into open and competitive markets, of authoritarian or Jacobin regimes into constitutional and pluralist democracies, and of monolithic and

---

[5] I have analyzed this convergence as regards France in *Le Droit sans l'Etat: Sur la démocratie en France et en Amérique* (Paris: PUF, 1985), prefaced by Professor Stanley Hoffmann.

conservative societies into pluralistic communities increasingly governed by the rule of law.

The principal threat to transatlantic solidarity lies rather in the insidious indoctrination of public opinion by politicians and the media in favor of the separatist argument. Differences of course exist, and they will likely intensify as a result of demographic, social, cultural, and strategic developments at work on both sides of the Atlantic. But these differences do not threaten the civilizational unity of the West. Rather, they make it all the more incumbent on Europeans and Americans to rediscover the abandoned paths of dialogue and mutual understanding instead of confining themselves to compiling an inventory of arbitrarily amalgamated and inflated areas of disagreement.[6] To that extent, prevailing media discourse on the transatlantic divide becomes a self-fulfilling prophecy insofar as it does not bring with it a critical and constructive reflection on the nature of specific differences and ways to resolve or ignore them.

Friends Again: Quick Fix or Strategic Shift?

Four years after the start of the French–American quarrel over Iraq at the United Nations at the end of 2002, both sides have learned their lesson. The second Bush administration, stranded in Iraq and faced with the dramatic consequences of this failure for American foreign policy and standing in the world as well as for global security, has had to recognize the limits of unilateralism, if not to acknowledge that "the French were right" on the hazards of invading Iraq. Likewise, Paris and Berlin have realized the tremendous political damage caused by their head-on opposition to U.S. foreign policy, both in transatlantic relations and within the European Union. Accordingly, both sides have made deliberate efforts to put Iraq aside and restore the relationship, with a fair measure of success.

Although the French and German governments have consistently refused to join the coalition in Iraq, they have toned down their criticism of the U.S. intervention and supported the political process leading to the restoration of Iraqi sovereignty. They have also stressed the paramount importance of the Euro–American partnership and realized its new vulnerability, which they seemed to have overlooked during the Iraqi crisis. The changeover from Schröder to Angela Merkel in Berlin helped that transition.

---

[6] For a systematic rebuttal of the thesis of a "clash of civilizations" within the West, see Cohen-Tanugi, *An Alliance at Risk*, pp. 119 et seq.

The second Bush administration, in return, made a point of recognizing the European Union as such (if not "discovering Europe"), with the newly reelected president paying a visit to the EU institutions in Brussels in February of 2005, soon after being sworn in. After the neoconservatives' contempt of the irrelevance of Europe and Defense Secretary Donald Rumsfeld's divisive line about "old" and "new" Europe, such a visit took on special political significance.

In practical terms, Europeans and Americans have continued to cooperate efficiently (as they always have) in the fight against terrorism, in Afghanistan and in the Balkans, where Europe is taking the lion's share. As the United States was stranded in Iraq, Europe also took the lead in dealing with Iran's nuclear program, in its own diplomatic way, but with the growing support of Washington paving the way for UN sanctions resolutions. In the Middle East, Paris and Washington have spoken with a single voice regarding Lebanon's efforts to emancipate itself from Syria, and France has regained its status as America's most effective ally in the region. Israel's withdrawal from Gaza and the landslide victory of Hamas in the January 2006 Palestinian elections have also allowed Europeans and Americans to put aside their longstanding differences over the conflict in favor of a common support of the path toward peace and the condemnation of terrorism and violence.

American and European views of the twenty-first century's world have also become closer, with Europe's awakening from its pacifist dream and Washington's rediscovery of the virtues of soft power. This new convergence does not guarantee the absence of another clash over one issue or another, but it should prevent such a clash from taking the devastating proportions of the crisis over Iraq.

The warming of transatlantic diplomatic relations is supported by public opinion on both sides of the Atlantic as if popular wisdom made it clear that the two allies had gone too far in their confrontation. The reality of the community of interests and values between Europe and the United States was indeed made even clearer after the terrorist attacks on Madrid (2004) and London (2005), the American military and political setback in Iraq, the derailment of European political unification caused by the French and Dutch rejections of the EU constitutional treaty, and the growing tension between the Islamic world and the West as illustrated, among other examples, by the orchestrated violence of Muslim reactions around the world in reaction to the Muhammad cartoons published by European newspapers.

Europe continues to depend on the United States for its overall security and standing in the world. The United States needs Europe's assistance, soft power, and legitimacy to share the political and military burdens of policing the planet and defending Western interests and values. Both sides and the world at large need transatlantic cooperation to confront the global challenges of terrorism, nuclear proliferation, global warming, AIDS, and other humanitarian and geopolitical hazards. The need for a closer transatlantic partnership is likely to increase, not decrease, in the decades to come, against the backdrop of the rise of China to global superpower status, the reassertion of Russian and Iranian power on the world stage, and the risks associated with the evolution of the Islamic world and Central Asia.

Conclusion

Looking back, the Iraqi crisis is likely to remain in history as the first transatlantic conflict of the post–Cold War era and, as such, as a case study of reciprocal disconnect and diplomatic mismanagement. Governments on both sides failed to recognize the new vulnerability of the Atlantic bond following the disappearance of the Soviet threat and the need to protect this bond from peripheral differences. Public opinion (and politicians and the media behind them) failed to understand each other's sensitivities. The Europeans underestimated the impact of September 11 on the American psyche and its role in the popular support for the war in Iraq and in the feeling of betrayal caused by the French–German opposition. The Americans simply could not hear that Iraq was an entirely different game than the "war against terror," especially as they were told the opposite by their own government.

After this inaugural fiasco, the lesson from Iraq, now understood by both sides, can be summarized as follows. America and Europe have increasingly different interests and identities (as opposed to "values"), which may lead them to have different views about the world and specific foreign policy issues. These differences need to be understood and carefully managed so as to protect from diplomatic incompetence, nationalistic excess, and popular acrimony a relationship that has become less natural while remaining just as vital as before. For the first time in decades, the basic message of Euro–Atlanticism – that is, the notion that Atlantic solidarity and support for a political Europe are not only compatible but reinforcing – is beginning to be understood.

But the Iraqi crisis may also well be the last transatlantic conflict of the post–Cold War years for another reason: The post–Cold War era may be already behind us. We are now entering a new, multipolar world that looks much different from, and more dangerous than, that of the 1990s. Since then, the West has suffered several major setbacks – the Iraqi fiasco, the crisis of European unification, the failure of the Doha round of multilateral trade negotiations – while new powers are on the rise in the Far East and in the South, and while the divorce between Islam and the West seems to be deepening. However disquieting, these long-term developments should cause the United States and Europe to strengthen the Atlantic community in order to reinforce each other and preserve Western democratic values and global leadership in the twenty-first century.

Paradoxically, the most problematic parameter in projecting a renewed Euro–American alliance into the future may be Europe's ability to provide a credible partner to the United States, particularly following the rejection of the EU constitutional treaty by France, the most vocal advocate of a political Europe influential on the world stage. Coupled with its unpromising long-term economic prospects and weak military capabilities, Europe's inability to unite politically may precipitate its marginalization in world affairs, which would undoubtedly undermine the transatlantic alliance, if not U.S. foreign policy.[7]

Nicolas Sarkozy's triumphal election as president of the French Republic in May 2007 is, therefore, positive news for both Europe and the transatlantic partnership. Mr. Chirac's successor has pledged to bring France "back in Europe" and to give the EU a new impetus. He not only shares key American values, but even more importantly does not seem to believe, as did his predecessor and many French diplomats, that France's and Europe's vocation is to serve as a "counterweight" to American power in a desirable "multipolar world." Together with Merkel's Germany, Sarkozy's France may well open a new, happy chapter in the history of transatlantic relations.

---

[7] See Laurent Cohen-Tanugi, "The End of Europe?" *Foreign Affairs*, vol. 84, no. 6, November/December 2005.

Index